Woozie
(GRANDMOTHER)
Wisdom
(ABOUT LIFE, SEX, AND LOVE)

LYNN HUBSCHMAN

WOOZIE (GRANDMOTHER) WISDOM (ABOUT LIFE, SEX, AND LOVE)

iUniverse books may be ordered through booksellers or by contacting:

iUniverse
1663 Liberty Drive
Bloomington, IN 47403
www.iuniverse.com
1-800-Authors (1-800-288-4677)

ISBN: 978-1-5320-6986-4 (sc)
ISBN: 978-1-5320-6987-1 (e)

Print information available on the last page.

iUniverse rev. date: 04/02/2019

Preface

This is my Woozie who I named and I'm scared to read what she writes. Everyone needs a Woozie!

— Ron

Most grandmothers spend the later years of their lives glued to rocking chairs knitting modest sweaters for their grandchildren, meanwhile, mine sends risqué lingerie to my freshman dorm, asks my friends if they're orgasmic and constantly reminds me that the world is much better after a glass of wine. I wouldn't want it any other way.

Alim

Woozie is a one-of-a-kind grandmother — sharp, lively, & frank. Her passion for sex & romance is contagious — so contagious that I now study sexuality myself. Enjoy her wisdom, it's rare!

Amelia

Contents

Dedicated To:

All the people that trusted me with their intimate lives in order to professionally help them

All the people I have loved who loved me in return

Introduction

What's a *Woozie*, you ask?

Well, it was a surprise to me too.

As mentioned in Volume One it was a name my husband, Emil, endearingly called me.

When our two daughters, Jody and Tracy had children I was identified.

After our first grandchild, Daniel, was born, he heard that name and thought that was my name.

As a result, he called me by that name, and the later grandchildren; his sister, Alina, and then Jody's daughter, Amelia, called me, *Woozie*.

Actually, it's kind of a cute name and nobody knows I'm a grandmother!

The wisdom part comes from my decades of experience as a counselor to thousands of people. Both my professional life and personal life have made grandmotherly wisdom available.

I know that we are not educated about the most important aspects of our lives.

My books are there to assist people with relationships and to help avoid problems. Grandmothers have always given advice; just from their life experience. Mine has a world of professional background.

My hope is that you will enjoy the manner in which it is written, and that you will learn from it and share it with others.

Life and finding love and having passion is not easy, but the more you know, the better.

This book is an effort to that end.

It's A Tough Life

"Tough times never last but tough people do." - Robert H. Schuller

How true. However some people do have a lot of tough times or live daily with tough situations.

There have always been terrible times throughout history and there are difficult times to live through in your own world, but the really hard times are those you experience personally.

Recently I was in a restaurant and a lovely pretty young girl was the server. She had tattoos all over one arm. When I asked her about it she told me they were dinosaurs. She then went on to explain that they were in memory of a brother that died at age five and she used to read to him about dinosaurs and he loved that.

She was a mother of a young boy now and he liked the same stories.

So, here she was working to help support her family and with her sad background being pleasant to patrons.

Now she is but one in a million of terribly sad stories out there and as a therapist I have heard my fair share of all sorts of horrible conditions people live through.

As a young family counselor, I will never forget the young mother who was a nurse and took care of a dying child for years.

How many families live with illness, lack of funds, crises that happen, and anything else that could make you depressed or feel you just want to give up? And we all know or have read about many who do give up.

It is indeed a tough life and the best and worst parts are always unplanned.

How many decisions have you made that didn't turn out well? How often have you been disappointed about jobs, friends, family, loves? No one escapes!!

The wounds can become scars and scars are *tough*. The wish is to not become so *hard* that you lose your humanity.

Being alone or having ambivalence takes a toll. Having more than one difficult thing in your life can bring you down. It's that proverbial straw that breaks the camel's back.

A lot of this has to do with your goals and hopefully they are realistic.

Having support from others helps. Humor helps. And having financial resources can soften many blows.

Now when it comes to love that's a big issue and often you may have to displease people in order to have and hold on to love.

Perhaps your family dislikes your choice, maybe friends disapprove and then, of course, there are a whole myriad of things you may not like about that person, yourself.

You may have to be *tough* to get what you want in a relationship. You may also have to be tough to end one or have someone end with you.

What happens is that these experiences show you that there is life that goes on,and all you have to do is keep moving and have faith and hope. If you survive one you know you can survive another.

At times it is impossible, and we all have our weak periods, but even then, we can push on.

People whom we respect that have lived difficult lives are often great examples to learn about and emulate. They are not us, but we can learn from them and also realize we are not alone. Someone else has lived through this.

Most of our troubles will not be on the eleven o'clock news, but for some people their problems are huge.

Insurmountable problems are out there, make no mistake about it. However, life does go on.

The question is; HOW?

In the end it is up to you.

In America we value independence and strength. What we need to teach is that sometimes we really need others and hopefully that will teach us how to be empathetic and caring when someone needs us!

"Making tough decisions that may make someone unhappy is something to get good at doing." - Phoebe Robinson

What You Don't Know Can Hurt You

"We are all born ignorant, but one must work hard to remain stupid." - Benjamin Franklin

What have been the things that happened that surprised you? How often have you thought, *If only I had known.* Most of us have a rather long list of things that fall into that category.

It is true that what you don't know can really hurt you and your life.

Schools do not teach the things we truly need to know. They do not prepare us for real life.

How do you make decisions? What facts do you have and where do they come from? How much *damage* has happened in your life and family as a result of *not knowing*?

Think about the areas that concern your daily life and your future.

Who taught you what to do with money? Did you have good advice about planning your future and investments? Managing money is a big deal and not easily learned. Often people learn only by 'mistakes' and then it's too late.

How do you budget and what is your expendable income? Savings? Taking care of your old age and your family doesn't happen by magic. Handling credit is a huge lesson to learn.

Who tells you about the large interest rates you can end up paying?

How do you choose your life's work? What should you have known?

The more you know about anything the better. And things do change so it is an ongoing process. Whom to trust and learn from is a question for each of us.

Rules and laws are often not given or misunderstood. Even simple things like parking a car can cause a lot of problems if you don't have the right information.

Medical issues can be life threatening. Who do you trust to give you advice or pills?

Being in a hospital and not being aware of what is going on and how you are being treated medically can be unbelievably destructive. Heaven help you if you are *foggy* or have no one to advocate and check on your treatment. You are a pure *victim*.

Legal issues are always a problem. Can anyone trust any lawyer? They are all in cahoots in my book and they always benefit from others' misfortune!

Jewelers are another area for lack of knowledge hurting and costing you. Sort of like car repair…

Who tells you beautiful colored precious stones are that way because they were heated? Who tells you some stones have been sliced and doubled to look good? Talk about a racket!

Whatever you pay, try to get that amount back if you want to sell it. Lots of luck!

Art and music and areas such as architecture can be appreciated the more you understand about what it took to get the finished product. While much is individually selective, knowing can give you an insight even if you don't like the end result.

What foods to eat and where to travel and what entertainment you choose again is an individual choice but information can guide your choices.

Insurance is another large area where money is spent, often unwisely. Often the devil is in the details that are glossed over or not explained in simple terms. Caveat emptor… buyer beware.

And simple things can cause a lot of disappointment and trouble. Did you think to measure the doorways and stairs before buying that sofa? Can you return … whatever, if there is a problem?

Buying things on impulse or from a *super* salesperson can be a big mistake in the end.

Whoever told you that you need to put a metal spoon in a crystal bowl before adding something hot? Probably no one which is why your favorite dish cracked and broke!

After age twenty or so we can no longer blame parents for our troubles. Taking responsibility is a big step and leads to reliable adulthood.

Now we all make mistakes that could have been avoided if only we knew…

That is one way to LEARN. Hopefully without paying too costly a price.

The real issue from my perspective is; you guessed it, relationships.

What exactly do we learn about being a person, a partner, and a parent? Think about it. The most important parts of our lives. Answer; very little.

We get better instructions about how to fix a dress stain and care for a plant than we do about how to care for a partner or child.

Let's change that!!

"The greater our knowledge increases the more our ignorance unfolds." - John F. Kennedy

Is Commitment Necessary

"Intensity of attraction is a beautiful thing. But to mislabel it love is both foolish and dangerous. What love requires on top of instant emotion is time, shared experiences and feelings, and a long and tempered bond between two people." - Stanton Peele

Recently I visited a prestigious college campus and had the opportunity to speak with a number of students. Naturally I was concerned about their love lives.

The girls spoke of difficulty with guys they were involved with, and the subject of commitment came up.

Being labeled *sexist* in a number of regards, has never altered my opinions about the genetic differences, that will never change, between males and females.

While we have all heard the mantra that the only things you can count on are death and taxes, many people need to 'count on' a partner, and they want them emotionally tied to them alone. That means commitment.

Now when young people talk that way, I get a bit concerned. To be tied to one person at young ages does not allow for a wide variety of romantic experiences. Those experiences will be helpful in the long run, in choosing someone to perhaps marry and have children with; if that is a goal.

What happens I believe, is that many young people have a sexual partner and are truly connected in a number of other ways, and then the female, usually, wants a commitment. Now that commitment may be that they only *sleep* with one another, or it may mean they do not go out with anyone else. This can be limiting, and in some cases, stifling, and in others an unreal expectation.

What happens with natural desires and finding others attractive? What happens with flirtation? What happens with exploring other people, maybe just as *friend'* first?

Guys seem to fear commitment more than females. Females want that 'security' knowing he is theirs and theirs alone. Especially when sex is involved. Guys do not seem to have that same need. But to be fair there are males that are extremely jealous and want that security as well.

The fact of the matter is that it takes time to be that secure about what you offer, and trust that YOU CANNOT be replaced emotionally and physically. Being young you can't know that .... yet!

The really secure and free people know that only with total freedom and being *chosen* does love survive and thrive. It cannot be ordered; legal documents don't do it either.

How do you get someone *tied* to you?

Easy. You offer what you are and the best and honest person that you are. Perfect people do not exist, and love will be blind in the beginning. However, by just being open and you, and trusting what the relationship enjoys, the truth will out. Enjoy and have fun. Share and communicate eye to eye; heart to heart.

He/she will want what you bring; the good and the messy, and the rotten parts. If not, you have a sham relationship anyway.

It is not easy to expose yourself with the warts and insecurities. There are yucky parts to all relationships, especially over time as the real you is there in living color and without filters. That's as it should be.

With time and experience you learn who to trust with what you say and do.

If you have been *burned* or duped, or just inexperienced, time will teach you.

Now is the time to learn. It is harder later

If the same problems keep arising, you may need to take a good long hard look at what you are doing and who you are getting involved with.

Maybe even talking to a professional counselor could shed light to prevent further heartache.

Hurt and pain are all part of this journey, so be prepared and not surprised. But also, do not be un-done by it. Do not let your self- esteem be threatened.

It is a big wide world out there with billions of people. You will find those that work for you. We fall in deep love maybe two or possibly three times in a lifetime.

All the rest is merely practice. Being loved and loving takes education and no university is teaching that… yet!

Exclusively yours is a lovely way to live; when it works.

"A little sincerity is a dangerous thing, and a great deal of it is absolutely fatal." - Oscar Wilde

Details Matter

So, the grandmother was beside herself as a huge wave knocked over her small grandson and washed him out to sea.

She screamed and then begged heaven to bring him back. She offered to spend her life doing anything to thank heaven for returning him.

After a short while a big wave washed ashore and lo and behold there was her beloved grandson. She grabbed him and hugged him tightly. Then she looked up and announced, *"But, when he went in, he had a cap on his head!"*

Some people are just never satisfied…

When we look around or even take a real look at ourselves, we can observe the attention to detail that we do or do not address.

Now in many cases the attention to detail is crucial. Surgeons for example better pay supreme attention and pilots and others who take our lives in their hands.

Then there are those who pay too much attention to things that we may not deem terribly important. Have you ever been to a dog show?

Look at the way owners and handlers deal with every hair on the animal's body. Often the owners look like they could use a bit of that attention themselves.

Then there are the obsessive ones who have to have everything in place and every *I* dotted and *T* crossed and spend countless hours getting things the way they want. Heaven forbid if you leave something out of place around them. They can be quite annoying. In relationships they can make partners crazy.

If the details become too much the stress is overwhelming and certainly not productive.

There are others who only see the *big* picture and can overlook details to get to the important aspects.

Often, they can be annoying as well, as they do not pay any attention to what they consider unimportant around them. Often, they are in La La land too.

With aging what *matters* becomes more clear. The things that bothered when younger are no longer what matters now.

With age and hopefully wisdom, the world and what goes on is put in perspective as you have lived through it all before.

Relationships take a more important role in life and compromise is easier.

You can get rewards too. It's like the grandchildren are the reward for not murdering your children!

When no longer a *player* you can be appreciated for cooking a nice meal for friends or family.

You don't have to be competitive; you can just be you.

Ever notice how older people say pretty much whatever they think?

The small gestures like small details take on a whole new role. A sweet look or word; a small gift from the heart, or something personal has meaning in ways that what money bought never did.

Having some fun, doing some good, finding and giving love, and being a responsible adult is what we all attempt to achieve. Whatever we accomplish toward those goals is put in perspective and we are grateful for whatever small gains we made in that behalf. Much of what is pleasant in life is from small details. The big things that occur are short-lived usually, but the small gestures linger and are called up over time again and again.

With mid-life heebie jeebies and worries of all sorts we sometimes lose sight of the small details that go on. While it is true that we have much to take care of and work and paying bills, dealing with children, aging parents, and the like take up most of our effort and time; we can learn to pay attention to those small details that are there giving life another dimension. It's that old, *stop and smell the roses.*

No matter what the circumstances we can learn to do that. We don't need drugs to make us happy; we can be *high* on life!!

"We think in generalities, but we live in detail." - Alfred North Whitehead

Go On Flaunt It

"Woman regard all other women as their competition, whereas men as a rule only have this feeling towards other men in the same profession…" - Bertrand Russell

Here it is another major difference between the sexes. Watch and listen and observe what individuals flaunt.

For men it can be their strength, height, achievements and success in their field, or money or power.

They will keep at it, as often the wish is to have or be or do more.

For women they are competitive with other women in looks, what they wear, how they live, and what their money can or has bought.

Men like being good at what they DO.

Women like being good in the way they LOOK.

That is because they are different and want different things from one another... it never changes.

She wants to attract a man and he wants to supersede his competitors.

How the message gets out that *'I am superior'* can vary. There are big homes, with all sorts of interiors and art. There are fancy cars. There is big jewelry. Designer clothes. Plastic surgery. There are expensive trips. Fine food and wine. You name it. If it costs a lot of money someone will buy it. Even philanthropy has a role. Ever see names on buildings?

Now I believe *showing off* can be fun and I believe we are all guilty of it at times. It helps to define us; makes us feel good and important and just goes with our competitive society. Nothing wrong with it.

It is when it is a constant or really making others uncomfortable that it can be a problem and even obnoxious. Some people flaunt their intelligence. Some with *boob* jobs only wear very seductive clothes. Some... you name it.

When we have a feature, (big blue eyes), or a special thing, (a Renoir), or expertise, (being famous), it is welcomed by others to share in what we possess. When you have to *force* others to notice; it is not pleasant. The Queen doesn't have to announce that she is the Queen. We all just know it!

I am convinced that cow dung could be made the most expensive item in the universe if the right marketers went at it.

All you need is for some movie star to buy a painting and the artist is now *made.* The next paintings will be very expensive. Just go to art shows and look at the *junk* that sells for fortunes... because some famous fool bought one. What do they know about art?

People who are genuine with basic good values do not have to continually flaunt what they are or what they possess. There is the story of a wealthy man I knew who was invited to a party where all the hoi polloi was also going. He drove up in his chauffer driven Rolls Royce and noticed all the other cars were Fords etc. With that he turned around and went home and drove himself back in his driver's car! He got the message.

When you are unique, or have something special, expensive, or new, it is fun to show it off.

If you have people around you who have good values and really care about you they will be happy for you.

If they are discontent with an aspect of their own lives, they will be jealous and not happy for you.

You will know the difference.

The important part is to look at your behavior and why you are doing what you do.

If you are flaunting material things it may be because you are not secure or feeling worthy of what you really are. That's a big problem. Things will never make you a genuine, lovable, desired person… except for superficial people like yourself! Being secure about who you are is the core. What you possess, even great intelligence and achievement, is only a shallow piece of a human being.

Right now, I'm going to a fancy dinner wearing my size two Valentino dress and Manolo shoes.

Let them eat their hearts out!!

"It is only through the approval of others that self can tolerate the self." Kingsley Davis

It's Complicated

"The indispensable first step to getting the things you want out of life is this; Decide what you want." - Ben Stein

When I work with people or read Facebook comments that say, *it's complicated*, I am tempted to spend time thinking just what those complications might be. With clients, they tell me.

There are innumerable areas for complication in our lives. We cannot avoid them. They are with us every step of the way. Like a chess game, we must think and maneuver around them. It is also true that some complications are overwhelming. Some complications cannot be moved, and they have to be dealt with in a different way. Most fall into a few major categories; family, relationships, money, values, work, friends, sex, decisions. There are a slew of others as well, but let's talk about some of the more prevalent ones that are suggested by the Facebook group which is mostly young adults, and about their relationships.

Without knowing these people, I can only venture a few ideas and hunches. I cannot be sure and can only conjecture, based on my decades of counseling in these areas, and my personal life experiences, with a wide assortment of people.

The first thing I would want to know is if they are in a relationship and for how long. What are the positives and what are the areas of problem or dissension? It may be that they are not feeling loved and appreciated as they wish to be. It may be another person has come into the picture to muddy the water. They may have differences of opinions based on values they have lived.

They may have drifted apart emotionally or intellectually. They may have friends who do not approve or offer support. They may have parental or step-parent issues that are unresolved or negative. Siblings can enter into this arena as well. How money is obtained or not obtained and how it is spent is a big one, often. Sexual desire and practice can cause major adjustments.

If they are or have been married before that can get in the way. Comparisons will not help. If children are part of the mix that can sever the tie.

Sometimes health related problems arise and that will change the dynamics between people.

One of the biggies is when a partner has been the one to make the major decisions and the other one allowed it but then *grows up* or becomes more independent and no longer will tolerate that former pattern.

If you feel you are doing your level best and can communicate in constructive fashion with your mate, then all else can be solved, if mature love is at the base. Even if at times the hurt or anger get out of hand, if you can then come back and talk in a rational manner you can probably work things through and have equilibrium, or a new way of relating.

The end game is to be united as a couple and get through the tough spots together.

It's ALWAYS complicated!

If there is a lack of trust that may take a bit of doing, including forgiving. Again, the base line will tell the outcome.

What are the reasons for being together? Question number one.

If the attraction and sexual drive got the thing going in the first place that's good. If there isn't much more added with time, that ain't so good. To have and keep a worthwhile person it takes more than exciting the loins!!

The thing about it all is that both males and females are responsible in all of this and no one has a free pass.

If it's complicated it took both to get it there and it will take both to get it over the hump.

Now if the complication or set of complications; and yes, there can be more than one area, are not resolved with a fair shot of trying, it may be TOO complicated to continue. No problem… learn from it.

Use all your experiences to help you grow and move along. Think what you might have known earlier. What you might have checked for. What made the situation undoable? Learn, so that the next venture into *love land* might be improved. Happiness is relative and comes and lasts in spurts. It is an accomplishment; not a given.

If you keep repeating the same bad pattern, you need to gain insight into what you are contributing to the situation. This is not pleasant or easy or fast often. Maybe a professional counselor can help.

Life IS complicated and people and relationships, especially the romantic ones, are NEVER easy.

Uncomplicated can be boring too!

"It is a good thing to have all the props pulled out from under us occasionally. It gives us some sense of what is rock under our feet, and what is sand." - Madeleine L'Engle

Nanny Versus Mother

"Parents are the last people on earth who ought to have children." - Samuel Butler

Today we see many women having children for whatever reason and then going back to work and hiring nannies.

Some of them leave their children easily but many leave with a heavy heart. What is especially interesting is that many of these ladies do not have to work or need the money. They are educated, talented, and want to offer something to the world.

Today they are able to work for the pure pleasure of it.

The women who have to work have a different path and many resent the role they have. Being the breadwinner is never easy and putting up with what work entails is not fun a lot of the time.

Coming home after a day at the office, or wherever means not relaxation for many of today's work force.

Coming home to children who want attention or need things done for them is not pleasant or looked forward to in many cases. Just the noise level is a problem.

If there is a partner he may not be helpful either. He too may want attention, or just quiet and its mother's job to do it all.

I happen to believe that a successful accomplished mother sets a good example for children. It also makes her a more fulfilled interesting person for a mate and the outside world.

Now what about that nanny business?

Well, today there are any variety of persons willing and able to take the responsibility of child care for mothers and in some cases fathers.

They can be old, young, American or foreign.

What I always tell clients, if asked, is that the only qualification is that they be kind and patient and really like the children. References are necessary. How nice it would be if there were courses to certify such people… other than those really expensive ones.

I also think a wife needs to be sure of her relationship with her husband before introducing a pretty, young, flirty nanny into the household. There have been a number of cases where the nanny replaced the wife in short order, in the bedroom!!

At any rate, the situation becomes muddied when the mother is away and comes home tired or not ready to play with her children or respond to their needs. Over time the nanny has replaced her emotionally with her own children.

The children go to the nanny for everything!

The mother can feel she has been marginalized… and she has.

Children learn to depend on, and yes, love the caretaker who responds to them on a daily regular basis.

There can be competition for the child's love, especially if the nanny has no children of her own. She consciously or unconsciously wants the child's heart to be hers.

You can't blame her; it's natural. Giving love means you receive it in return… in all relationships and especially with children.

The early years set the tone and the child connects for life.

One of the best examples to read about is the story of Gloria Vanderbilt and her nanny.

What gets imprinted at young tender ages stays for life. Feelings get imprinted. Just seeing the same face, and smelling that person, and feeling their touch day in and day out has meaning.

While the bond of mother and child is one that cannot be broken, the relationship may need attention at some point. The best way to handle the situation is to stress what family means and show love in any way possible when with the child. A child, like an adult, can love and learn from more than one person, and in different ways.

Both mother and nanny can be important influences in a child's life and be loving and showing it in their unique ways. Each needs to feel important and secure in their role and that may take a bit of understanding and work. Mothers should know only they are the mother, and nannies need to know they are important and cared about.

We can all be number one in different arenas!!

"Women should remain at home, sit still, keep house, and bear and bring up children." - Martin Luther (1483-1546)

The Authentic You

"Be yourself is the worst advice you can give to some people." - Tom Masson

Who is the REAL you? Who knows the REAL you?

As humans, we all try to put out the best message we can about who we are.

We look a certain way, we dress in a particular manner, and we act according to our background and personality.

No one who is sane puts it all out there when they first meet someone; no matter who they are.

If they are famous their biography precedes them and no need to announce who they are.

Often a façade is presented and only with time and comfort and trust can it be put aside.

Sometimes there are big surprises about who the real person is. The old story; a wolf in sheep's clothing, is but one example.

Usually time will cause the real you to present itself.

It may take a crisis or something that angers you or it may in fact take an incident that exposes you; either in a positive or negative way.

A show now on Broadway, *Dear Evan Hansen* is a huge hit. The reason in addition to beautiful music and voices is the story.

It revolves around a young man in high school who is trying to be accepted and loved. He goes to great lengths to achieve this both within his personal family and his peers and others.

It is what we all want; to be accepted and loved for who we are.

At times, we wear masks. With Halloween around the corner this whole issue is most appropriate. I have had both gay and transgender clients who can feel free to dress and for the moment be free to be who they are. Halloween releases them. Many of us put on the costume and mask of who we might like to be or how we wish we were seen.

Many play at *Halloween* all the time.

The question always is, 'Can I be accepted and indeed loved with all that I am, the good and the bad?'

A very few try to get it over with early on and do 'gross' things as a test. Some rare people really just don't give a damn, or so they say.

At heart, I believe after decades of working with individuals of all stripes and backgrounds, that the majority of people truly want to be accepted and cared about and feel they 'matter.'

It does all begin, you guessed it, at the beginning with a mother and parents caring and loving you. They may change with time and that will hurt. Peers also have to include you. Just look around at the people dressing the same, often weirdly, or having tattoos or piercings, or green hair! They want acceptance. They want to be noticed.

At times, we ourselves may be evolving and not sure who we are or what we want to be, but that's okay. Being a full blown YOU takes many turns and many experiments.

How many people put on an affectation, or are very reserved and don't let you get close?

Just disclosing information is not intimacy. Intimacy involves feelings and vulnerability. None of us wants to be rejected, or hurt, or feel unlovable. The teen years are especially challenging in all of this.

People with disabilities, or who don't feel comfortable with their looks or bodies are especially vulnerable to self-hate even.

We all have *tender* spots emotionally. We all have wounds that grow scar tissue and we all have to deal with our authentic self. The question will ultimately be, 'If this person knew this and that about me, would they still care about me?' Frightening business to be sure.

The only way to know is to test it. Test it with someone who has tested some of all of this with you. If you are very brave just let it out with words or deeds. All you need is one person to NEED and WANT you!

Love that is real needs a REAL you; an authentic YOU!

"Whatever you may be sure of, be sure of this- That you are dreadfully like other people."- James Russell Lowell

When Your Children Become Alien

"Children are a great comfort in your old age---and they help you reach it faster, too." - Lionel Kauffman

That's right. If many people really knew what having and raising children was all about many would opt out. Today young people do question having children where other generations took it as a given and necessary expectation.

At some point and maybe at many points your children will become alien to you.

That of course, is appropriate if they are to become their own person.

It is easy when we want a child and then have that dependent adorable new life we created. Whatever we want to say, or do is up to us. We can dress them as we like and feed them what we want and take them wherever we wish. We tell them what to do and what to think and how to behave.

We have all heard and perhaps lived through the proverbial *terrible two's* when the child says, *no* to many things we want a *yes* to. But they are still under our control.

It is again a battle when the teenager begins to experiment with life and what their generation is accepting that we again feel our power threatened. The normal rebellion helps the young person begin to separate in many important ways from their parent.

The differences in opinions and behavior can be mild or fierce. Sometimes the battle causes a real breach in the love and relationship that was formerly shared. The testing out that can go on can damage the young person, sometimes for life. Parents often feel helpless and lose many battles at this stage.

The real alienation occurs in adulthood when the child, is no longer a child and can be totally independent from the parents.

Here is where the hurt to the core can manifest itself.

Often it is the differences in basic philosophy. The young adult can have values that are held that they know really matter to the parent and they don't agree.

It can be a difference of how they choose to live, what religion or lack of it, they follow.

It can be their educational choice, or career. How they spend money, and the really big one; whom they choose to marry or be with.

The child knows how to hurt the parent in a way that no one else can.

The parent then has to decide if the love and bond is strong enough to tolerate the difference and *allow* the child, who is now an adult, to be who they are.

In my many years of counseling I have had numerous cases where the rift became so great and the schism so deep that it was irreparable. The relationship was broken and neither side would give in to accept the differences. Many families have drifted apart and that wound is an open one that does not heal.

Not seeing or talking or being involved in each other's lives is a hurt that is always there even if it is never spoken about. How sad!

To see your flesh and blood be so different from you or what you wanted from them is no easy task.

Many parents feel their child owes them something; doing what they want. This is a fallacy to begin with. Children owe parents little more than respect. As adults the joy is sharing life, perhaps grandchildren, and having loving family times together.

While it is true you may not want to be together too much, the times you are all together should be at the very least pleasant and fun. Often there is tension between some members, or siblings, but that can be put aside to enjoy a holiday or special occasion if the family really has love as its' history and roots.

Old feelings and discord doesn't vanish but as adults much can be put aside for a dinner or time together.

I often ask clients if they would like the person their child has become if they were not their child. It is a question many answer with a, 'No, BUT… they are mine and we share a history and I love them.' The trick is can you respect their difference and then accept and continue to love them?

It is a two-way street as are all relationships. Some children lose respect for their parents and find it hard to deal with them; especially when the parent is older and may need them. Tables get turned.

Each generation has to move on with new ideas and behaviors or we stand still and there is no growth or personal development.

At any rate, the job of parenting is fraught with some of our most difficult times AND some of our most beloved times. Make a decision about how you choose to live in your family!!

"There are only two lasting bequests we can hope to give our children. One of these is roots; the other, wings." - Hodding Carter

Will Millennials Change This World

"You have reached the pinnacle of success as soon as you become uninterested in money, compliments, or publicity." - Dr. 0. A. Battista

We hear a lot today about this millennial group; those born from 1980 to 1994. The iGen group is from 1995 to 2012.

As with every generation before it, the older people say the new one is going to hell in a hand basket.

The values of each succeeding generation are different, and the world moves on in a variety of complicated ways; some visible like dress and appearance, and others unseen like values and some behaviors.

Current books abound about this new group. Some interesting observations and studies show promise for real change in America's values. Maybe some that are long overdue and quite apparent in coming elections.

Because of the digital technology they are freer to work in non-traditional ways; many in pajamas from home.

They do not want to *kill* themselves for the almighty dollar. Some people see them as lazy, but the bottom line is, they figure out how to get their results with minimal effort. Smart?

Their views of education and advanced formal degrees is not a priority. They believe in learning the tasks required and continuing to learn within their own lifestyle. Often, they learn from sites like Wikipedia where the best minds and information is readily available.

They also like to learn from others' experiences in real life or fictional.

They are not always engaged face to face.

What they value is their standard of daily life; not work, work, work, and that old measure of *success.* Greed is not the be all and end all, and family and community matter to them.

How refreshing!

Now the area I like to explore; you guessed it, love, and romance including sex, is most fascinating.

With all the dating and other sites like Tinder, getting to be with someone for whatever purpose is easy today. So how come the study from the Centers for Disease Control stated that 41% of high school students had sex in 2015 and that was DOWN from 54% in 1991, the reason proscribed is that they are too busy texting, watching YouTube, and using Snapshot The online forms of communication have replaced getting together in person! Saying that they want to watch Netflix or Chill may mean only that; not an invitation for sex.

Pornography is readily available and many in this age group actually prefer that to having a live person with them... imagine!!!

They are putting off marriage and becoming adults is taking them longer. Many are living with parents; not exactly conducive to a romantic evening.

This generation is focused on itself to be sure, but it is also true that they are very individualistic, and many choose not to have sex. They are careful. In a related statistic, they are careful in other aspects and have fewer car accidents and homicides. As a careful group, sex is included in that mix. Love and sex are 'messy' emotionally, and many are not interested; at least not yet.

While this group is freer sexually and sex in the twenties is wonderful, waiting until ready is not a bad pattern.

Again, it's an individual matter and they are, if nothing else, their own individuals.

We will wait, as with all generations, to see what they do for our world. So far, WE haven't done a great job in many areas!!

"He that is not handsome at 20, nor strong at 30, nor rich at 40, nor wise at 50, will never be handsome, strong, rich, or wise." - George Herbert

Uber Me A...

"So we, who are united in mind and soul, have no hesitation about sharing property. All is common among us---except our wives." - Tertullian

Nice sentiments.

Today we live in a throwaway society. Whatever it is, there is a new model coming out and we want that updated version. If what we have breaks we don't bother to spend money to repair it; we get a new one.

What our parents collected is now too bothersome to keep and polish and take care of. This generation wants it easy, and simple.

The message seems to be; don't get too attached to anything… or maybe anybody!

With robots on the way to take care of much of what we do and what work demands what will the role of people be?

If we don't want to collect antiques, or live with lovely gracious things or beautiful art work, what will our lives entail?

Moving at the drop of a hat is possible. Attachments with things or people may be on the way out.

Food is there for the asking; all kinds at any time.

And how about renting a pet before committing to one?

I have been of a strong mind for decades that we should be licensing people for the two most important roles in life; partner and parent.

You have to do more to drive a car or be a lifeguard than you have to do for those other roles. For one of them you don't even have to get out of bed!

What would it look like if we had standards that guaranteed you would be a fine partner or a wonderful parent?

It isn't difficult to set the attributes down.

True, people can and do change but we could do a bit of a job when people are reasonably mature and test them over time.

Uber has set a great example of what we can do without owning cars. It's like having a private chauffer when you want it to go wherever you choose to go at any time.

What if we could *Uber* our lives in other ways?

You can rent dresses for special occasions-a la the Oscars. You can borrow jewelry to promote a designer. You can buy and sell things on E-bay and Craig's list for temporary use. Baby things are a good example. You can rent homes and vacation places.

What, just what would be the response if you could rent or Uber people and experiences?

There are dating sites to be sure but suppose you just want a particular type of escort for the evening or for the class reunion? Why not have that service available?

There are temporary employment agencies why not temporary children, or mates?

You could *try it out* so to speak. What about this idea of checking people out first?

The *mate* would have to be certified in a number of areas including, you guessed it, sex.

Catherine the Great had that figured out. She had her ladies in waiting try out any proposed lover to see if they met her criteria. Good idea?

As far as parenting, there could be a whole slew of expertise that any prospective parent would have to be knowledgeable about.

The fact of the matter is that we could check out a number of situations that we now are just thrown into. Instead of merely *winging it* to discover that you were ill equipped to deal with many issues that came up, you could have had things tested.

Even with dating I can envision a whole realm of possibilities to enhance that whole mine field.

Uber me a great one and then I can compare!!

My whole premise is that we can improve our lives and relationships with the knowledge we have. It's not reinventing the wheel; it's just making sure it is a good one that does the job necessary!!

"It's possible to own too much. A man with one watch knows what time it is; a man with two watches is never quite sure." - Lee Segall

The Killer... Anxiety

"The natural role of twentieth century man is anxiety." - Norman Mailer

Having worked for many decades with people around their lives and relationships, and in just viewing the world I believe that most people suffer from anxiety. This can be in spurts, due to real or imagined threats, or just a steady state of being.

A certain amount of stress or worry is always part of life. It is usually short-lived and contained. It is when it becomes out of hand or extreme that we need to be concerned.

Just look around at the number of young and old people taking drugs for their moods. Look at the amount of alcohol consumed on a regular basis. Look at the displaced anger that goes on. Just look....

As humans in America we are 'supposed' to seek happiness and self-fulfillment. No problem.... PROBLEM!

The problem is that being content really only comes when we are emotionally connected to others. Finding that 'someone' can be a big source of anxiety. The problems then arise because being emotionally connected also means we are open to and subject to another's desires and wishes which may or may not coincide with our own. PROBLEM!

Anxiety can come from our own unrealized expectations. These may be faulty to begin with.

Many students get in a bad way over getting into the *right* schools or passing tests or being popular. The young students taking serious drugs on a regular basis at some of our prestigious schools is alarming.

How we look is another source of concern and a huge amount of money and time is spent in this area. Cosmetics, plastic surgery, exercise to the extreme, and clothes all fall into this category. It is stressful and we are bombarded with images that we try to copy.

And money issues cause a lot of worry.

Being happy with who you are, how you look, and your relationships, is a huge goal and not easily attained. The lucky few who get it and live comfortably for the most part are somewhat rare.

Now there are real crisis that cause anxiety. Natural disasters, accidents and health.

Just look at a medical testing waiting area and observe the people's faces, and watch as they rub their hands together, or jiggle their legs. All signs.

If you ever saw a mouse put into a tank for a snake's dinner you will never forget it. It knows what is going to happen and it rubs its' little paws together frantically. It is a sight that will stay with you.

So too with people. They exhibit their anxiety in a variety of forms and try to relieve it with a variety of coping mechanisms. Sometimes talking to a professional can give insight and help. Change is not easy, and the real task still has to be worked out with the actual people or situation involved.

How many people are frustrated at work and come home and take it out on their spouse? Many. It is safe there they believe, and the spouse is not going to fire or leave them.

How many angry people are frustrated and live miserable lives? Many.

All of this needs attention and only being secure in oneself and all that it takes and having a loving relationship will help relieve the real issue.

Whatever it takes should be employed.

Sometimes getting over the *hump* will allow you to see that you can *manage* and indeed not only survive but grow and learn to recognize the problem. It will allow you to become stronger for the next challenge that is sure to come. No one escapes anxiety. We all have our Achilles' heels and we all face danger real or imagined at some point in our lives. Some unhappy ones face much real anxiety on a regular basis. This can wear you down. Ever look at the homeless people on the streets?

Some people are done in by the situation and retreat literally or figuratively. They withdraw and if they do this emotionally, they are doomed to a life of loneliness and much unhappiness.

Some people get very involved with activities or causes and do not confront their anxiety directly. They try to *mask* it, if you will. For some that works. Again, whatever works for the individual is fine. No one can judge or tell anyone else how to live.

Having worked in a hospital for years I can tell you that anxiety is the cause of many illnesses. It will cause your body to react and that will make your defenses compromised. And yes, it can cause death. Look at who gets sick, with what illness, and what was going on when it happened. Now that doesn't mean that some people have genetic or body conditions that are not in this group; some people are prone to certain medical conditions through no fault of their own. Often conditions can be exacerbated due to anxiety.

Just having a *condition* is anxiety producing.

In the end, we are all responsible for ourselves. The trick is to get through this life in the best way possible; FOR YOU!

"If I knew what I was so anxious about, I wouldn't be so anxious." - Mignon Mc Laughlin

A Slap In The Face

"When we hate our enemies, we give them power over us—power over our sleep, our appetites, our blood pressure, our health, and our happiness. Our enemies would dance with joy if they surmised that they worry and lacerate us. Our hatred is not hurting them at all; it only turns our own days and nights into a hellish turmoil." - Unknown

There is no truer statement. But being human we do at times *hate.*

We are subjected to others who may do or say things that hurt us. Often it can be rather innocuous or in the form of a joke or sarcastic remark. Sometimes it takes the form of overt or subtle competition. It can be from anyone or over any issue.

While *copying* you in any form is said to be a form of flattery not everyone enjoys that form of praise.

Since we all have different tolerance levels what may rub off one person's back may be a mortal wound to another.

When hate is on a larger scale and people act it out in violent manners that is another story.

On a grander scale we have many problems in America and while homicide and violent crime is way down some statistics are rather interesting. This is especially true in today's climate of anti-immigration in some circles.

From a ten-year study of averages up to about 2014 there are interesting results.

Number of Americans killed annually by:
Islamic jihadist immigrants........... 2
Far right-wing terrorists...............5
All Islamic jihadist terrorists and US citizens...9
Armed toddlers........................21
Lightning.............................31
Lawnmowers...........................69
Being hit by a bus....................264
Falling out of bed....................737
Being shot by another American...11,737

What does this say about our country and its' values? What does our government do about any of it?

So, we go from a slap in the face verbally to actual killing. All in the name of human relationships and how we deal with one another.

Now on an individual case and a relationship problem, it can also be a slap in the face or a killing.

Just look at the news! There is always someone being hurt or killed and more often than not it is involving a close family member or love partner.

How many cases have I counseled where, usually a female partner, talks about an abusive situation? Often the male has been drinking or taking drugs, but not always.

Sometimes it goes on for years.

Whenever I hear these stories and the female tells me how apologetic her partner is later and how he says it will *never happen again*, I warn her; it will!

If someone needs to be in control and you are not, you will be taken advantage of. Lately our news is full of stories about powerful men doing just that with subordinates. Often it is sexual in nature.

But that can also be in intimate relationships at home.

Why would anyone put up with that?

Lots of reasons. Not counting the newsmakers who want to get ahead in a career, there are a plethora of reasons why.

We do not have to go over the list; you know it.

The natural reaction to any sort of *slap in the face*, is revenge. That too can take many forms; subtle or overt.

In this life there are victims and people who are brutes. They seem to find one another.

Just being *nasty* can suffice to get the hurt or anger out. Learning how to deal with it without physical resorts should be taught in schools. Hit the pillow!

Lynn Hubschman

Women have changed and that is helping all of this. This generation of men and women may indeed relate in more positive ways and still keep flirtation and all that goes into a relationship more positive.

"Violence is counter-productive and produces changes of a sort you don't want. It is a very dangerous instrument and can destroy those who wield it." - John Gardner

Once A Loser…

"The fear of failure is a realistic one because, in general the chances of failing are much greater than those of succeeding, and because failures in a competitive society entail a realistic frustration of needs. They mean not only economic insecurity, but also loss of prestige and all kinds of emotional frustration." - Karen Horney

We all know them; the losers among us. They come in all stripes and colors.

The old adage that 'once a loser, always a loser' holds true in most cases. It can start in childhood when you don't have what other kids have, you don't dress like them, you are not popular or with the *in* crowd. The message begins.

Now it may be worked through, however, if by the thirties and certainly by the forties you have not *made* it, you are a loser. You may have been a *loser* in an important relationship. You may have screwed up your early jobs, or you may just have drifted into loser land.

Losers are not always immediately identified. They may have bad resumes that they doctor up or they may come across as really trying to succeed. You may buy that for a bit. However, in pretty short order you will see it for what it is. The loser may try to get money from you or be a parasite on someone else. They are ALWAYS in need of money!

They may seem very *busy* but it's like a dog chasing its' tail; it goes nowhere.

They can try to be sociable and smile a lot but it's all vapid. There is no substance to them. They make bad decisions, and are not competent or accomplished.

I have worked with some who have a fine education but never got it together to earn a living. Like everyone, they find their level. They are not the *A* list or even the *C* list. They are way down the alphabet. There are some entrepreneurs who go up and down and some do succeed. They are a different category. There are creative people who just don't get 'discovered.' They are also another group. Today's technical world has young bright people taking over the fast- moving world they inhabit. They are fabulous. The older group here quickly can fall into 'loser.'

Luck may play a part but that will merely open the door. Meeting the challenge is the test. Losers like to blame others or become negative putting others down to feel better about themselves. Inside they know the truth.

If you are emotionally involved with a loser you may choose that to feel *needed* and important. That usually doesn't last forever. You will recognize your *mistake*. You cannot delude yourself.

As a professional we see these people but their limits are so crystal clear in short order that if we are well trained and legitimate we do not continue to see them as they are *hopeless*.

With aging, they become even more *pathetic* and can turn to other sources for a bit of relief. Age only compounds the problem they have had for years.

So, beware the losers as you do not want to be identified with them in any way. Do not be fooled!!

"Since modern man experiences himself both as the seller and as the commodity to be sold on the market, his self- esteem depends on conditions beyond his control. If he is "successful" he is valuable; if he is not, he is worthless" - Erich From

Not Crazy Enough

"The mind is its own place, and in itself can make a heaven of Hell, a hell of Heaven." - John Milton

That's right. We can think all sorts of things and many of them do not serve us well or make us lead better lives.

Often, I have had clients ask if they were, *crazy*.

Now crazy is a bantered around word.

Real *crazy* needs a diagnosis from a professional. Then we know who is schizophrenic, paranoid, bi-polar, clinically depressed, borderline personality and so on. There are pretty clear definitions of these disorders.

Sometimes people go undiagnosed for years. Some commit terrible crimes or horrible behavior that gets them labeled.

But, by and large, most people have moments or periods where they think and maybe even act bizarrely.

Now we are not speaking about drugs or alcohol and the reactions that temporarily, for the most part, make individuals do *crazy* things.

Losing inhibition can take a variety of forms, but most are basically harmless.

Sometimes people have passing thoughts that frighten them. I had a client who after giving birth would look at the tiny baby and think, *I could kill this child, easily. It is so small.* She thankfully never did anything but care for the baby. The mere thoughts frightened her to come to me and make sure all was well. It was in her head.

Then I have people talk about being in a high place and thinking they could jump over the balcony, cliff, et cetera. Passing thoughts.

Passing thoughts or occasional *funny* out of the ordinary behaviors can be managed and tolerated.

When it crosses that line you and especially others will notice it and maybe be alarmed.

Being a 'bit' different makes you unique and in many instances quite interesting.

If it is a put on or an act to force that it will be seen as a sham.

Most people have *quirks* that set them apart or make them annoying to say the least.

Many are compulsive behaviors that mean you say the same things over and over or do things obsessively. In many cases I just call it being responsible and taking care of business.

Today especially, no one seems to care to do a job well. We HAVE to go over things many times to be sure they are done correctly. That is not crazy, it's getting the job done.

Psychiatrists are sought for many reasons. Most of the time they are seen for a short-term problem or difficulty in life. When they get their hands on you, many make it a lifetime annuity. I had several clients tell me they were seen regularly at high fees for problems that eventually righted themselves. I have even had some tell me the doctor told them not to get married or have children, only for them to do just that and live happy lives. That's criminal! I have even had several tell me the doctor had regular sexual relations with them. Totally unethical. I encouraged them to tell the licensing board about that.

There are some wonderful *helpers* in a few professions; psychiatrists, psychologists, and social workers, mainly.

They can help you gain insight into your behavior, see where it originated from, and help you change behavior that is not working well for you and your life.

The main thing to look for is someone that you like and relate to well. It is always helpful to know their background and that they themselves have figured out how to live well.

Sometimes medication can help over a hump. Only MDs can write prescriptions.

Some people can contain their *craziness* and can compartmentalize their issues.

They may have a responsible job but at home they let it all hang out and behave badly.

Sometimes an event or reminder of a childhood problem may resurface, and a person acts out briefly and wildly. It is short-lived, and they may apologize. All in the normal range.

We can control our thoughts and we need to in order to function well.

In the end however they are merely thoughts. It is when behavior gets in the act that we need to be careful.

Many great things happen as a result of our dreams and thoughts. Many wonderful behaviors started out as thoughts. These are the good thoughts and we can program ourselves. We can put up a *stop sign* when we go down the road to bad thoughts. Many times, these thoughts are figments of our imagination and not reality. We believe someone or something bad is going on. We can make ourselves, *crazy* over things that never happened or never will happen. We have vivid imaginations. The thing is to use it for our welfare not our distress.

A psychiatrist asked a young man what he did with his time. He responded he just sat around. The doctor asked if he had no desire to go out with girls. He said he did. "Why don't you, then?" asked the doctor.

"My wife won't let me," he said. Ha, Ha, but there it is; get the facts!

The expression *crazy like a fox*, has different connotations. There, it is using your thoughts for manipulation purposes. Conniving is not crazy.

So, be crazy once in a while… it can be freeing!

"A neurotic is a man who builds a castle in the air. A psychotic is the man who lives in it. A psychiatrist is the man who collects the rent." - Jerome Lawrence

Not My Problem

"You often get a better hold upon a problem by going away from it for a time and dismissing it from your mind altogether." - Dr. Frank Crane

Nice words and quite frankly, easier said than done.

As a therapist for decades I can let you in on a well-kept secret; many problems are solved in just that way. However, for many people talking to a therapist and working through a situation better equips them for future difficulties.

It is not easy to *just forget* about what you see, and feel is a problem for you.

Problems come in categories. Those that are real and current, those that are totally out of your control, and those that you manufacture.

The real ones are usually right there in your face. They can be financial or health or individuals who upset you.

Those that are out of the blue can hit you and knock you over.

And then there are those that you think about that *might* happen.

It is truly amazing the number of people who think about all the *what ifs* and get worked up, sometimes to distraction, over probabilities that may never occur.

I have had people get physically ill in this manner.

Yes, life is fraught with all forms of unpleasantness, and things that happen to us that we do not wish upon ourselves. It takes strength; emotional strength, to survive and surmount much of what we experience.

What happens to us as individuals naturally takes precedence. We want to be free of problems.

As a result, we try to live out our lives trouble free as best we can.

If we lose our job, have a car break down, fight with our friends or spouses, or have a health issue we are in the midst of a personal problem and attempt with all our resources to make the situation go away or get better. We all have problems of one sort or another; no way to get around it.

Yes, if you are financially secure many problems are easier to get through. Some however are just situations where you are in better surroundings to have a fight or get a car repaired.

Money, while a big problem in a whole slew of areas, is not the total answer.

Now when it comes to all the things that we worry about and make a problem, many of these if not the majority, may never happen.

The other big issue I hear are all the *alleged* problems that people take on that could well be handled with the phrase, *Not my problem.*

Think about it. How many times have you heard and gotten upset over someone else's difficulties?

When it comes to children it is true we try to make things better for them as they are too young and inexperienced to handle many things.

If we know of bad things that affect our friends or people, we care about we can empathize and that's a good thing. We could use more empathy in this current world. *BUT* and it is a big, *BUT* we need not take on the emotional baggage when it is not necessary. How can we separate?

For some it is not easy but for others you can learn and practice, and mean it, when you say,

Not my problem.

Try it; repeat after me… Not my problem.

Those things we have no control over make it easier, but those things that happen to people we are involved with make it hard.

You can try and be helpful while distancing yourself emotionally and really not taking the situation on emotionally yourself. If you are a sensitive and caring person, it is harder.

You do care and that again is a nice quality. If it takes too much out of you then you are paying an unnecessary price for being understanding and loving.

Perhaps you can let it *bother* you for the short term but quickly learn how to move on with other aspects of your current life. For in truth, it is not your problem and the resolution will come without your involvement. Time does heal, and many helpful *suggestions* will not solve it in the long run.

A good way to practice is with current events that you have no control over but do bother you.

While in truth some may indeed affect you in the end and become problems the immediate situation is, not your problem.

I once had an elderly banjo teacher… yes I love the banjo and wanted to start an all-female Mummer's band for the New Year's parade in Philadelphia, who said, "Lynn, there are no problems…. only solutions."

Never did learn to play well and much too cold to march in skimpy costumes in a parade!

"The best way to escape from a problem is to solve it." - Brendan Francis

Mothers Set The Stage

"The successful mother sets her children free and becomes freer herself in the process." - Robert J. Havighurst

True, true, true. But how to get there… that's the issue and big question.

Mother's Day is coming up and we all know what that means.

It is giving or sending a card, flowers, candy, a gift or a visit.

There are brunches, lunches, and dinners galore all over the place. It's a big deal.

For those that are not *blessed* with being a mother you may be *like* a mother to someone and feel that glow and warmth.

It's a big money-maker day, to be sure, and it is only one day, but it sends a message.

Now if your relationship is honky-dory, great. You celebrate a lot of mother's days all year. If it ain't so hot this may be a bittersweet day, and if, in fact you have a bad or non-existent relationship with your mother it is painful.

If you were adopted, or lost your mother early there are other feelings you get caught up in. There is no perfect to be sure but whatever you received in mothering sets the stage for the rest of your life.

If the relationship is a good one and you like or admire your mother, you will gladly follow in her footsteps with a bit of personal variation and generational changes. If you did not like the example you were given you may *fight* all your life to be different. Now that's for females.

For males you have a different road to travel when it comes to *mother*.

In most cases you had to fight the mostly unconscious feelings that you lived with from birth about wanting to be close and loving her OR hating her and wanting to get as far away as possible emotionally from her.

But guess what? You will more than likely marry or be connected intimately with a female just like her. True. Scary, right?

The pattern gets in when you are not even aware and by the time you realize what you are dealing with it's too late to change. She is your idea of female. She represents what women are about.

You can change some of it to be sure, but the real nitty gritty is in you

As a marriage counselor for over three decades I can tell you that looking at couples and taking the histories I know it before they tell me.

The guy who has to lie to his spouse all the time had a domineering, controlling, demanding mother. Her anger frightened him, so he avoided, almost at all costs, displeasing her. Turn that into, *wife* and you have the same pattern repeating itself.

Then the really big issue; he has to choose another woman to be close to that is NOT his mother. His *mommy* may really not like that idea. She may even try to sabotage the relationship… forever!

Letting a child mature, grow up, have their own ideas, and ways of behaving, making choices contrary to your own is a mother's most difficult task.

The process normally begins in adolescence, but it may not, and it may never be done, or finished well. It means that *mother* has to retreat from being *mother* and that is very, very difficult; especially for controlling women who have ALL the answers.

Look around on this Mother's Day and see how children, of all ages, relate to their mothers.

Look at you and know what you really feel for your own mother.

What do you share and tell? What do you still want from her?

If she is no longer with you what do you remember and miss?

Do you have any guilt about anything relating to her? Where does it come from?

I have not mentioned sharing a mother with her spouse, or other siblings, or step-families, but that can also be troublesome in your mind and feeling.

There are also mothers who are *competitive* with their children as they themselves age. Not a pretty sight.

No relationship is easy and this one colors a lot of who you are, who you will become, and how you will relate to others. The best advice is to become aware early on and try to change what doesn't work for you. It is not an easy task, but many have been successful in the long run and it is certainly worth the struggle.

So, on Mother's Day mothers wish to be acknowledged for what they brought into the world and appreciated for all they gave. They can be honest, hopefully, about the other side as well, but with it all; make it a joyful day!!

"My mother was dead for five years before I knew that I had loved her very much." - Lillian Hellman

Money Doesn't Care Who Has It

"When I was young I thought that money was the most important thing in life; now that I am old I know that it is." - Oscar Wilde

Anyone who is foolish enough or not living in reality to think that money doesn't matter just hasn't had to deal with real life.

The fact of the matter is that money is not just a necessity it is what makes your life what it is.

Yes, you don't want money to be your god, but you need enough to live the way you choose.

As a young person it is easy to live very modestly and just *get by*, but with time and what life dishes out you had better have the where with all to not just survive but to really enjoy what life has to offer.

Now it is true we all have different needs and expectations, and that's fine. We all need to learn how to stand on our own two feet and be responsible for our own lives.

Today both men and women have learned that.

There are circumstances where some people are indeed incapable of working or making a living.

This can be due to illness, mental or emotional incapacity, or wanting to be creative without being paid for it.

Those circumstances can be addressed in other ways, usually by government subsidies.

But we really do not learn how to not just earn money, improve our employment opportunities, or manage money or invest it well.

I know a college dean who told me he could never balance a check book until he was well into his thirties with a family to support!

While our way of living may be meager as young people, as we get older, we need money. If we have children, we need more money to make their lives pleasant.

Learning what it takes to make money is a lesson well learned early in life. There are many very wealthy people who make their children work at menial tasks to earn a dollar. Good lesson.

What is interesting is that many people who make a lot of money later in their lives remember what it took and are rather tight fisted. Believe me there will be children who know how to spend it when they inherit it!

Inherited wealth is another story. That comes easily usually, and the value of hard work is often not learned. Sometimes that money is squandered as well.

It's a game and has never been different throughout history.

Money and power that goes with it are what makes governments, and tall buildings with peoples' names on them!!

Beyond the basics it is nice to have enough money so that if you need a new car you don't have to lose sleep at night. Money is nice in order to do gracious things for your family and others.

Some people need a private jet to go places, others are happy just to be able to sit in coach and go someplace. We all have different standards and ascribe to different goals.

There are also hypocrites and parasites that talk a good game while using others' resources.

And do not kid yourself, with aging, money is extremely important to look good, not have to work hard, and to have good care, medical and otherwise.

True it doesn't cause happiness but it sure as hell makes unhappiness less and in better surroundings.

And, true; it can't buy love, but it can and often does buy substitutes... watch the current news!

I have a friend who often said he frequently has big arguments with his wife and he is grateful that they can occur in first class gorgeous hotel rooms. It makes it better...

It is nice to have *disposable* income to do whatever you want with it. See something you want and bingo... it's yours. No worry, no fuss, no after recrimination.

Learning the value of money when you are young and learning how to invest and use it and then earning it at something you enjoy and then spending and saving it as you wish are good goals.

Living within your means is a hard lesson and many do not. There is too much out there to buy, or upgrade to. It takes discipline. It can make people unhappy to not *have*.

Being competitive can be a game and there are a lot of very successful people who never have 'enough;' not for the money but for the message it conveys.

All through history, no matter the society, money matters. Go to Pompeii and see the houses of the wealthy that remain. Look at the art work there. A very clear message; *I was important, and this is how I lived.* So, in the end, you and you alone must decide what is realistic for you and then go achieve it. Then look at your bank balance and empty your pockets!!

"Money is a terrible master but an excellent servant." - P.T. Barnum

Let Me Stress This

"Worry affects the circulation, the heart, the glands, the whole nervous system. I have never known a man who died from overwork, but many who died from doubt." - Charles H. Mayo

We all have it; stress. It may come and go, and the reasons are as varied as are the individuals who experience it. It can be a killer.

Sometimes it takes the more innocuous form of a worry. At times it can be an annoyance. Other times it is an inconvenience or a bother. It can come from our own set of standards or from an outside source. Family, friends, work, or just life in general.

We know it when it occurs as it usually is a visceral response. Our body signals us. We can have headaches, a tight throat, a welling up of anger or any other series of bodily reactions.

When we FEEL it, we are able to respond. How we respond is usually in proportion to the threat we feel.

It is fascinating that the stress we place on things is exactly the reason we feel STRESS.

It is a double-edged sword, so to speak.

What *matters* to us affects us when any of that is challenged or lost.

Of course there are the actual physical things that normally can occur; body changes, accidents, property damage, and so on.

Then there are the emotional relationship aspects that cause us bad feelings. The main one is loss of a spouse. The second most troubling thing in life is said to be a major move of your home.

If we put it in perspective you might think about the fact that dinosaurs were wiped out over 60 million years ago by an asteroid in the Gulf of

Mexico, it is believed. The gases released went around this earth and killed off all but the really strong.

Being *strong* will help. What do we mean by that?

Basically it is being able to withstand the vicissitudes of life. By experiencing things that go *wrong* and not succumbing we can learn to go on and survive. It can even make us better in other areas as a result. The 'strong' often have professions to help the *weaker.*

Many people attempt to treat themselves to lessen or rid the stress. There is a huge problem with alcohol, drugs, anger, and even suicide. People hurt, and they try anything to alleviate that horrible feeling. Today there are any number of stresses in just daily life.

The individual tolerance level varies, and the reactions follow.

If children learn that parents solve their problems and frustrations, they do not learn to handle stress.

Much of life is routine and quite frankly, boring. But when things are not the way you want them, or things happen out of the blue stress enters. There are in fact people who like stress and look for it or cause it as that makes them feel alive.

It is better than having no feeling for them.

The real stress that causes the ultimate of this feeling I believe, comes from the ending or fear of ending in a romantic, love relationship. There is no emotional pain like that. You feel dead and may wish or actually cause your death. It happens more than we might like to believe.

Many murders occur around this fact. It's the *If I can't have you no one can.*

Look at what ticks people off and how they handle it. Many times, it focuses on the lack of control over a situation or person. We don't like that feeling. However true love demands just that.

It can be what appears to be minor *offenses*. He didn't call. She looked at me funny. Something I don't like was said. He or she reacted in a manner that I don't appreciate. You name it; it happens. The best way to deal with any stress is to share it and that will lighten the burden. Having a caring ear and soothing response will help. Find it!!

"When I look back on all these worries I remember the story of the old man who said on his deathbed that he had had a lot of trouble in his life, most of which never happened." - Winston Churchill

It's ALL Bullshit

"Life is an onion which one peels crying." - French Proverb

A young man I know recently had a conversation with me and we were discussing difficulties in relationships. At the end of part of our talk he turned and said, "Well, everything is finite."

In contemplating his early wisdom, I was struck by how right he is.

Everything is so temporary and we as humans really do not take that into consideration as we sleepwalk through life.

It is only as a person comes to the point in life where the days left are so much fewer than the days lived that many even realize it's really a short walk.

Now don't get me wrong, and you know what I think about life and especially love; there is much to rejoice in. But it is in spurts and moments.

We are our worst enemies and we do most of it through a waste of time on nonsense and bad feelings. We can work on it. We can push ourselves to be better. It is up to us and us alone.

The main thing and it's a biggy, is to check our values. I recently heard a Charlie Rose program where he spoke with both Warren Buffett and Bill Gates. What a pleasure. Both of these hugely *successful* men said they value their family and human relationships above all else. This is great news for the majority of we humans who will not be in their league with talent and achievement. It is the core of what brings joy.

It is NOT money, power, fame, or influence.

Interestingly when I read the book about the Dalai Lama, he expressed the idea that man's ultimate goal is to not *suffer*. Think about that. How and why do people *suffer*?

What are our goals and desires? How do we go about obtaining them?

Well, my title says it. Most of what we get caught up in is *Bullshit*.

What is that you ask?

Well, it's the not feeling worthy or appreciated the way we want. It's being envious or feeling *less than* someone else.

It's feeling we can't rise to the occasion.

We fill our lives with anger and hate. We don't forgive. We want revenge.

We want to be in control, and we want our desires met and little or no responsibility for our behavior.

Bad stuff.

The trick is to have it like a bank account and have *emotional currency*.

That means building up a reservoir of good feelings. Good thoughts. Good relations with others. AND… you got it; learning how to truly give love.

When you get *outside* of the YOUNESS you are in another realm and dimension. You are there for the 'other.'

If the other is a *we* then that can always be built upon. History together will assist but that's not the whole story. It's the day in and day out and dealing with all the crap that life is about that needs attention. That's there and won't disappear and that's part of the bullshit but that's not where the joy will come from.

Transitory, yes, finite, yes, but those moments can be built upon and remembered and become the stuff that makes this life worthwhile.

Behavior has consequences and we have all had our own share of bad behavior. But you can't buy TIME. It is fleeting and what is gone is over and what you waste today doesn't come back.

And no, it can't be all hunky-dory, but it can be enough so that at the end you feel you lived fully and well.

There is enough in this life that we cannot control and enough really yucky stuff out there. But if we are able to be loving we can get through all the bullshit and have a *successful,* really *successful* life in the most meaningful of ways.

Recognize bullshit and then move on to AUTHENTIC!!

"Life is a dream, and it is well that it is so, or who could survive some of its' experiences?" - Isadora Duncan

Is There Really Free Will

"He who can follow his own will is a king." - Irish Proverb

We have been led to believe that we have a free will. Do we, really?

I think it is a very limited concept and not so free at all.

Think about it.

We are governed by our society, our class, and our immediate values.

We have to care about what our wants entail and how far we can go with expressing them. Who among us is so free, spontaneous, and uninhibited to allow ourselves to do just what we feel like doing whenever we choose to do it? No one!

There are cultures where it is common and indeed acceptable to relieve one's bodily functions out in the open in public when the need arises. Not so in our country.

There are places in this world where free sex is not just tolerated but welcomed. Not so here.

There are places where... fill in the blank.

How *free* are we?

We are free to follow the mores and laws that surround us.

It is true people break these all the time and most get 'caught' and pay a price, or jail sentence. Some do get away with *murder*, real or imagined.

As far as the physical aspects; your freedom ends where my nose begins!

It is nice to believe we are *free* and indeed we are in many respects. We can speak our minds, except for yelling *Fire* in a public place when there is no fire.

We can dress pretty much the way we choose. Unfortunately, that can raise eyebrows in many instances, but no harm.

We can move about pretty freely, and we can choose our professions and mates. This is not true in many parts of the world.

Often poor choices are made with this so-called freedom. But here again, we can use the experience for our future learning. Hopefully the poor decisions do not damage us for life. That is free will at its' worst.

If we are acting freely under the influence of drugs, or alcohol, or another's will we may make very bad decisions and act on them in harmful ways.

Recently, I watched a news report where a young man, a teenager, was out drinking and then drove his girlfriend home and had a traffic accident that ended with her dying. While he was punished and remorseful, he ended up starting to speak to groups of young people about his experience and hoped they would avoid what happened to him.

That never would have happened without his bad decision to drive under the influence of alcohol.

Sometimes it takes a tragedy or horrible life event to get people to look at their decision-making process.

A totally free will would never be possible.

If it was, we would have a chaotic world.

Sometimes the problems occur when one's concept of freedom is at variance with another's background and rules of behavior.

If I am free to do such and such and go about doing it and you are not, that can be a great disconnect.

This happens frequently in dating and relationships.

It might be a good idea to spell out and discuss the forms of behavior we want to tolerate and maybe even respect. At times we can change our own views when we think there is a better way.

What I would like you to understand and do may be quite different from what I am used to doing or expecting from a partner.

There is much to be said for being *free*, and we enjoy a lot of that as Americans. We often lose sight of the fact that many people in this world do not have that luxury.

In many places the laws, role, and family you come from dominate your life choices. Here we can develop and do pretty much whatever our wishes and talents allow.

If I am *free* to be me, then it is easier for me to allow you to be *free* to be you. BUT that takes a good bit of acceptance and understanding.

It is fun to be silly at times and to allow that part of your self expression.

Those people who are always in control and checking every angle are often missing out on the fun of life.

They are responsible people true, but looking at everything that could go wrong, like a lawyer, makes life a bit tedious. That's not really freedom.

Some people are too willful just to be stubborn or stand out. That is not a good thing.

As children we are under our parents' authority and we submit to their will for approval and to avoid punishment. As adults, a lot of that remains and we have the same standards and behave accordingly. It is hard to shake those early messages. Some may be good but to be ourselves we need to evaluate the will we alone can exercise when we are responsible for ourselves. We also need to be aware of what we do as parents and how we force our will on our children.

If our will is out of sync with the rest of our society, we may be creative in an effective way or we just may be different, and a bit crazy!

"If it's got to be a battle of wills, I'll fight the devil himself, as long as the necessity lasts. But it's not my idea of life." - D.H. Lawrence

Is Patience Still A Virtue

"Prayer of the modern American: Dear God, I pray for patience. And I want it right now!" - Oren Arnold

Right NOW!

If we look at our lives today they are filled with a lack of this thing called patience.

Nothing is done slowly or with ease. Everything is at a frantic pace, and most of it for no reason at all.

We live fast.

We drive fast. We eat fast.

Our attention span is minimal.

We watch TV, and the news in sound bites.

We are on the cell phone and on the computer with instant results.

Who has written or received a hand-written note lately?

Who has cooked a special dish that took hours?

Instant answers are there on Google. Finding people is available with a click of the mouse.

Getting services is often our undoing.

Have you tried to get information from any service provider lately? They put you on hold or on an automatic non-person system. When you do get a live human on the other end or at a counter they are basically retarded or with an attitude or in Asia and not understanding or speaking English well.

Is it any wonder Americans are on Opioids?

Frustration and anger loom large in our daily lives. We want what we want when we want it... period!!

Recently in a bank, I saw an elderly man in front of me talking to the clerk. He had something he wanted done and he kept telling her, getting louder and louder. His voice rose, and he looked like he was having apoplexy or a heart attack.

Finally, she did what he needed and calmly turned to him saying, *Have a nice day.*

I thought he was going to jump over the counter and choke her.

It goes on everywhere.

Being patient has pretty much gone by the boards.

What do you wait for? What does take time and attention?

How patient are you, really?

How about those inconsiderate people who are always late?

Can you allow time to pass? Easily?

Recently I had a client who talked about being furious with her partner and carrying on and on about what was bothering her. She was totally exasperated when he finally turned to her and said, *Can I have a kiss?*

It diffused the situation and brought in humor, but it did not solve the problem That would take time and understanding… patience.

When it comes to relationships things cannot be worked out in an instant. Sometimes it takes a long time to have change occur.

With communication often partners want their other half to have the same thoughts and ideas and be able to express them right away. They want the problem solved immediately. Men perhaps more than women. They are ready to move on quicker.

Now with intimacy that definitely takes patience.

It can be slam, bam, thank you M'am but how much better is it when there is time to talk, share feelings, touch, and slow movements?

Patience is definitely a virtue here.

Women do NOT achieve orgasm quickly. It takes time.

As men get older, they too need patience enacted in their behalf. Some clients talk about just getting IT over with and how long does it have to take? Not a good attitude to please oneself, let alone a partner.

Often, we have patience with young children understanding their limitations due to age. Why not try to keep that same perspective in other areas? Tenacity can really pay off in a lot of situations.

A lot of what we hurry about doing is so very useless and unnecessary. Think what has given you the best part of your life. I'll bet it wasn't anything fast.

Instant is good in making quick Jello dessert but not for most of what gives pleasure in this life!

"The first virtue: patience. Nothing to do with people waiting. It is more like obstinacy." - Andre' Gide

I Will Survive

"It is not clear that intelligence has any long-term survival value." - Stephen Hawking

Listen to the song with the same title, *I Will Survive* by Gloria Gaynor and you will get the idea.

Survival is an accomplishment not a given.

We all go through periods and certainly history has shown that survival as an individual, country or world doesn't happen by *magic*.

There are any number of people, places, and even our own planet, that have *given up*. From time to time, or even forever; some do not go on or continue.

Our planet has *died* several times before and today many fear that happening again. Some through human causes and some just nature's evolution.

Countries have gone through destruction and many have not survived or not survived as they had done before. Resiliency may have a lot to do with it. Changing the way things were done before can help in many instances.

And so too with we humans.

How many individuals and families have gone through not just *tough* times, but horrific times and come through, not unscathed but maybe stronger or bent.

Even in concentration camps some women gave birth. That's really hope and faith in a better future, if it wasn't an accident.

But today we are faced with a number of facts that are disturbing and give cause for concern.

The suicide rate for females is dramatically higher. People are using opioids, other drugs, and alcohol, to a dramatic extent.

Our infrastructure is deteriorated to an alarming degree.

Our educational system is not producing learned people. Well, maybe it is better to survive happily if you are dumb!

People are not *nice* for the most part and being an individual who is independent and making money seems to be what matters.

Forget politeness and looking like you care about how you look.

Robots may soon be taking over a lot of what we think of as *humanity*. The prediction is that by 2020 you will spend more time in contact with a robot than with your spouse! That may be a relief for some, as a matter of fact…

HOWEVER, the other side of the coin is that it does take gumption, strength, and maybe just a sliver of hope to get through.

There are some great positive things happening around us. There are wonderful researchers, for example, at places like the Cleveland Clinic working on a vaccine for breast cancer.

There are creative writers and just decent people struggling to make this a better place to live and work, and have the planet come together for the good of all.

There are sturdy families helping one another and sharing good and bad times together.

There are neighbors reaching out to offer a helping hand.

And there are individuals struggling to find deeper meaning in their lives with one another.

Of course, you knew I'd get there... there is only one course for action; learn how to really LOVE!!

Without that, you as an individual, cannot offer much to another or to the community or to the world.

It is the most difficult learning in the world. For some it may come easily because they were loved from the start and learned to love themselves first; but for many, it is a slow painful process. There is always rejection, hurt, betrayal, and despair along the way.

The trick is to survive all of that and keep pushing ahead. Do not give up as long as you breathe.

Find a way to care... about anything. Then work on caring about another human being. There are always people out there who need caring and love. It is up to you to reach out and find them. They will not come floating through your window. YOU go out and find them!!

Just surviving is not enough… it is how you survive!

"Life comes from physical survival; but the good life comes from what we care about." - Rollo May

How Much Stuff

"And when you die, have everything buried with you. If the next wife wants it, make her dig. I'm going to have a mausoleum. More closet space." - Joan Rivers

What do you have? What do you *collect*? What do you keep?

The now deceased comedian George Carlin did a routine about our, *stuff.* He talked about it all in a humorous fashion, but the truth is our *things* matter… to us.

What do you have in material things? Your home, your furniture, your car, your art works, your jewelry, your clothes. They all tell something about you, what matters to you, and who you are.

Certainly, the place you live in tells what kind of person you are and your state of finances. This is also a sign of the type of people around you who are in the same class and speak the same language and have similar life styles and experiences.

There are people who live *below* their means and like that. They perhaps grew up there or just feel comfortable surrounded by people who are a bit different from them. Where you live determines where you meet others, usually where your children go to school and so on.

Some, and this is perhaps a large group, live *above* their means. They are ascribing to a *better* life for themselves and their children. Some just like to have others think well of them and this is a means to that end. Many end up in debt and others forfeit their dreams and have sorry ends as a result. Some go to extremes and often ill-gotten or illegal ways to fund their life style.

How you furnish your *place* also sends a message. In years past, families collected beautiful antique pieces, and lovely table ware and silver for entertaining. Today young people want minimalistic everything. Ikea, straight simple lines, and bland colors are the norm. Not many people are throwing dinner parties with imported china, Baccarat crystal, and sterling silver flatware. It all needs attention of which they have little interest or time for.

Recently, I attended a talk by one of the country's leading auction house personnel. He was very emphatic stating that your children will not get anything for all those beautiful antiques you spent a lifetime collecting. No one wants them!! So, you just enjoy them....

Cars show the outside world what you can afford. Strangers can take notice. On the Internet and Facebook many guys are showing their cars. It's a way to impress some females. Again... can they afford them or is it a debt they really can't afford?

Jewelry is a biggy for females and also for a certain group of males. It is in your face!

Clothes used to tell a lot about you but today that's not the case. Blue jeans, shorts, tee shirts and so on are de rigueur for the whole world. Wearing and displaying a designer's name is often the case. Wearing cute sayings on your shirt is common. Today only women usually know when another woman is wearing an expensive dress or shoes!

Collecting art, books, rare items, antiques, and so on still goes on but it is for the owner's pleasure and usually not as an investment except in very few cases.

Then, how much do we need or in this case, want? Up to the individual. How much can be used? All very personal questions.

When it comes to *stuff* in relationships, that's where it can get sticky.

Your *stuff*, versus my, *stuff.* What is OUR money spent on?

He wants sports tickets or memorabilia. He wants electronics. She wants clothes, and a vacation. And so on.

Who decides? Maybe take turns? There are many arguments and even breakups because of all of this.

Many couples end up in huge credit card debt with all this going on.

Everyone wants what they want; when they want it. The mature have to learn discipline and financial responsibility and fiscal information.

Maybe the best *stuff* is a good education and money invested wisely.

How often do we read about famous people; sports figures, movie stars, and so on who have made fortunes and either squandered it all or had people take advantage of them? How many have found that the money and *stuff* didn't bring them happiness and they turned to drugs and so on?

Handling money is a big responsibility and like everything else in life it takes knowledge and experience. Again, we don't teach any of this in schools for the general public.

Perhaps being and attracting intelligent, creative people is the best *accumulation* in the end.

But don't get me wrong; it all takes money!

Not sure I agree with this but here it is;

"Happiness consists not in having much, but in being content with little." - Marguerite Gardiner

Heaven Help The Millennials

"It's hard for the modern generation to understand Thoreau, who lived beside a pond but didn't own water skis or a snorkel." - Bill Vaughan

That about sums it up.

If you are or live with or work with a millennial you will know exactly what they are about.

They think the world is their oyster and they can call the shots.

Nice work if you can get it, but for most that just ain't the way this world works.

While every generation thinks the next one is going to hell, this one is not unique.

They really do believe they are special and can write their own ticket.

Where did that attitude come from?

Probably from the homes in which they grew up. Because their grandparents or great grandparents had to toil from dawn to dusk at any menial job just to feed their families, this groups' parents wanted life to be easier for their children.

And easier they made it. They made them think they were god's gifts on earth, bought them everything they wanted, gave them every opportunity with lessons, education, and showed them the good parts of the world. Why not come out with an inflated ego? That in itself is not a bad thing.

Why not then want everything handed to you on a silver platter?

Watch the Facebook piece titled, *The Millennial's Job Interview.*

While it is truly hysterical it is not off the mark.

She is not coming to work at eight o'clock. She is having her coffee at Starbucks first. No, she doesn't have specific technology skills. The person interviewing her is not saying nice things to her, so she wants to know if she can speak to the HR person, and so on.

I have spoken with a number of people who offer jobs and they have all said that the millennials are a real trip. They want to come in, be paid top dollar, and not work hard or long. The attitude is different from other generations.

While their parents probably sacrificed in any number of areas to provide well for their families and many became professionals working hard, their children do not want to follow that path.

Now there are groups that do want to work hard and become *successful* in that old definition. Many are foreign born or come from poorer backgrounds and they want to *get ahead*.

What is good and maybe even redeeming and endearing for the millennials is that money is not their be all and end all. They want to have time for other pursuits. They appreciate nature in a new way as a group. All of this may be good for our society.

The real changes are in my areas of interest; marriage and family, and just relationships in general.

Most of the couples date for a long period of time. People aged 25 to 34 knew one another and dated an average of six and a half years. They want to be financially secure, want to develop themselves, and see the world before settling down.

They marry later; 29.5 years for men, and 27.4 years for women. They want to avoid divorce.

Age does not necessarily do that, but it can contribute, especially if the individuals have matured and are responsible.

Learning how to be a partner doesn't happen automatically; hence my work and book.

Commitment is a BIG step!

When questioned for a study about 70 percent of single people stated they wanted to marry. So, marriage is not disappearing and that is necessary for any society to go on, but it is changing; perhaps for the better.

Today all sorts of diversity is accepted and today the idea of having children is carefully considered; not a mandate. Again, probably good.

Therefore, enjoy the millennials and their values and let's see what they produce.

The *hippies* worked out pretty much okay in the end, and just remember what their parents thought!!

"In case you're worried about what's going to become of the younger generation, it's going to grow up and start worrying about the younger generation." - Roger Allen

Giving Thanks

"Are you fond of lobster salad?" asked the hostess of the doctor. "*No,*" he replied, "I'm not fond of it but I'm grateful to it."

With the approaching holiday for giving thanks it is a good idea to take a look at what we are thankful for. Pity that for many this only occurs when it is forced; like on that holiday.

There are, of course, people who are thankful every day for something. Look at the news and you can see why many are grateful just to return home at night!

We all show or do not show appreciation in many ways and at various times.

One of the hardest and best is to accept and respect another's right to behave differently than what you might like or prefer.

How many do that? Even in the best of relationships there are areas of disagreement and contention.

What is interesting is that if you begin to practice certain behaviors, over time, they can become automatic. For instance, if you start or end each day or week, or whatever with saying something positive and kind about the person, or persons you care about, it will become a habit. That behavior will trigger good feelings and positive reactions.

The opposite is also, unfortunately true. Keep picking on the negative aspects and that will also become habit. You choose!

Everyone contributes to the whole. It can be like bacon and eggs. They go together. The chicken contributes to be sure BUT the pig sacrifices!!

At that Thanksgiving table much goes on. The old patterns and feelings are there. They do not vanish. The bad ones resurface.

With alcohol often, the outcome is not pleasant.

Many times, there is a peace-maker who tries to keep things going along in a good way.

Sometimes this just buries the real feelings. Real feelings cannot be denied.

What you do about them however is the bottom line.

At my own such dinners I asked each family member to say what they were thankful for. Every year they did it until one year they rebelled. Most said the same old hackneyed remarks about family and so on.

Some even mentioned being lucky and thankful for being an American. Whatever. It just got to be anticipated and routine.

Then I decided to be a 'counselor' and be creative. I found nice cards that said, *I am thankful for...* and I gave everyone one to write something;

anonymously. They did and then we guessed who had written what. Some were clever, funny, or sarcastic. Most were guessed correctly.

After that they all agreed NOT to have to say anything, so I alone made my little speech about what I was thankful for. Too bad; my house, my rules!

Being *family* correct is a lot like being politically correct. You think you have to say the *right* thing.

What we are thankful for does change with years. The twenty somethings see things very differently than the seventy somethings. Wisdom? Experience?

Another aspect of being grateful is that the recipient of the gratitude then comes to expect it and might feel awful if they do not continue to live up to that standard. That can be a burden.

If you are always thanking someone for something that can get to be a bit much. Also, what do you give back?

Are you the chicken or the pig?

Basically, we should all deliver what we want to. We should feel free to be ourselves.

If, however you are a *taker* and do not give back or show appreciation that can be a problem. It will not lead to happiness and feeling good about yourself.

There are all levels of takers and givers.

This holiday will be a good time to take stock and see where and how you fit in.

Give thanks then and more…

"It is a great mistake for men to give up paying compliments, for when they give up saying what is charming, they give up thinking what is charming."- Oscar Wilde

The Great Equalizer... Hospitals

"Going to a hospital is rather like going to an alien planet." - Quentin Blake

Having worked in a hospital for years and at times being a patient I know what goes on; on both sides.

From the perspective of the medical staff they want to be helpful and use their knowledge to make you better. They also want you compliant and not a *bother*.

They, especially doctors, do not want their opinions challenged. They tell you all the details about what is going on and protect themselves from law suits. They often make themselves seem like they are your *savior*. They want to be important.

When I first worked in my hospital, the staff worn crisp white uniforms and nurses wore caps signifying where they trained. Today they run around the place in scrubs and other *lovely* outfits. Respect came with how they dressed and presented themselves then; today, all different.

What patients do not think about is that these are human beings who, like you, have issues, personalities, families and good and bad days. Some deal with life well while others act out their problems even at work.

As a patient you are there with poor people, and rich people, and everyone in between. You all need help and care. You are equal to one another in this sense.

There is nothing more undignified than being in a hospital gown, usually open in the back and not feeling well enough to close it.

There is no room for shame in your position.

Your bodily functions are there for people to see, address, and deal with.

If you are scared of what will happen or a diagnosis, true or not, your anxiety level will soar. That doesn't help the situation.

The question is always; would you rather have a sound mind and poor health, or be *out of it* with a healthy body? It isn't up to you, of course, but it is an issue.

Watching someone you care about suffer is so very difficult. You just feel helpless and their pain becomes yours, in some fashion.

If illness becomes a way of life or if there is a chronic disorder, you, as well as others around you get just plain worn out and tired.

Heaven help those people too incapacitated to make good choices or good judgments and have no one to advocate for them. How many sick, or sick and elderly, have been taken advantage of when they are diminished and unable to really fend for themselves?

I personally have heard and seen families torn apart, often over the patient's will or money, or who gets to control them. I know of a few medical people who were magically put in patients' wills. The story of Brooke Astor is a famous one. Read it.

There is no way around getting older or having down times. It is part of life.

Final decisions, sometimes about life or death take place in hospitals.

The joy of new births is also there. When I was working there was a room next to a new mother's where a young woman had delivered a still born. You could hear the two women and what they each experienced. I had that changed and yet in many instances in hospitals the cured are close to the dying.

If patients need after- care that needs special attention. Often once a patient is *out of danger* they are somewhat neglected. It is hard to *fight* for what you need when you don't feel great.

Another wrinkle today is information on the Internet, for example. Much is fine but often there are conflicting opinions or just *bad* information. Someone not trained in the field can really get things messed up.

Getting second opinions is always a good rule of thumb. The best *experts* can *screw up.*

In the final analysis you should check out the people that you trust your life with and then…. get a four-leaf clover!!

"I became faint and nauseous during even very minor procedures, such as making an appointment by phone." - Dave Barry

Go… Ask Santa

"It is dangerous to accept gifts, for two days after come requests" – Henry Cardinal Manning

Ho, Ho and Ho… It's that time of year again.

We are now in the Holiday season… And maybe even in the spirit. For children, it is magical and fun.

For those, not children, it can be a variety of feelings; happy, or sad, remembering other happier times.

The history of Santa is a real story. In the fourth century in Myra, now Turkey, there lived a Bishop who came from a wealthy family. He was kind and gave secret gifts to needy people. Legend has it he started the *hanging of stockings* tradition.

He was named *Saint* Nicholas and died around 345. In 1087, his bones were stolen from Turkey by Italian merchant sailors and they are buried in the Italian port of Bari. He was said to have aided sailors.

In the 16th century, the stories became unpopular and in England, Father Christmas was the one to deliver presents to children. Dutch settlers in the early United States had Kris Kringle and St. Nicholas became SinterKlaas who then evolved into Santa Claus.

In 1823, *Twas the Night Before Christmas* was published by Clement Moore. *Rudolph the Red-Nosed Reindeer* was written in 1949. Actually, Rudolph may be female as they keep their antlers in the winter!

In 1863, he is seen in different outfits until 1881 when Harper's Weekly published Thomas Nast's image that we still have. He was used in Coca-Cola ads since the 1920's.

Now that we have him the question is what do we do with him? How nice to have someone to tell what we wish for. How great would that really be? Kids sit on his lap or write him letters and parents try to fill the requests.

It's really fun to hear what they ask for. Ads from technology, help give them ideas. You can learn about family values from all of this.

Looking back, my older daughter, when held up to Santa at the Thanksgiving parade, said she wanted a *fuh coat*! She got it: a red one that rotted trying to be saved for her daughter one day, in my own parents' attic.

If we adults could ask for stuff what would that sound like? Two older gentlemen did just that. They visited Santa, and they were told they could have any wish. The first one asked for peace in the Middle East, the second asked for all sorts of sex with his wife of forty years.

Santa contemplated a few minutes and announced, "It's only the first wish I will be able to deliver!" Would we want instant gratification, even if *only* once a year? I think so.

The use of *Santa* as a means to control children or their behavior often works. To believe someone is all knowing and all seeing is a bit scary. Think of some religions.

People ask for things from that source too, but often not material things. How about psychics who can answer prayers of other sorts?

Wishful thinking and *magic* can be comforting and certainly hopeful; putting it in someone else's hands. If we must do the work, that's too hard, risky and frustrating.

My idea would be to make this a better world and teach children from a young age about compassion and that joy comes from *giving*. We might do this by asking Santa for things in another way.

Do yourself a favor this season and read O. Henry's, *Gift of the Magi*. It's perfect.

I would teach children that they first have to ask for something for someone else before they can ask Santa for anything for themselves. Dickens' *Christmas Carol* would be played out a lot earlier in life than it was in the story. Wouldn't that be a nice start to changing this world?

Happy Holidays!

"No one has ever become poor by giving" - Anne Frank

Diamonds Are Worthless

"I remember thinking as a child that diamonds were stars that fell from the sky as shooting stars. You can only imagine my disappointment at learning the truth of them. I still prefer stars." - Barbara Lieberman

The truth is diamonds are not rare or intrinsically valuable. It is a big hoax exacted on the consumer. Take a look at the history.

Cecil Rhodes had the biggest mine, originally looking for gold, in South Africa in 1889. He found diamonds and immediately decided to control the supply as well as the perception that they were valuable. Diamonds were and are not scarce! He formed the De Beers company.

Another massive mine was found and owned by Ernest Oppenheimer. Rhodes died in 1902 and in 1914 Oppenheimer merged with De Beers and they agreed to price fixing of diamonds. Diamonds are actually a really compressed variety of coal!! All the diamonds on earth were formed about a hundred miles below the earth's surface about one billion years ago. There is probably an inconceivable amount still down there.

So, how did we get to this point; believing they are valuable and everyone has to have them. The diamond engagement ring has a great story… enhanced by DeBeers, of course.

In 1477 eighteen-year-old Archduke, (and later Holy Roman Emperor) Maximillian proposed to his great love; Mary of Burgundy. He gave her father a ring for her with tiny diamonds in the shape of an 'M.' It was faceted, which had just been invented in Bruges. Mary's father owned the land there and thought this was a great idea. When Maximillian married Mary, he bought the Low Lands which were most of Belgium and the Netherlands and gave it to her as a dowry.

Earlier the ancient Greeks and Romans gave betrothal rings; a circle which was a promise. In the eighth to eleventh centuries when the Vikings swore allegiance to their king or made a vow, they did it with a metal arm ring. In the Far East and especially in Hinduism a married woman always wore a bangle bracelet.

The Romans used the fourth finger of the left hand as the vein of love that went to the heart. The truth is all the fingers and veins lead to the heart!

Early on in Western culture men exchanged pledge rings of metal. The Catholic church then entered the picture and Pope Innocent III in 1215 decided to institute the law that there should be a waiting period before marriage and that became the *engagement*. This was the beginning of real engagement rings. Both men and women wore them, and Christian marriages had to take place in a church.

At this time, the wealthy could flaunt their status by the expense of the ring. Diamonds were not used often as they were not thought pretty.

New technology, like Mary's ring, was invented recently and the diamond, called the Shawish Geneve, was cut by laser in Geneva and it cost seventy million and was cut from a single hundred and fifty carat stone. It took a year to do it. It has a hole in it where the finger fits; there is no metal on it.

In 1946, DeBeers did a study and hired N.W. Ayer advertising agency to market diamond engagement rings to the American public. The message was that a man had not proposed unless there was a diamond engagement ring. The size of your worth was seen in the size and cost of the stone!

Everyone wanted what everyone else wanted.

Ninety percent of brides here have such a ring and recently Americans spent seven billion dollars on these rings!! Now the rare diamonds are red. Few are seen. Pink ones are next. The yellow or canary are not rare. The brown or black are close to coal!!

Try to sell one and see what you get for it. The beauty may be in the design or a unusually fine one.

The celebrities who sport them at Oscar parties or other events have them on loan frequently to keep the allure and appeal going. It is all a game!!!

The association of diamonds and love made the case. Can you buy love?? Not on your life!

Most jewelers can't tell a cubic zirconia from a diamond so maybe put your love in a better thing and know that real love isn't measured in stones!

This last quote is just for fun.

"Diamonds are a girl's best friend." - Carol Channing in *Gentlemen Prefer Blondes*

Face It... On Facebook

"Every man ought to be friends with a nun and a whore and while talking with them forget which is which." - Brendan Francis

Recently I have been on Facebook for the first time ever.

Now you have to understand I know nothing about this Facebook world and what I discovered blew me away.

While technologically *retarded* I thought it a good idea to let the world know about this blog and my book with the same name, on Amazon.

As a result, I went on Facebook.

How people came on a list to be my 'friend' is a world I cannot explain but there they were; hundreds of them.

It became a challenge to look at the names, see the faces, read about them, and then decide whether to make them a *friend* or not.

They came from all over the world, men and women and all walks of life.

Deciding who to add on my list was a full-time job. The only criteria *was* whether or not I believed they would like my blog and book and benefit from it.

Soon I discovered men were flattering me and others were 'liking' my work. How nice. It could be almost intoxicating. It could become addicting!

Now, as a therapist I know a bit about people and their motivations. What you cannot know is who is telling the truth.

I began a small research project asking people, mainly young people, about their own experiences on Facebook.

There were a variety of responses both positive and negative. What really became apparent was that you need to be selective about whom you connect with beyond that first exposure.

What really shocked me was how sad and lonely people are and how, as I knew, everyone is looking for emotional connection.

The other thing that truly bewildered me was how many young beautiful females think that exposing their bodies, especially their breasts, many artificial ones I might add, makes them desirable. What does that lead to? Now, let's think...

The guys show off their muscles and cars.

So, again, my premise has been correct; females use sex to get love and guys use love... and money, to get sex. Does it work in the end?

Well, I have known several couples who met this way and have found love. And I have known several couples who met on dating sites and happily married or got together. This is a whole new world for meeting others.

The trick is what after that initial meeting?

One very wealthy divorcee' I know met a man she liked through Facebook. Before giving her heart away she put a private detective on him to verify what he had told her about his life and past. It checked out and they are together now for four years.

Another guy met a girl from Sri Lanka and went there and ended up marrying her and he is extremely happy. Go figure! When could that have ever happened before? Answer... never!

Today I have learned how to *delete* most who are inappropriate and cannot benefit from my work, and I accept others who seem right. Only three people out of thousands have sent comments that I have answered personally. It all takes time and effort. I *invite* people to *like* my page and most do. That is comforting and rewarding.

Face, it; Facebook is what you make of it!

"It takes time and a kind of power in oneself to know another just as it does to get anywhere in one of the crafts." - Sherwood Anderson

First Year of College; Neither Fish Nor Fowl

When Dr. Charles Eliot an educator at Harvard was asked how Harvard had gained its' prestige as the greatest storehouse of knowledge in the nation he replied," In all likelihood it is because the freshmen bring us so much of it, and the seniors take away so little."

That may be a truer statement than many would like to believe. You are truly not fish or fowl after that first year at college.

What it takes to get into a *good* college today is unbelievable. The competition is fierce, let alone the cost.

I happen to interview prospective students for my own Ivy League university and out of twenty-five years only four have gotten in; all the people I see are outstanding young people.

You just never know what the institution is looking for to round out a class and diversify it. Then there is the issue of legacy and money. All adding up to fierce competition and a lot of disappointment. It is a strange business and nerve racking for the student and their families.

The truth of the matter is that I believe a curious, hardworking, good student can thrive and get what they need from a wide variety of educational experiences. The thing about college, and especially a liberal arts background is that it gives you a cultural expansion. College also lets you experience a wide range of people and ideas.

But most importantly, it helps you define yourself.

You are on your own; you make your own decisions, both good and bad.

You have friends who may be like you or from different backgrounds which can expand your horizons. All great.

You learn about being accepted, being popular, finding new skills and a big issue; your sexuality.

This is where many young people try on alternative behaviors and come into their own in this most important area.

Many discover they are able to act out their impulses and attractions. Indeed, many claim their homosexuality or transgender leanings at this time. They are free of parents and all that they have grown up with.

The heterosexuals can act out their desires in a variety of ways and do.

Now after that first year there is a boomerang effect.

The student goes *home* again.

What a shock!

The camaraderie of friends around all the time, the *love* object, the decision making, and the parents asking questions and setting rules is a BIG jolt.

Seeing old friends will take on different feelings and adjustment. Seeing old boyfriends or girlfriends will not be the same as before.

It will all need to be emotionally worked through.

You are not fish or fowl. You are not a child and not yet an adult.

In a sense it is the best of times because it's all fun, and no real grown up responsibility. Well, yes, you need to study and have exams and that stuff but you don't need to earn a living and support yourself... yet!

It seems young men have a longer growth period to maturity. They really don't get there these days until almost thirty, for the most part.

Young females seem to have less of a struggle.

When kids go home for summer after that first year they revert to being twelve years old again. The parents take care of them; laundry, meals, money and so on. It is always the same even when you are fifty! The old patterns stay there, and we all want to *please* our parents. However, with all of it you have to buck them, challenge their ideas and life, in order to be your own person, in your own generation. If they come on too strong you have to fight harder and be stronger. You have to suffer their disapproval for a while, and maybe forever, BUT it is necessary for you to be whatever you are to become. Tell them I said so!!!

In the end the college experience will be a learning one and in ways that you never expected... Enjoy!!

"A college education is one of the few things a person is willing to pay for and not get." - William Lowe Bryan

Family... As A Sporting Event

"Families always have these unspoken dramas, and at holidays, everyone is supposed to sit down and pretend that none of that is going on." - Richard LaGravenese

With the holidays approaching we all have issues coming up.

The Norman Rockwell happy family smiling around the turkey is just that; a pretty picture taken in a moment in time. The reality of most holidays and family dinners include much more.

With sports, people train and then practice, and finally have a test to see who wins.

It does not evaporate. Family history is in you.

Whatever it was, or is, will probably be with you forever.

The *training* that took place growing up is pretty much ingrained by adulthood. Even if you hated it; it's in there.

You were loved or not, had most of your needs; physical AND emotional met, or not, and you learned about being a male or female and how they relate to one another in that training period. You formed an image of yourself that was reinforced at home and later on the outside.

You negotiated within that family system and related to everyone there, including siblings.

The *practice* part came later as you tried out what you learned at home on others. Most people repeat what they have lived as children with the other people they engage with. This is where the rubber meets the road. Maybe it works well, and then maybe it doesn't. What you do about it at this stage is crucial. Keep practicing what doesn't work well or try to change it. That ain't easy. It can be slow, and painful.

So now come the holidays.

Most families do get together and try to have a good time.

Some succeed. Many do not, and some have a really up and down occasion.

Often alcohol can unleash things that were better left alone.

The old feelings are there and resurface.

The *team* will organize itself around old patterns. Then the game is ON.

Who brings up what and who *sides* with whom will become immediately known.

Old rivalries will come to the fore. Hurt feelings will want to be paid back and so on.

Often the meal will end with people having headaches and indigestion. And it won't be because of the turkey and stuffing!!

Who will come out the winner?

Now it's fine to have disagreements and old sores and memories that may not be good, BUT, and it's a big BUT; you should be able to handle family in a mature responsible manner.

That means not neglecting the past and the feelings BUT moving in positive territory and getting along, perhaps just civilly to make the holiday, at the least, pleasant.

By not giving in to the old bad stuff you can move on to new and happy areas of conversation and that will change the game plan and make for a good holiday event which will in turn lead to happy memories and a desire to repeat it again next year.

The choice is yours and even if some family members choose to be bitter or angry or resentful, only you are in charge of you. Do not take the bait. You have nothing to prove at this stage of the game. You need only talk to yourself and then have the family engage with one another in positive ways.

Yes, some people remain angry for life and want others to be miserable. That need not be you.

There is so much to discuss in this life that you can find topics of interest that do not stir up unhappy feelings. And that does not include politics or the world situation!

"Happiness is having a large, loving, caring, close-knit family, in another city." - George Burns

Class Will Tell

"Gentility is what is left over from rich ancestors after the money is gone." - John Ciardi

What a nice way of explaining what real *class* means.

It is indeed a matter of gentility. It is a manner of being that gets into the bone marrow from early years. It becomes a part of you. It is a way of relating to people and the world. It is not *taught* or *put on*.

It is like so many other aspects of this life; you know it when you see it. You recognize it and feel the difference from those that are without it.

While it is true that growing up in a family with money you learn certain behaviors and ways of acting, that is not the whole story. You do take for granted that money is not a problem and the fear or need to earn money is not a big concern as it is for most of the people in the world. That alone allows for an attitude of comfort and ease.

It shows you the world and how to see it through travel. It sends you to the *right* schools, and has you meeting and being comfortable with people like you.

It shows you how to set a table, (no ketchup bottles on it), and what silver ware to use with what foods. Cloth napkins are there; not paper. You learn about wines and foods and how to converse with ease.

You are above all else taught manners.

All of this doesn't mean you cannot learn over time, experience, and observation how to do all of this, but it is not ingrained automatically from the start.

Now it is true there are some people who can *affect* class and come across as if they were *to the manor born*, however with the right questions you can learn it is an affectation and not the real Mc Coy.

Certain clubs will only admit people who come from a certain background with the *right* ancestors. I had a friend who was listed in the famous *400* but was dirt poor. She had the right name! That can also be a problem.

Being *elite* is easier in America where money can buy you *in*. Some other countries do not have this luxury.

It is also true some born into a certain group choose to reject it at some point in their lives; for a variety of reasons. These can include rebellion, a partner, or a feeling of discomfort.

While most people with true *class* are egalitarian, polite, and kind, many are *hung up* in a number of areas. They can't let loose a lot.

Others can abuse their station in life and look down on others, be condescending and behave nastily. They can do gross things and behave in really awful ways. They have the *name* and think that's all they need.

Most people who are *classy* are cultured and know about the world of literature, art, and music. They have been exposed and it has gotten into their skin, so to speak.

Being refined is dignified and respectful. You even dress the part. Years ago, a particular group came to dinner in evening dress every night! We are a LONG way from that.

Today's working women have no time to cook, polish silver or write personal thank you notes with a fountain pen...

This generation can't even spell and uses computers for that among other things.

What is observable in little gestures is obvious to those *in the know*. It is the behavior that is 'instinctual' as it is part and parcel of the individual.

Once at the beach I saw a man I knew who was extremely wealthy stand at the water's edge and watch a woman he knew casually, struggle to get out of the ocean. He never offered a hand to help. That said it all.

Little things show it all the time.

When you have it; you have it… that's all there is to it.

Sadly *class* is missing today in so many instances.

It requires caring and being there for others when it counts. It requires discipline and not saying whatever you think, or hurtful things intentionally. It is a *manner* that exudes and lets others know you are not spontaneous and out of control. Yes, that takes a lot of fun out of life, but it is not for having fun that people with *class* hold on to it.

Can you have *class* and be a free spirit? You can but it takes being aware and balancing the two aspects.

The other part of this is that those who have this quality don't have to struggle and fight to be successful. They don't have to push or claw their way up; they are there.

Class will always tell, and you know what it is and you know how people with it act. It can be an acquired taste and that takes time and attention.

It is quiet and never outspoken, gaudy, or in your face. It just IS.

"Society can exist only on the basis that there is some amount of polished lying and that no one says exactly what he thinks." - Lin Yutang

Comfy and Convenient

"Comfort is the great social tranquillizer." - Philip Rieff

Today everyone wants to be *comfy*.

Just look at how people dress; worldwide; how they speak and how they relate to one another.

It's all very *comfy*.

It's also sloppy and easy and shows a lack of caring.

I do not want us to go back to corseted females, and dandies dressed up as men, however I do think we have taken it a step beyond repair.

Go to the theater, even in New York, on a Saturday night and look around at the audience; especially in warm summer weather.

What do you see?

You see men and women in shorts, t-shirts, sneakers, or flip-flops and so on.

It looks awful as far as I'm concerned. Now I'm no prude or stickler for dressing up but really does that make a person feel and look good? I think not.

Even if they are wearing other clothes, they are often so mismatched you can barely look at them.

Do these people know they have no taste and show they do not care how they appear?

Now some young people, especially females looking to attract men do dress up. They wear flattering nice skirts and dresses; sometimes very tight fitting or low cut. That is okay as they show they put some thought in the process and looked in a mirror before exiting.

Comfy is fine but being in gym clothes all day and night conveys a message; I am being comfortable, period.

When I see really pretty dresses and men's suits and ties in stores, I wonder who is buying these things and where are they wearing them. Funerals? Weddings?

And the language… it's also *comfy*. Fine grammar and politeness have all but vanished for so many people. It's almost like a new foreign language has replaced it all. Texting and the brief ways to express oneself is amazing.

I've come to think that without the word, *fuck* a lot of people could not express themselves.

There is nothing basically wrong with being comfortable and that's fine, but how about *nicely* comfortable. It is possible.

What it shows, and I am not an old fuddy-dud, is that nobody cares how they present themselves. I have heard tales of people even applying for high level jobs dressed as slobs!

And how about everything having to be *convenient* today. No one wants to exert themselves.

Nobody seems to care if a job is well done. There is no pride in accomplishment.

How often do people today have to repeat a task that was not performed well or at all?

How often do people want everything at their fingertips?

We have convenience stores everywhere. We advertise that whatever you need, or desire is readily available. What do you have to work for? What is worth achieving?

Even when you pay top dollar you often cannot be assured that the task is well done.

What is especially scary is when some of these matters involve your wellbeing as in medicine and health care or repairs to homes, bridges and so on. That is a whole other story; life threatening.

All of this says a lot about what we have become as people and what our culture has tolerated.

Who are the examples?

Listen to the language on TV, or in the movies. Hear what *celebrities* have to say and how they say it. Not pretty.

Role models are dressing the way we all emulate, and role models say what we think and how we talk. It is for me a bit sad to look around and listen to all of it. It is frustrating to try and get anything done well and competently without having to check and go through the same requests many times. No wonder we are angry and fed up. No wonder we are looking for comfort in other fashions. Is it any wonder that we drink, take drugs, and yell a lot?

And in relationships too comfy and convenient makes the whole business short lived!

Maybe, just maybe, if we had better standards and we set better examples for others to follow, politeness, and curtesy, and a sense of pride might be the norm rather than the exception.

Being comfy and having things convenient is fine... after you are eighty!!

"Nothing that is worthwhile is ever easy."- Indira Gandhi

Feminists... Many Shot Themselves In The Foot

"Many men admire strong women, but they do not love them." - Elsa Schiaparelli

So, what's this all about?

Women being *strong* is not a new concept, and what does *strong* mean?

As far as physical or brute strength men are the stronger.

As far as intellect or accomplishment they have become more equal and the feminist movement of decades ago certainly did help that; especially with women's educational opportunities.

But today women are not in the lead with power and money in the workplace, for any number of reasons.

The real differences are evident in the relationships women have with men both in and out of bed.

They are not just needing a man in their lives although most prefer that. They still dress for men and wait for the phone to ring or the text message to occur.

Women are more assertive today in all areas of relating to men. There is a difference between assertive and aggressive, however.

The difference as I see it is one of politeness. It gives room for the *other* to respond and engage. There are ways to ask for what you want as a female. How about, 'I would like it if you would...' As opposed to a demand. That makes men run the other way or give up. Women also do not need to have men being aggressive with them. Just look at the news lately about sexual conduct.

The roles of female and male are still basically the same and no amount of *feminism* will ever change that. We are just DIFFERENT!

I recently had a couple come for counseling and one of his biggest complaints about her was she was too assertive.

When I asked for an example, he gave an interesting story.

They were out driving and at a stop light she saw an attractive man about forty. She has a daughter who is divorced in her thirties.

Her husband said she pulled up close to the other car and asked if he was single. He replied he was. Then she asked his religion, and it was the answer she wanted. She then said she had a single daughter and pulled out a card and wrote the daughter's name and phone number on it and reached over and gave it to the other driver.

Her husband was shocked and embarrassed and not happy. He said she is just too *pushy*, especially with him.

While we have to take advantage of our opportunities, we all have to decide when to reach out and when to restrain ourselves.

Men still like to take the lead and they like the role of being the one to make the first move even if it means rejection. They like taking the 'strong' man approach to protecting a woman and being the *thruster* in bed.

Woman can and have learned how to be satisfied in bed and teach their partners what they desire without being overbearing. Men do not want to be intimidated or *rated* in the bedroom.

Masculinity needs to be all male in its' basic sense. Stereotypes are there for a reason for centuries.

Different cultures have ideas that may not mesh with today's American woman; that's fine in some cases but awful in others.

Free choice and connecting out of passion and love makes relationships that are what they should be; no matter for how long. Serial monogamy is the wave of the future I believe.

A recent book; *Sex Matters* by Mona Charen talks about all of this in a clear sensible way.

Her theories include the fact that feminists have dismantled courtship and the dating culture. They have made men the *enemy*. They have created a war between the sexes.

And the bottom line is that they are not happier at work, or at home.

This is the pity of it all.

Men are fearful of showing they are interested, attracted, flirtatious, or wanting to be close to a woman. Lawyers have certainly helped fan that fire!

Women still like to dress so that men notice them, but they are on guard about where or how a relationship should be carried out.

Who makes the first move? How? Where then?

All not easy today.

For my money women should be soft and loving and men should be more assertive and interested. That is nature, damn it!!

"The major concrete achievement of the women's movement in the 1970's was the Dutch treat." - Nora Ephron

Carrots Versus Cocaine

"Today more than 95% of all chronic disease is caused by food choice, toxic food ingredients, nutritional deficiencies, and lack of physical exercise." - Mike Adams

No news here. Who doesn't know this? Well, it turns out knowing and doing are two different things.

Have you looked around these days? There are fat, really fat, people everywhere. All ages, all races and men and women. It is a national emergency. Don't people care? What is the problem?

It turns out, I believe, that people have been *addicted* to bad food. Companies have made fortunes selling unhealthy foods for years. They start with babies who become used to sugar and fat and crave it.

Another fact is that poorer people are kept poorer by governments for a purpose. They live in areas where all their neighbors eat the same *junk*. They are trapped and it goes on from generation to generation. They are less healthy, have more stress, less education and shorter life spans. It's by design!!

What should be rights are now considered privileges.

Who goes to the best schools? Who has the best health care? Who lives in good crime free neighborhoods?

Now I am not saying everyone is equal in all areas; we are not. But the basics and the reward for talent is not always there.

We need all the thinking and innovation we can get in this entire world. However smart kids are not given the same opportunities if they are poor. It's a real uphill battle and only the very strongest can survive the accident of birth and where they are born.

The smart ones do eat carrots! They have a healthy diet and exercise and do yoga. They are disciplined...They like things to be natural; even not using make-up!

Now there are some weird things out there and the saying is that if you can't pronounce it, don't eat it. If you live on kale that may not be the best thing for you.

Again, it's education and knowledge that will help. Vitamins? Maybe?

You can go crazy with all the information too. One day coffee is awful for you, and the next it's good. Eggs? You can go through a whole list and then try to decide what works for you.

Now when we talk about drugs that's a whole other story. There is addiction and then there is ADDICTION.

While the list of drugs is long and the reactions varied we all probably use some drugs from time to time.

Lately the numbers of young people using marijuana is huge. The numbers of older people taking Opioids has been declared an American dilemma.

And rich kids at elite colleges using cocaine is out of bounds. I hear it all the time. Lots of people with money find cocaine a choice they enjoy.

When I worked at a hospital the numbers of health care professionals using illegal drugs was well known; including many physicians.

For poor people; they are using crack, and a number of other substances, and doing all sorts of things to maintain their habits. Crime and prostitution are big on the list. What a pathetic life these people lead. What it does to a society is another matter.

They are sad, and have huge problems with money, health, sleep, paranoia. anxiety and so on.

We see them, all ages, as homeless sleeping on the streets and don't bat an eye. We are inured.

What does that say about a culture?

Then, of course, there are the creative people who say drugs help their talents and they have used them for years. They are not the ones who overdose and die.

Drugs are rampant and we use them and keep big money flowing to other countries and people without formal educations. What would happen if that *talent* and conniving was put to worthwhile use?

The use of drugs and the people who are addicts will never go away. Some places have given them freely to the people who use them and have eliminated the crime element. Knowing what the drugs contain and taxing them might be a better course for law enforcement and governments. The money and tragedy involved is immense.

These people from grower to recipient and all the middle men take up a huge part of daily life for countless numbers of people.

Then there is all the effort in law enforcement and prisons and so on. Talk about a Fortune 500 company!!

So, yes, we can eat carrots and we can use drugs at the same time in many cases.

Human beings are complicated and universally unique. We find our cohorts and agree.

The bigger question is what becomes of us, our children, or families, and our larger society?

"Reality is just a crutch for people who can't cope with drugs." - Robin Williams

Crazy Stuff

"No one can drive us crazy unless we give them the keys." - Douglas Horton

That's right. Who or what drives you crazy?

In our world today, there are a lot of crazy things going on all around us. Most of them are not in our control; the political situation, some aspects of old religions, world horrors, and just the mass of people.

Now there are, to be sure, bona fide crazy people. They have psychiatric diagnoses. And yes, some professionals are themselves not all that sane!

But by and large we know when we think someone is crazy. I'm not talking about the *whack jobs* out there. They are just temporarily not behaving in a rational manner. I'm talking about all of us that at one time or another have had crazy thoughts or behaved in a bizarre manner.

There are people who follow the rules and never are out of control. They are not the *fun* people.

People who are in love are always a bit crazed. It is usually a temporary condition. Watch couples before they are married and used to one another and watch those married and see the difference.

Some really crazy people have been creative in a wonderful way. They have produced art, music, literature, and food to name a few. Some suffered as a result and many committed suicides but that aside, they were crazy and productive.

Most jobs won't tolerate crazy. They need workers to follow the rules. But there have been a number of companies that have allowed and even encouraged employees to think outside the box and come up with new ideas to try. The risk is often a good one and pays off big time.

The fact of the matter is, reality sucks a good bit of the time.

Getting out of your brain and your own life experience and being wild can help make it tolerable and even pleasant.

Being an eccentric is interesting and not boring. It's just this side of really crazy.

People who push it in an artificial manner are not what I am talking about. I'm talking about the real unusual but not the ones that are insane. That's the legal term for true crazies.

Just acting out from time to time, looking different, or having a free-wheeling episode here and there can be exhilarating. It also makes this world tolerable and helps keep you happy.

The bad ones think bad thoughts and then act on them. How often do we hear the neighbors saying, "He was such a nice quiet, polite boy. I can't believe he murdered his girlfriend and then cut her in pieces."

Not so far-fetched. Listen to the news.

Some insanity runs in families and may be genetic. It always a good idea to get a family history before connecting with someone long term.

Barring that, being a unique individual is great. Being uninhibited at times is good for you.

Just thinking crazy thoughts off and on, won't hurt you, or others.

Sharing those thoughts with someone can be tricky. Will they understand? Will they run away? Will they then share their crazy thoughts with you?

It can be a fun exercise.

None of us, runs on radar. We have to talk and talk plainly. And maybe say the same things over and over to be understood. A test I give couples about communication is to look each other in the eye and say something important and meaningful about yourself. Then ask the partner to repeat what was said and then say what they believe their partner was really saying to them. I am always amazed at the misinterpretations I hear.

Just because you think something and even after telling it you cannot be sure you are understood.

Schizophrenics have an uncanny ability usually to know what people are about. They have no filter and get to the core of the person they are in contact with. It is quite fascinating.

Most of us, however, get by with our own brand of crazy thoughts or actions and for the most part survive well. We like to remember them or have others remind us of them. It usually comes with laughter.

"Here's all you have to know about men and women: women are crazy, and men are stupid. And the main reason women are crazy is that men are stupid." - George Carlin

As Luck Would Have It

"Most of us regard good luck as our right and bad luck as a betrayal of that right." - William Feather

Are you lucky? With what? Maybe you feel unlucky at times. It's all part of the human condition.

Think about it… what part does luck play in our lives?

Turns out, a lot.

The family into which you are born sets the stage for starters.

Was Prince William lucky…

Having good parents who love you and meet your basic needs gives you a stable beginning and that's all just plain dumb luck.

There is a myriad of other elements to this thing called, luck. Being born healthy with all the *marbles* in place is a feature of luck.

As we individuals grow and develop luck comes into play in a whole variety of ways.

The element of *chance* is always a factor in life.

Not having calamity occur with parents, the elements coming down on you, a whole group of, *accidents* and continued health and well being are taken into consideration.

I like to look at the things people do to ward off bad luck. Some pray to religions, some buy voodoo dolls.

Others go to soothsayers ala Alexandra of Russia… Some say special prayers, look for four leaf clovers, spit on dice, take chances with lotteries and gambling and so on. How many people rely on the stars and consult their horoscopes, as did Nancy Reagan? How many check the stars for their right mate connection? Many, many.

I once had a friend who had a fabulous sense of humor. One day at a wishing well I saw him leaning over and not throwing coins in. When I got closer, I saw that he was dipping his American Express card in!! Very clever.

Whatever it takes to ward off evil and bad luck.

It is always a matter of luck when out of the blue awful stuff happens and you have absolutely no control.

Think of all the people in car accidents, fires, terrorist attacks, and so on.

Wrong place at the wrong time… Bad luck!

Getting a horrible disease, or mental breakdown; very bad luck.

Some people seem to have a bad luck life with all sorts of unpleasant and unhappy things occurring. It is not unusual for this group to believe they are being *punished* for something *bad* they did. They feel they deserve what happens to them. Others seem to lead a charmed life with good things happening all the time through no fault of their own.

Making money in a whole variety of ways can happen through luck.

This group also believes they deserve their good fortune for the way they have lived and the good deeds they have done.

It can be disheartening to think that luck is not the result of intellect, hard work, and fortitude. That can really make you mad!

And now to the topic I specialize in; love.

Does luck play a role here?

It can.

Being in the right place at the right time can mean you meet that special person.

Meeting them when they are ready to follow through on that initial happening is another factor of good fortune.

After that it is not luck but knowing what to do that will make or break the relationship.

I have devoted my entire career to helping people have fulfilling partnerships.

Luck will then be what happens in your lives.

The best part is that when two people are really connected whatever befalls them in the way of good OR bad luck, they get through it together and help one another emotionally.

In the end; cross your fingers, say your mantra, buy a lottery ticket, check the stars, and I wish you… GOOD luck!

"Give me, mother, luck at my birth, then throw me if you will on the rubbish heap." – Bulgarian Proverb

Let's Do A Budget

"Money may not buy love, but fighting about it will bankrupt your relationship" - Michelle Singletary

It can. What we do with money says a lot about who we are and how we relate to the person we are closest to.

First question has to be; who has the money? Who earns the most and how is it handled?

The decisions about where it goes is more frequently than not, made by the person who has the most money. This however may not always be the case and sometimes it is the more vociferous and aggressive partner that becomes the decision maker. If one is *wiser* about money that person may be anointed to handle the dispersion.

Any partnership will have something to do about money.

Today with so many temporary relationships, not bound by law, a variety of patterns occur. Even with marriage today and prenuptial agreements, patterns fall into place. Who pays for what?

Some people are spontaneous, even with money. Others are careful and responsible, while others are cheap or withholding. A lot of this depends on your early life experiences. It may be easy come; easy go.

Some relationships use money to get what they want; sex, gifts, and so on.

But let's concentrate on a mature couple who work together and decide how to spend their money jointly.

What kind of budget would they have?

Well, for starters they would have to put down the necessary expenditures first.

That would include housing, transportation, food, and things like medical and other insurance. Taxes are always there. You need to decide what portion of income is to be used for necessary things like housing, cars, food etc.

I have had couples for therapy that wanted fancy cars but ate out of tuna cans to do it. Up to them!

Phones, medicine and drug store items, and items such as repairs, and haircuts would also need to be included. If there are children, clothes and maybe school would be on the list.

Then comes discretionary areas.

They would include, clothes, entertainment, hobbies, sports, and travel.

With credit cards, many young couples get into trouble wanting to have it all and not being able to afford it. That will catch up with them in the end. Living beyond your means is a bad philosophy. It is easy to do, and we are all subjected to ads for fancy cars and so on. We have friends or neighbors with more than we have and that becomes a sore point.

I am always reminded of my parents who as they got older had an issue with my father complaining about not having real soft towels. I went out and spent a small fortune to buy them fluffy wonderful ones.

When my dear mother died, I saw them in the linen closet, never used and with the price tags on. I guess she was saving them for *company* or a special occasion. Well, I'm here to live differently. I use the nice towels!!

Yes, having things we like, and need is important, but just accumulating and not being able to afford some things is a problem. Very few people have ALL the money they want whenever they want it.

The old adage; saving for a rainy day, may still hold water. No pun intended!

There are always unexpected things happening that cost money. Heaven help you if you don't have it. Being dependent on others; parents, friends, or banks, makes life stressful and makes you feel badly.

With recent horrible events; hurricanes, fires, earthquakes, and so on, watch what people take with them if they have a few minutes. Usually it's things like pictures and sentimental items.

So, don't be afraid to fight it out with a partner because money and how you use it and budget it is crucial. All you have to do is look at the divorce courts and see how much anger, and despair is tied up with the money situation.

Being able to stand on your own two feet and support yourself should be mandatory.

It is always a good idea to have some portion of money in your own name and then decide what should be jointly held and used.

If you married for money believe me, you will get what you deserve… and it won't be a happy life!!

"They say love is more important than money, have you ever tried paying your bills with a hug?" - Nishan Panwar

Phooey On Getting Old… er

"Youth is a blunder; manhood a struggle; old age a regret." - Benjamin Disraeli

Now the real question; when are these milestones in order?

Well, it's a very individual matter.

Now, those of you who follow my blog know I write about the first world, and people who want to improve themselves, and mostly educated and responsible. That does not negate the fact that other groups have issues around aging and indeed some cultures do care for and respect their elderly in better fashion.

What we usually see are individuals who in youth take everything for granted about their looks, health, strength, and capabilities. They are looking ahead and coping just fine for the most part.

Middle age, which can be about forty begins to set some new challenges. And again, age is how you look, feel, and behave. Not to mention the grandmas in ultra miniskirts!

I have known people in their thirties who were 'old,' in their manner. And I have known people, especially these days, in their eighties that are youthful, and great to be around.

It seems to boil down to attitude and of, course, physical and mental wellbeing.

Now again some people with minor health problems succumb to complaining and making their Medicare card a trip to Disneyland in the form of doctors and hospitals. It is a constant activity and topic for conversation. They find one another and jibber-jabber all day and night about the idiosyncrasies of their bodies, pills and treatments.

Aging occurs if you live long enough… no news here.

With men, first signs may be loss of hair… devastating for many. Some lessening of strength. Bones may ache, and wrinkles can occur. Pot bellies are rampant.

Women, on the other hand suffer in different fashion. If once beautiful some of that may change and again wrinkles and lines while they may make a man look distinguished make a woman feel less desirable. There do seem to be many more good-looking women than men and not just from face lifts and make-up. Men do get face work done more these days but they do not have the benefit of make-up.

Coloring hair is common with women, and some men Some of it just looks awful!.

They all like to exercise and eat right and keep in shape.

Men usually continue to work and some women as well and that is stimulating and helps with being involved and vital.

Many women continue their roles as homemaker and caring for the family so they do not change role as frequently as men when they retire.

A man alone seems to need a woman more than a woman needs a man, with aging. And there are a lot more widows.

When the AARP card comes it is a shock for many and is a message. True there are some benefits but they do not outweigh the fact that time is moving on. The message is now not how many years I have lived but how many years do I have left to live.

People do a variety of things during these phases. Men find younger women and fancy cars, to feel virile and women make themselves *needed* to others.

Sex is a big change and can be non-existent for many which is a *biggy* for men. Some women never really enjoyed it and even the thought of 'toys' or vibrators is abhorrent.

Knowing what the inevitable is for all of us we make plans and think about these issues. Many just block that whole business out and let the children or lawyers or others do the planning. The roles are reversed in many cases with children taking care of elderly parents. That's a whole other story.

In the end, we all do it as we have lived. We are the culmination of our life's experiences and we have matured, become compassionate, and wise or we can be bitter and nasty.

Being as lively as we are able in whatever areas we can and doing things for others seems to soften the blow. We are here until we are NOT!

"Giving up is the ultimate tragedy." - Robert J. Donovan

Shh ... Don't Even Mention It

"Death tugs at my ear and says; Live, I am coming" - Oliver Wendell Holmes

With the end of yet another year approaching this might be a fitting topic. Endings are a chapter unto themselves.

While young, most endings offer new beginnings. When older, endings can be fatal!

That's the thing about it; it is very final!

Now, like sexuality many people do not discuss the topic at all.

It is often like, 'If I don't think about it or talk about it, it doesn't exist.' Well, guess what? We all know no one gets out of here alive.

Knowing that, many choose to disregard it and that may work for them. Others have religious faith and believe that a better existence awaits them in a heaven where they will have virgins waiting for them, or they will see loved ones that have already died. That helps.

But for the pragmatic or atheists, that doesn't work. Those that are cremated also have another path.

Those that dwell on death or fear it usually have not enjoyed life or accomplished what they hoped to achieve.

Those that have little or few regrets do not fear death. Indeed, most of these people are in the process of doing and planning when death arrives.

Being responsible means that the knowledge is there that the end will come. Hopefully after a long and fruitful life.

Those that suffer and linger, or those that die young are tragic and awful for their loved ones. All those recent terror deaths or war deaths are really sad to observe. It makes no sense. We should all have a *pill* if and when we need it.

But for the majority of people a plan for disbursing of one's accumulated assets takes place.

Now I have known many successful people who did not either leave a Will or discuss their wishes with a spouse or children. Reasons abound as to why this is the case. Usually it's because they know someone will not like the plan.

There are any number of people who do really nasty things and cut out family members because of some past grievance or hurt. Leona Helmsley left a huge amount of money for her dog's care! Nasty, nasty, nasty.

Too bad people cannot make peace with those that are related or close to them. There are, on the other hand, people who leave money to strangers they met along the way.

Some people are very thoughtful and write lovely things to those they leave money or things to. It all shows the nature of the person and how they have lived.

When my own father was way in his eighties he was in the hospital. The doctor came in to tell him how well he was doing and talked about how this and that test came back fine.

He looked at me and said, "See, I'm dying of improvements."

Humor helps.

When I worked in the hospital there were huge arguments and shenanigans over a dying parent and what certain siblings, for example, wanted. Lawyers have written and had dying patients sign documents that they never understood.

I had a client whose husband was well to do and when he died she went to the vault to see what he had left her. What she found were gambling debt receipts. Tragic.

Then there's the story of the woman who as she became elderly had her portrait painted. She insisted the artist paint her in a lot of jewelry and many diamonds. When he said she was not wearing these things she announced, "I know. I want the second bitch he marries to go crazy looking for them!" Sweet.

Some partners pick out the second or third partner for their spouse. Some want them to remain single and pine for them. We are all different.

The old adage that if the partner remarries it is because they had a good experience the first time. Not always the case. I know of many who were relieved and glad to be rid of their partner.

The hard part is that losing someone with whom you have shared life with and truly loved is extremely difficult. It is final, and you are left with memories and an empty pit in your stomach. Certain things can trigger unhappiness and sadness. Keeping busy helps. Being with people you care about helps. Doing nice things for others really helps. But in the end, we are alone without that person.

Every parent, especially mothers, remember every detail of a child's birth. And, every child remembers every detail of a parent's death.

Where resources and money are involved, whether large or small amounts, there is concern. A fair parent tries to do justice and divide equitably among children. The poorer ones may need more but successful ones should not be *punished* for their hard work.

Also look at the billionaires that leave their fortunes for charities and good deeds. Leaving too much to a child can make them lose ambition.

There are any number of legal battles that have been waged over family money and they are not pretty to learn about.

In the end we will all be 'gone.' The trick is to live so that we enjoy the life we are given. Before age fifty it's how long I have lived, and after fifty it's how long do I have left to live. Who knows? So, do it well!!

"To live in hearts we leave behind is not to die." - Thomas Campbell

At Times Mourning Becomes Us

"You never realize death until you realize love." - Katherine Butler Hathaway

This is a very true statement. If you have really loved, you know how your heart responds to another person. When or if that loved, person is no longer a part of you; you experience a death inside.

Now this can happen in any number of situations.

It can be the loss of a parent. Usually after they have lived a long time and hopefully not suffering from an illness.

It can be the loss of a close friend.

It can be the loss of a child; young or mature it is an impossible grief.

And the one I will focus on is the loss of a lover.

If it is because they have decided to end a relationship with you, or even if you are the one realizing they are not good for you; it is a heartfelt loss.

If it occurs as a result of death it hits with a terrible finality; no matter the circumstances.

Elisabeth Kubler Ross wrote about the five stages of grieving, thirty years ago, they are: denial, anger, bargaining, depression, and acceptance.

You can be 'stuck' in any of these stages, and there is no timeline for any of it.

You can also cling to the sorrow of it. You may hold on to an unrealistic idea of what the relationship actually was. You can stay isolated and not engage with people. You can create a 'fantasy' person as opposed to what the person really was in actuality.

Any or all of this is possible.

Living with the happy memories and what you shared is helpful. Knowing you were the source of happiness is also healing.

The thing is to move along, and you are still alive.

What you do with the rest of your life is what will now matter.

Our loved one would want us to go on in a good way.

For some they are *buried* with the departed.

We can forgive and forget the down or *bad* parts emotionally, anyway.

Your age will determine some of this. If you are toward the end of the life span it may be the end of love in that special way. If you are younger there should be a future to share your love again.

It will never be the same as each love is special in its' own way.

We only fall in deep love two, possibly three times in a lifetime.

Recently I was with a friend who had just lost an adult child. The sorrow was unbearable and not only that; twenty-five years ago, she lost another daughter in a car accident. Now she had one son left. When we talked, she said the only peace she had was knowing her child no longer had to suffer in this difficult life. That helped her to carry on. It is hard to imagine how a mother can continue with this difficult life herself with what life had handed her. But life is for the living and go on we do. We can go through the motions and carry on day by day.

We can have other people around us who care and are understanding. We can love and be loved in many ways; albeit maybe not the deepest one with passion.

I know several people who have transferred that feeling to a pet dog!

We can remember what we gave to our beloved and how we made them feel.

To have had that is a blessing and what this life should be about. To have shared ourselves in this most significant of ways is what we can keep alive in our hearts and minds.

Not easy and there are times when we will be overcome with unhappiness and the hole in our hearts but carry on, we must. We are still HERE!!

"I think we had the chief of all love's joys. Only in knowing that we loved each other." - George Eliot

Grieving... For Life

Westley: I told you I would always come for you. Why didn't you wait for me?"

Buttercup: "Well... you were dead."

Westley: "Death cannot stop true love. All it can do is delay it for a while." - William Goldman

While this is a time of year when people are *supposed* to be happy, many are not. The fact of life we all have to contend with at some point is that there is misery, abject misery, that appears in everyone's life at one point or another. Watching others rejoice only exasperates your grief. Now it is true each of us has a variety of things that can make us feel badly. We all grieve in individual fashion.

Having worked closely with all sorts of individuals and families I have seen the gamut.

We all have different tolerance levels and we all stand alone to get through parts of this process; it is a process.

If a loss occurs early in life, we learn to mourn. We usually have parents, siblings, friends and others to assist in this.

Losing a pet for example can have a ritual of burial associated with it that makes it more bearable. Replacing a pet can help.

If, however, the loss is of a major person in the child's life the grief can be overwhelming and inconsolable for a long time.

As young adults, we may have a person we believe we love to discard us for another. This is also grief.

All of this is leading to the main event; the final loss of a genuine love, when we are adults.

Most people as adults suffer a plethora of losses. It can be grandparents, parents, money, possessions, a body part, or prolonged illness. All things to grieve about to be sure. How the spirit 'fights' back depends on a number of factors.

The history and having survived other losses will help. The strength emotionally that each individual possesses will tell part of the story. The support system of family, friends, professionals can help. Being with others who have gone through the same type of loss will bring some comfort. They will understand, but still they are not YOU! But, in the end, the final *push* to go on must come from you, and you alone. There are people who get ill, take drugs of all sorts, and there are suicides, to be sure, but barring that, most go on.

The beginning of grief will cause an empty hole in the pit of the stomach. Things that remind you of happier times will trigger sadness. Tears can flow at any point and be a river.

Being upset and just going through the motions of being alive, without joy, can last a long time.

For some they have a shrine to grief and they wear it like a badge. Even if someone dies and is no longer in pain the final exit hurts those behind who care.

It is not easy to get over the hurdle that life demands if you are to go on and LIVE.

No one wants to be around anyone who is unhappy, morose, and not truly engaged. You cannot be interested in anyone else's life if you are wrapped up and 'stuck' in your own unhappiness.

There is no time limit, and no one way to get through this part of life. You can tell yourself that you are still alive, and that life is for the living. You can tell yourself that life goes forward not backward. You can tell yourself that you should get over the *blockage*. You can remember the happier times and know you did all you could and brought happiness to a loved one, for example. All good thoughts to keep in mind and keep repeating.

BUT, the feelings will not just dissolve or go away. The *sting* will lessen, and you can help yourself by *policing* your thoughts and not ruminating. You do not have to *cling* to sorrow.

Some of this depends on your stage in life and what time you perceive you have left to still enjoy… whatever.

Some people in the face of a final awful medical diagnosis, for example, rise to the occasion and make every minute count; address things they might never have, and make their ending unbelievable in many ways. That opportunity would not have been possible without the circumstances. I saw it often when I worked in a hospital.

We are all a compilation of our personality coupled with our experiences.

The real trick in life is to make the things that happen to you… work in your behalf.

It's ALL learning. AND you show children, if you have them, and others what can be done. You are the example for living and dealing with grieving.

While you may want to *die* as well, you didn't... YET!

"Some love lasts a lifetime. True love lasts forever." - Anonymous

A Better World... A Better You

"Bad times have a scientific value. These are occasions a good learner would not miss." - Ralph Waldo Emerson

Do you think this is the worst of times? It can seem that way.

Watching the local, national, and heaven forbid, the international news can make you crazy.

There is murder and mayhem all around. Nothing is working well, and people have given up.

The world however is probably in a better place than it has ever been.

Believe it or not things have improved in the larger picture.

For example:

People are living longer

Wars and deaths are low worldwide

Poverty is about ten percent in the world; much lower than before

Children are literate in larger numbers than ever worldwide

We do not see these statistics and relate to them on the grand scale.

There are wonderful things going on to make life better in many ways.

What we contend with is our own little world and that view is quite narrow and limited. Naturally, because we live it day to day.

Money, (power), and sex rule as they always have since time immemorial.

Those things cause individuals to behave in bizarre ways at times.

People who serve as, *leaders* have proved they are not immune and no longer are seen as examples to follow.

What's a person to do?

Can we be better if we think the world around us is crumbling and falling apart?

We can indeed, IF we study history.

There have been far worse times in history throughout the world and certainly in our own country.

Depression, lynching, health hazards, and on and on. If you know about the fiasco at Los Alamos, you want to run for cover right now!

As individuals we strive for what we want in this life. And this life is tough.

I recall my own dear mother, when I was about ten, saying to her sister as her husband was dying, that it was a good thing to get out of this world. I could not believe my *happy* mother said that.

Then I had a friend whose mother became a great grandmother and when she called to tell her she was shocked that there was not happiness in her reply. All she said was, "Oh, now there's someone else to worry about."

Yes, when you have lived long enough you know there is a whole mess of *junk* to go through in life. It helps to know we are but mere specks of star dust in a huge galaxy out there.

Sometimes I believe it might be better to not be smart. Thinking too much can get you down. Actually, I wonder if that Rodin sculpture of, *The Thinker* might just be having constipation!!

All these kids going to college wasting time and money, going into debt, may not be a good thing. When I was in college, I knew that certain fraternities were spending a lot of time having parties with members getting drunk and bringing in prostitutes one night a week. It is learning of a sort.

Then there was the experiment in zoology which I hated and never used where we swiped our cheeks for analysis under the microscope.

One girl had sperm discovered. Needless to say, she became quite popular!

We need vocational schools and then college and graduate work for specific professions.

This world needs all the talent it can get; from rich, and poor and every background.

Opportunity is the name of the game.

Let's hope hate and pitting people against one another for stupid reasons will one day be gone, or maybe just easier. Happy contented people enjoy one another no matter what. Only the unhappy are hurtfull.

Find your happiness in any world!!

"I was very famous as a young man and I celebrated both the good and the bad times with drinking." - Glenn Hughes

Give The Gift... of Sex

So, a couple from Mars asks an Earth couple to exchange places with them for a night to experience what each lives. They do and....

The man from Mars undresses and the Earth lady says, "is that it … disappointing in size" He then tells her to wiggle his right ear and lo and behold the organ increases in length. He then tells her to wiggle his left ear and then it gets wider. Needless to say, they proceed to have a fabulous sexual night. Next morning at breakfast her husband asks how her experience was and she tells him it was fantastic. She then inquires about his night. "Not so hot," he responds, "all she wanted was to wiggle my ears all night!"

Recently I had a darling young couple for marriage counselling. In one session, she said she didn't want to, *Give him sex,* as she was not so happy about something he did. WOW!!

While this is a holiday season again, and we like to give one another presents; sex is not a commodity and you surely don't go to Bloomingdale's to buy it!

Actually, my own idea of a gift is something shiny that I can wear around my neck.

When sex is used as a bartering tool you are in trouble. It is not a bestowed gift. It is a mutually shared experience. That's it! I often find sex being used as a method of control. Again; BIG mistake!

While we have defenses to protect ourselves sex should never be one of the barriers we put up. There are any number of defense mechanisms.

Some include:

Rationalization; Trying to prove your behavior is sensible and justifiable

Denial; Refusing to accept or face the reality

Projection; Placing blame on others

Reaction Formation; preventing feelings from being expressed by exaggerating the opposite feeling

Compensation; making up for real or fancied inferiorities

Displacement; Discharging usually hostile feelings on others rather than the person involved

Regression; Going back to less mature behavior

Identification; Identifying oneself with someone of higher standing

Fantasy; Imagination

Sublimation; Putting frustration into socially accepted behavior

Undoing; Counteracting what is felt as *bad*

Acting Out; permitting forbidden desires to be acted upon

Emotional Insulation; Withdrawing

We all need defenses and usually choose one more than others. It is our, *armor* emotionally so that we are not *wounded*.

No one can be without defenses. Some people have thick iron walls around themselves and others are more trusting and have tissue paper. It all depends on our personalities and life experiences. If we have been close emotionally and hurt by someone or repeatedly hurt by others, we build up our walls.

It's sort of like a *feeling protection*.

Now when it involves close relationships, and that means including sex, we can be very cautious; or in today's world not cautious at all, and just have sex. We all must choose what makes us not just comfortable, but happy, and feeling good about ourselves in the end.

It may take a heap of experience and time.

My own idea is to have three marriages.

The first with a responsible person to have children with.

The second for mad passionate love and fabulous sex.

The third for companionship.

Now maybe one person over time fits all three categories. Maybe not.

We are all different with different needs. We all make compromises.

The idea of giving oneself should be total and mutual or else... what's the use?

So, yes, sexuality is a magnificent gift, BUT it is a gift we are all given, and the thing is... how is it used??

"My wife is a sex object---every time I ask for sex, she objects." - Les Dawson

Enjoy Sex... Fake Love

"If passion drives you, let reason hold the reins." - Benjamin Franklin

In today's world where so much is *instant* it seems there are drastic changes in both how couples relate to one another; both in and out of bed. Nothing new here but... everything! Sex is readily available and can happen with total strangers. Go on line and say what you might enjoy sexually and there it is. Love however is a whole different story. You can indeed enjoy sex and fake love.

For some, particularly females, there may need to be a feeling of love; being loved. Is it necessary for good sex? No. Is it necessary maybe to make believe you love your partner or more importantly, that he loves you? Perhaps. It is curious how many couples can engage in a sexual relationship and one or another can tell themselves they are in love with their sexual partner. That's the head talking, holding the reins.

Sex and even good sex can happen and for many it is easy. They have that relationship and do what they want when they want, and love is not discussed or really felt. That's fine for many young people and fine for learning about sharing their bodies and achieving orgasm, hopefully. BUT, when we talk about love, that's a whole other story.

Can it be faked like an orgasm? Perhaps. Many people can talk themselves into things and delude themselves. Many view certain gestures or behaviors as signs of love.

Even if it is said, 'I love you' can mean different things at different times.

So, how do you know the real McCoy? The real deal happens over time and testing. It includes more than sex but doesn't exist without it in the manner I am speaking about. There are small gestures, there are *looks* and there are words.

We live in moments and the moments that matter are those shared with intense intimacy. Waiting and longing for someone only adds to the desire to be together and to share oneself. Touching, gazing, pleasing the partner in small ways makes the wanting to be close a visceral experience. When apart there is an *emptiness* inside, and the feeling that you can only be content in your lover's arms. Does it last forever? Love does... even after death, in the truly loved.

Passion is necessary for life to be well lived. Too many people are hemmed in by guilt, doing the *right* thing, being judged and so on. It takes courage, real courage, to be free enough to love completely. It is a very risky business. Sometimes one or the other waits to say the words, 'I love you' first. Not necessary. Risk it if you feel it. You can fake an orgasm, but you cannot fake true love. Both are feelings to be sure, but one is more easily accomplished and repeated. Both make you feel good in different ways. Both make you feel desired, and both make you attached and vulnerable. Thinking about the one you love lights you up. You glow in a way that nothing else can replicate.

Being in love can make that sex you share more meaningful, and heavenly. It can be *down and dirty* and with abandonment. Love covers all the bases and is worth waiting for, fighting for, and living for. *Fake* whatever you like and *need* to, but in the end your heart will tell you the real story!

"I don't regret how much I love, and I avoid those who repent their passion." - Rumi

What's Your Sexual ID

"I'm not lesbian; I'm not bisexual; I'm not straight. I'm just curious." - Alice Walker

Are you?

Today, in America, we have a *fluid* concept of sexual identity in many respects.

Almost twenty years ago my book, *Transsexuals-Life From Both Sides*, was groundbreaking. When I appeared on many TV talk shows the issue was either unknown or ridiculed. Today there is a better attitude as people have been educated.

People today have a wide range of choices in many areas including sexual preferences.

The ability to experiment and try a variety of behaviors is more available and opportunities are at your finger-tips. The Internet has certainly changed the manner in which people are able to meet and become involved with one another.

It is not just young people either. There are sites for older men and women to engage with one another in all sorts of ways. If you just want a *friend*, that is out there. If you just want sex with someone who lives close by, that is also available. Whatever your preference is sexually, you can bet there is a place for you to find a like- minded individual, or group.

While much of this remains private and known only to you, some people, or couples, discuss their likes with one another and they either agree and accept the partner's desires or reject them.

It is still not easy for individuals to share the fact that they are gay, bisexual, transgender, or whatever else, with family or friends, or the world.

We still have judgments from a lot of places. We still have not changed society to automatically be open and loving.

There are still people who think they can *change* you if you are not conforming to the norm or majority.

Young people today are exploring their sexual identity in many ways. Some of it may indeed just be temporary. Some of it may not be.

When it comes to that most important of all drives; sex, we are driven to search for satisfaction. Hopefully, in the end, it will include love; but not always for some.

All of the intricacies of how you look, what name you use, what pronoun is assigned to you, do not happen easily or quickly, or without drama and pain.

When *famous* people come out as gay or whatever, they can often help others. It's sort of, *If they can do it, so can I.*

Millennials are marrying later, and their divorce rate is down. Having experience before marriage helps.

Marriage itself is different. The rates of both men and women not wanting to stay in an unhappy relationship has caused many to try different sexual activities. Many have affairs. Some tell or have their partner's approval. Often variety helps a relationship that has dulled over time.

There are groups like the Skirt Club that has 7000 members worldwide and are in places like New York and L.A.

These groups are composed mainly of professional married women who come together for same sex adventures for a night.

Like I said, you can find ANYTHING today, at your finger-tips.

In 2010 only, 51 percent of adults were married.

It is no longer the same old story. Women have been shown to have a sex drive equal to men. The bonobos, pigmy chimps, are closest to our DNA.

They are matriarchal, and the women are the ones *demanding* sex, all the time with any mate, both males and females! They are also one of, if not the most, non-aggressive group of primates. Is there a lesson here?

However, in our society anything outside the norm, whether hypocritical or not, is seen as, immoral.

Many are left with fantasies and secret lives as a result. It's the behavior that counts!

Being accepted and happy when you are *different* is still a road less travelled. Where are the pioneers and examples of courage?

"Love has no gender-compassion has no religion-character has no race." - Abhijit Naskars

Used Or Abused

A woman in a boat was stopped by a maritime police officer as she cruised in a lake.

When she asked what the problem was he announced he was giving her an expensive ticket for her violation. "What violation?" she asked.

"You are not permitted to fish in these waters," he said.

"But I'm not fishing," she replied.

"You have lines and poles here so you could use them," he said. As he proceeded to write the ticket she screamed, "*Rape!*"

Other boaters came to her boat.

"What are you doing," the policeman yelled.

"Well, you have the equipment and you COULD use it," she announced.

Enough said.

Recently I have had a number of people tell me about their bad experiences of being used by men in a sexual fashion. Some of the situations are indeed what I would deem beyond *used* and become *abuse*.

One woman who was in her fifties told me about a married psychiatrist who was romancing her and having sex with her regularly. She learned this went on with other patients as well.

There is no other word for such behavior other than *exploitive*.

It is taking advantage of a vulnerable person for one's own benefit. How awful.

Yes, she felt *chosen* and, in a sense, *loved* but at what expense, and was it genuine?

And did she have to pay for these *sessions*?

Another woman also about sixty was in a relationship with a man a bit younger. She was educated, successful, and worldly; all the things he was not. He was, however, good-looking and sexy.

He took money from her and had a number of other women he was buying things for, she found out. She allowed this situation to go on, as did the former woman I wrote about for a number of years. WHY??

The fact of the matter is that sex does make the world go round and women are particularly vulnerable in this area.

While it is true that the sex desires and drive for women, in many cases, reaches the level equal to men they are able to deal with it differently. They do the promotional work behind the scenes while men and their sexuality is literally *out there* for all to observe! Once ignited it is more difficult for a man's response to be squelched.

There are PREDATORS who look for women to USE and ABUSE. Yes, women can seduce and many have used men in their fashion but sexually it is the men who usually prey on women.

They use their powerful positions; does the name Clinton ring a bell? They use money when they are short, fat, bald and boring! They use whatever will *get* the female to bed. Flattery is a big one. Just look at Facebook and the comments from strange men to women whose pictures they like.

It starts out with a *Hello beautiful*, or something like that.

The thing is they are willful and make the female feel *chosen*. She sees it as exciting and an escape from the daily tedium of life. Nothing beats feeling special and cared about. Needing sex is what ignites it. Sometimes she uses sex to get the emotional needs met. In that sense she too uses a man.

No one has the right to tell anyone else how to live; except parents of small children.

No one can decide what any woman should tolerate or accept. No one can live it but her. My own advice is that when the *pain* outweighs the *pleasure* you will want to move along. And there are women who accept and tolerate great ABUSE for years and years. They need something from that man and will do whatever it takes to get it.

While outsiders can observe what is happening and deplore it, it is meaningless to say anything because nothing will work to end it. The head knows what is happening, but the emotional part will always trump that.

Do both parties get something they need in the end… you bet! BUT and it's a big BUT, being exploited is an unequal relationship that is really unfair.

Whoever said life is fair, anyway?

"Illusory joy is often worth more than genuine sorrow." - Rene' Descartes

Viewer Discretion Is Advised

"We are most alive when we're in love." - John Updike

Recently there was an article in the New York Times about *What teenagers are learning from porn, by* Maggie Jones.

It turns out they are getting a lot of what we would call *sex education* in this manner.

As a sex educator for over 30 years I was not surprised and also a bit disappointed.

It is true that most of what we teach at home or at school is sterile about the body parts, menstruation, and the like. Or, we are giving information about all the bad things that are associated with sexuality; venereal diseases, and pregnancy, and sometimes, about morality.

Who teaches that sex with a partner we care about and hopefully, love, is the best that life offers?

Well, I do, and my book does, and my blog does.

When young people view pornography, they see acts; many of them, but not a relationship. They don't see caring, and they certainly don't see romance.

Now there is absolutely nothing wrong with ANY form of sex, as long as both partners agree, but some of what these kids or adults watch is not everyone's cup of tea.

They see porn from the ages of 13 and 14. In a study; there are lots of studies, 93 percent of boys and 62 percent of girls said they saw online porn before age 18.

A lot of it includes many forms of abusive or violent behavior.

As a result, some colleges offer courses about not being addicted to it, or how it might warp their libidos, or ruin future relationships.

The most popular site is Pornhub.com with 80 million visitors a day!! These sites in total are among the most visited sites in the world. That's a message.

Most parents have no idea that their young adolescents are watching these sites. So much for family closeness and communication.

It is true that talking about sex is touchy and most parents shy away from a great deal that kids are interested in. Problem is what facts do they get. What ideas do they get? What do they try out?

They are learning all sorts of *stuff.* They end up thinking that's how to behave and please a man or woman.

Some of the videos include men ejaculating on a woman's face. It's not what I call a *facial.*

They see bondage and sadomasochistic behavior. They view more than one partner having direct intercourse. They see objects being put into genitals. Some see choking as a part of the act. They watch anal sex.

Some see this as a safety against pregnancy.

There is the belief that all of this leads to a generation of men being sexually assaultive and helps shape how teenagers think and talk about sex and how they think about masculinity and femininity. Just watch the news these days!!

Not surprising is the study that found that in 2016 teens at ages 16 and 17 said that porn was their primary source for information about sex. Great!!

Not great!!!

Getting accurate information medically, and scientifically, is necessary, but the more important information is left out. What people need to know, and what they are curious about is in short supply.

While there is no scientific evidence that porn is addictive it can be compulsive.

What about technology today and people sending naked photos and sexting? All very easy and what happens as a result?

An unknown fact is that the *actors* in sex videos are not paid much. Blow jobs are $300, Anal sex is $1,000, double penetration $1,200 and gang bang $1,300 for three guys and $100 for each additional male.

Guys are paid less than women; rare in most professions! They often use things like Viagra to keep an erection.

For my money one of the *nastiest* performances involves putting the penis into the anus and then directly putting it into the female's mouth. YUK!

In another study, 70 percent of females said that anal intercourse caused them pain.

In all of this it is usually the male pleasure that came, (*literally*) first.

So, how to have great sex and learn about that?

There are some courses in colleges such as Starr Strong, and Porn Literacy that help give the whole picture. There is a site; tube8.com, that helps teach about values as well as technique. Learning about masturbation and how to achieve orgasm is a good thing. Knowing that it is the clitoris that allows orgasm for the female, is important for both sexes to learn about.

Knowing about lubrication and what that is and does is important for both sexes. *Toys* and vibrators are not bad things.

With all of this, the question of pursuing and showing you like someone and how to relate out of bed is the key. Who teaches *courting*?

Being complete is more than sex.

It's the values that matter and porn is only a small part of what good sex can be about.

It can be a stimulant and it can open eyes to a whole world of behaviors, but it is not teaching mutual pleasure and connection and the biggest goal; LOVE!

"Sex, on the whole, was meant to be short, nasty, and brutish. If what you want is cuddling, you should buy a puppy." - Julie Burchill

Unzip His Heart And Pants

"If it happens that you do want peanut butter in bed while you're having sex and your partner doesn't, in the long run the thing to do may be to find another partner." - Dr. Ruth Westheimer

Well, maybe, but not necessarily so.

What two people do with their sexual selves can vary but they should both enjoy and agree to whatever.

You can have great sex without love to be sure but to be able to combine the two is indeed magical. Now, not everyone wants that or is capable or willing to risk that.

It means you can be hurt mortally; emotionally, and you have to give up power and total control.

That is scary. Men in particular, but not exclusively, have a difficult time doing that.

There are sensitive men who do offer their hearts, more easily. But for many men they can have sex; be orgasmic and enjoy a partner but LOVE; that's a whole other story.

To have him unzip, so to speak, his heart takes a woman that knows what to do.

He needs to really trust her and that she won't *hurt* him where it counts; his heart.

It is the woman who leads him to do this. She has to feel confident and want and show her love for him to believe it. That takes time and testing.

It may happen as part of the sexual life and that's fine. He has sex as his display of love, truly.

For him total surrender is sexual and total surrender in love takes a lot. He needs to be able to be 'weak,' and maybe even be dominated. He has to be relieved of his *pressures.*

He relinquishes his will to his woman's care.

He needs specific sexual guidelines.

Criticism is the sexual kiss of death.

He likes touch usually and he gets pleasure from seeing you having *pleasure.*

Sex is not something anyone does *to* another if it is with love. It is a shared mutually good experience and includes foreplay that begins all day long with words and gestures. It is shared with communication.

It is sort of like eating. Not too fast, variety, new experiments, and a gourmet meal is definitely different from a hamburger on the run at McDonald's!

To be immersed and savor the moment is the goal to exquisite pleasure.

Unzipping the pants can be the start of something wonderful to be sure, but nurturing the heart takes a different course in order to unzip it. So much is involved in the whole process; from how you think your body looks to knowing about his body and what to do with it.

There is a great book with exact details about this; *Passionista* by Ian Kerner PhD.

Nothing is left to the imagination and he gives step by step guidelines to pleasuring a man.

There is another book by him regarding pleasuring a woman; *She Comes First*. I recommend them both.

Orgasm is a journey not a destination he says and we all know that; those of us who do know.

Pornography, fantasy, and every conceivable form of sex is discussed. You cannot be shy or embarrassed to get through the book or a great sexual life!

What has been your best sexual experience so far? Why was it the best?

The answers will be important to your continuing or future encounters.

Only three percent of mammals are monogamous. Why?

Probably because lust changes over time, and familiarity and loss of excitement and unpredictability take over. You know; BORING!!

A wise woman knows how to make it stay alive. No need for Viagra!

Interestingly, young men are turning to things like Viagra to make sure they are virulent. Too bad.

The hormone Dopamine gets released with love and makes you feel good and wanting to repeat the experience. The best drug!!

It makes you want to be attached; literally.

With orgasm women release oxytocin and that is sort of the *cuddle* drug.

With men, they release vasopressin and that allows them to relax and touch. We are different creatures, and nothing will ever change that so get used to it, revel in it, relax and enjoy it! You can learn to slow him down and he can learn how to speed you up; but you are in separate cars!!

"One makes mistakes; that is life. But it is never quite a mistake to have loved." - Romain Rolland

Sex Goes To The Dogs

So, Billy's digging a hole in his garden when his neighbor looks over and asks, "What are you doing, Billy?"

"I'm digging a hole to bury my goldfish who just died."

"That looks like an awfully big hole for a goldfish."

"Well, it's because it's inside your stupid cat!"

We all love our pets and there is a small fortune spent each year on them. The real reason we like them so much is they give unconditional love and companionship, and the main reason; we can project any thoughts or feelings we wish on them.

So, I'm in London with my guy and left Beaucoup, (cute huh?), the small yorkie home. He was a friendly but not so bright Yorkshire terrier who went everywhere with me. There was always a bow in his hair, (it's OK for male dogs) and he attracted a lot of attention.

After running all over London we got the bright idea to look for another yorkie.

On Kensington Church Walk, there was a pet shop that said they had a female dog for sale, so we ran over there and of course fell in love at first sight with the tiny puppy. We bought her and brought her back to the Savoy Hotel and left her with the coat lady while we went for lunch before going to the airport. Plane ride home was a mess and we remembered the lady had given the puppy a bowl of warm milk when we picked her up. She was sick the whole way home and my lap was not exactly fragrant. She was named Princess Maggie Scratch and we told her all about the two girls at home that would be so surprised and that Beaucoup would just love her. The anticipation was wonderful.

Once home, she went into the room where Beaucoup was; he growled and snapped at her. The girls were thrilled and we all said it was just a period of adjustment that was going on and that it wouldn't take long before they were best friends and later making adorable puppies themselves.

Next day Beaucoup was no friendlier and the day after he almost bit her causing us to keep them separated.

Lots of theories were espoused and finally an appointment with the veterinarian was made.

Now he was an old family friend and knew our dogs over the years. As a matter of fact, I had been his marriage counselor at one point and had done a sex ed. class at his children's school.

After examining the puppy and giving her shots he asked her name. I announced, Princess Maggie Scratch.

Then I went into a long story about how we found her and brought her home and as a matter of fact were having a hard time with Beaucoup accepting her. Maybe sibling rivalry, I suggested?

With that he held her aloft and turned her around and said," Perhaps you should change her name to Prince."

What?

Yes, we had been sold a male masquerading as a female and no wonder poor Beaucoup hated her on sight.

It is difficult to tell the sex of these tiny dogs when they are so young, but the store must have known and wanted to make a sale. I wrote to all the authorities in England about it and never received a reply. Caveat Emptor!

The two dogs never did get along and eventually Beaucoup was given to another family member. We kept Prince!

As a marriage counselor and sex educator everyone heard the story.

I'm still working on convincing some I'm really good with people; dogs not so much!

There's Sex And Then There's SEX

"There are things that happen in the dark between two people that make everything that happens in the light seem all right." - Erica Jong

This is true. And it is only true when there is a real connection and an emotional attachment to the person you are having sex with.

You can have great sex without love, to be sure, but you CANNOT have great love without sex!

My old line is that females use sex to get love and guys use love to get sex. Different approaches with different goals.

I don't care what changes have gone on and what this generation is experiencing, some truths are there for ALL time.

If I am not interested in sex and being sensuous or being that bad phrase, *a sex symbol,* I don't want to be here.

Women want to be attractive and have bodies that attract men. Men want to be masculine and attract women, and that's all good.

In order to really connect and be intimate, you need to be a person, but one who can merge, if you will, with another. You have to communicate and share feelings. You have to feel desirable and derive pleasure from your body and his.

Eroticism and passion can wane over time and it takes being able to be curious and responsive to your partner to keep it going.

How many times have I heard couples complain it was the same thing all the time? They only wanted to get the act over with.

Everyone has insecurities and issues about their body and their sexuality. Men more than women have fear of *it* not working. Will *it* go up? Will he be able to satisfy her?

Women, because of their anatomy, can hide their responses. They however do emit a warm fluid with orgasm and a knowledgeable man knows it. His response is right out there in living color.

When you accept another with all they are and you long to be with them they matter in a special unique way. You give up yourself in a total fashion.

Listen to the sounds of a deep orgasm. It is like nothing else. It is a total letting go.

The reality of maybe losing love is scary, so, many people cannot get to that point of total lack of control and sharing of themselves completely.

The more attached you are the more you have to risk or lose. You cannot have *rapture* with any holding back.

To keep excitement, you have to give up control.

You need to experiment with each other sexually.

Females use words for closeness while males use their bodies.

For females, eroticism is more diffuse. It includes smell, and skin contact, and not just the genitals.

It is a mind-body experience.

If there is any negativity it makes the sexual experience difficult. You need a clear positive approach to have it be fully erotic and vital.

Different positions; sixty-nine, where you both have your head, hands and mouths on each other's genitals is an approach that helps you connect with body parts. Having sex on a plane; the *mile-high* club offers diversity, and pornography is stimulating for both sexes.

Denying to use one's body in a fulfilling sexual life is sad.

We have the equipment and it's ours to use.

Some people are *hung up* in many areas and that is too bad. Sometimes alcohol or other things can help loosen people up. Sometimes it is just the strong pull to someone that lets you be free.

While the act itself, even with time to build up to the act, does not take a long time the after reaction and longing to repeat it will stand you in good stead. Happy cells are healthy cells.

There is NOTHING like being in love and showing it with your body and being responded to.

There is a power in being irresistible.

Look at history and how sex has overridden reason and all sorts of social barriers. This is not included in rape or when one partner is not a willing participant.

Being serene in a long-term relationship is fine for many, but to live with passion is a whole other ball game!! Play Ball!!!

"Sex which has been acclaimed by too many misguided poets as an utopian activity, seldom attains that status in the human race." - Anita Loos

Talk About The Big O

"Of all sexual aberrations, chastity is the strangest." - Anatole France

As a therapist for decades, I am always curious about the people who choose not to engage in sexual activity… it's not natural.

The most potent human drive is to connect bodily with a partner who excites you and hopefully one you share loving feelings with. You need to talk about that big O.

Now I am not talking about people who have medical conditions that prevent their expression of love physically, or the really old people who are not interested or capable of enjoying sex. But even here just being naked and close and touching; hugging and kissing is lovely. It is the basic human connection.

Sex rules the world and people have done EVERYTHING to have a good and meaningful satisfying sexual life.

When it comes to orgasm the question is; does the couple talk about it?

The closer two people are with intimacy the more they share verbally about the things that truly matter to them; FEELINGS!

Young people today are less hung up about the issues. They experiment and have a variety of experiences. All to the good. It is like anything else in this life; the more you know, the better. The more practice the better you are at what you do. The more you are involved the better you can ultimately decide what you need for a long term relationship. It takes time and a lot of ups and downs.

No one is happy all the time. No one is responsible for your happiness but you. You cannot manage your life when it comes to love. It chooses you. You can have great sex without love but you cannot have great love without sex. It is when the two of you are joined that *magic* happens. You want to be together, and you want to please that person in and out of bed.

If you have been hurt before you will be cautious but try and try again.

Females tend to get *clingy* and are often put off or angry about *stuff.* Guys just want to be left alone and happy to have a good sexual partner.

You have to kiss a lot of frogs to get the prince!

When it comes to orgasm talking is needed.

You need to say what you don't like and more importantly what you do like.

Where to touch, how to touch, and what you share verbally is NECESSARY!!

There should be NO faking it! A good partner knows.

Females especially need to know their bodies and what makes them feel good; a hand, a mouth, a penis...

Where they enjoy being touched and the lightness or strength of the touch matters. It also matters for a guy but he is ready usually at the sight of her. With time and familiarity, he could benefit from the same discussion as she needs.

Orgasms begin long before you hit the bed. They start with the endearing words that are shared. You cannot go from being busy with work, household stuff, children, bills etc. to putting it all aside to be ready for the big O.

Couples who can communicate about intimate feelings can usually talk about that most sensitive subject; their sex life. Those that cannot are probably not close in other ways as well.

When he or she is *irreplaceable* emotionally you have the real deal.

Many couples live in a loveless fashion forever. They are the *walking dead*. You can see them all around you. Years together mean nothing. Endurance contests or just habit. Not good enough for this all too short life. It takes bravery and insight to achieve that higher level of being. Once there you cannot really live without it. You are alive!!

Bringing one another sexual happiness makes you want to do it again and again. Even if you don't get to the big O, no problem from time to time. Not to worry... just talk and be close.

Lynn Hubschman

Over time you can incorporate *toys* and a variety of surprises. Just put your creative imagination to work! All you need is one another and that magic feeling to get it going.

Because we are a goal oriented society we have to teach people that the big O is not always necessary or possible. It is not a problem. Have fun with each other in bed.

And as for *simultaneous*; who cares. If it happens fine, if not also fine. The big O is a feeling that cannot be duplicated any other way, so learn how to do it and relax.

It will keep you young, happy, and vital. Feeling desired is the best!!

"If you aren't going all the way, why go at all?" - Joe Namath

And Then There's Pillow Talk

"Sharing pillow talk with the wrong people can make a hard bed to lie on and will surely lead to nightmares in your relationship." - Carlos Wallace

He said: I like you
She said: I like you, too

She said: Sometime let's have coffee or lunch and talk
He said: How about Tuesday

She said: Hey, not so fast. French kissing is not something I ever liked
He said: (Nothing)

He said: Let's go to a hotel
She said: Never, ever, never
He said: Do I take that as a maybe

She said: Okay next week I will go with you to a hotel. I can't fight this
He said: I'll pick you up on Tuesday

She said: I am both nervous and excited
He said: I know the feeling

He said: Let's meet at one next week at the hotel
She said: You bring the wine and I'll get sandwiches

He said: To us…. forever
She said: I'll drink to that

She said: You are my gorgeous man
He said: If you say it often enough, I'll start to believe it

She said: Tell me about your mother
He said: You're like a dentist's drill digging down all the time

She said: You make me furious because…
He said: (after a long pause) Can I have a kiss now

She said: You are an incredible man
He said: You are an incredible woman
She said: Doesn't count, you copied me

She said: I don't love you…. I adore you
He said: I love you. You are under my skin

She said: Do you think I have the best of you
He said: No question about it

She said: I'm done with him. He can't call in three days.
He said: It's not right or intelligent and I tried to test it and failed.
I miss you, want you, need you, and love you

He said: You are the best thing that ever happened to me
She said: Even from when you were young in love, had kids, and were
successful in business
He said: Yes

She said: What is the difference between this relationship compared to
another
He said: This is the real McCoy

She said: I didn't even behave this way as a teenager
He said: Me either

He said: I wish you were the mother of my children
She said: They'd be the same children

He said: Marry me
She said: We're more married than anyone

He said: I'd like to die in your arms
She said: Don't die. I'll be really mad if you do

He said: I don't think we could be together 24/7
She said: If we were both free, we'd be together

She said: I love you so
He said: Me too

Conversation over many years between a couple over 70 married to other people.

It's the same whether you are 16 or 86!

"You are so gorgeous. Please tell me you don't plan on talking the whole time.

You don't like talking?

There are much better things you could be doing with your mouth...." - Elizah J. Davis

Sex Ed. 101, Sex Ed 102, Sex Ed 103

"Is it all a matter of hormones? Oestrogen uber alles? Nature gives us thirty years of blindness to male bullshit so we can make the maximum number of babies." - Erica Jong

Recently I had a discussion with a very bright college student about what she learned about sex. Quite a lot actually. That's the good news. But there is another side to it all; the bad news.

Early in my professional career I was doing sex education in schools. You have no idea about the problems that were created. Some of us, we were very few at the time, had car tires slashed in the parking lot, while others were jeered at. School administrators were shaking in their proverbial boots, lest parents complained. We even did classes for the *retarded*, in institutions, and found that the people who truly needed the education were not the *inmates* but the caregivers.

It is a funny business this form of *knowledge.* We who live in America are bombarded by sexual material constantly… but guess what? We are a very uncomfortable people with this subject.

As a counselor, for decades, I can tell you, people will tell you anything, including what's in their bank accounts, but they have an extremely difficult time sharing information about their sexual lives.

Have you ever just looked at couples, and imagined what they are like, *in bed?* I do that quite often. Most of the time I want to laugh or… throw up!

Anyway, back to what goes on today with this so-called education. There are courses for high school students and college age kids, and there is a lot of information. However, many questions that are highly personal and *embarrassing* do not get answered.

Today there is the Internet and people of all ages, turn to it for information and also for stimulation, in many cases. That's fine but there is also a wide variety of faulty information. It is a tricky business.

I still think the old adage that guys use love to get sex, and females use sex to get love, is true.

Both young and old people are having sex a lot. Good News. How many are orgasmic and find love? You tell me.

People are experimenting with a wide variety of activity. That's good too. Practice and exploring are indeed beneficial.

There are dangers out there; like diseases.

Some of them include:

Human Papillomavirus, (HPV) Genital warts

About fifty percent of sexually active people will have this. Some forms can cause cancer. It can clear up on its' own or a doctor can treat it in a variety of ways; freeze it off, gels etc.

There is a vaccine and the virus is spread skin to skin.

Chlamydia

This a leading cause of infertility. It is treatable but if not, it can cause pelvic inflammatory disease.

There may be no symptoms but if there are, in the female, there may be a vaginal discharge, pain when urinating, or occasional bleeding. Latex condoms can help prevent it and there are antibiotics.

Syphilis

This is spread from open sores anywhere and during sex. If caught early it is curable with antibiotics, or penicillin. Interesting that some symptoms may be a rash on the hands or soles of feet. Condoms again may prevent it.

Pubic *Crab* Lice

These are parasitic insects that feed on blood and can be found in any hair including pubic hair.

There is itching and blue spots. Special shampoos and cleaning clothes and bed linen will fix it. Again condoms do not protect against infection.

Hepatitis B

This can cause liver damage. Often there are no symptoms but there can be joint pain or skin eruptions. There is no cure and can be spread through sexual fluids, shared needles, tattooing, and piercings. Condoms can reduce risk.

Gonorrhea

This is fairly common and sometimes treatable or preventable. Symptoms include genital discharge and pain urinating. If untreated it can cause infertility. Condoms and antibiotics help.

Chancroid

Females have no symptoms, but males get ulcers on the penis. Spread skin to skin and rare. Antibiotics and condoms.

HIV

Symptoms may not appear for years. If they do, there will be fever, and rashes. There is no cure but there is medication, especially PEP right away after exposure. Condoms help.

Herpes

Saved this for last as it is common and no cure. It is spread skin to skin and symptoms include blisters on the genitals or anus. Condoms do not prevent it.

So, back to my college student. She said the best advice is to get tested and maybe colleges should demand that for every student, at least once a year. She also felt one person for a good while was a good idea.

As an aside, I know many people who want that done before they *sleep* with any new partner. One woman had a detective even check a guy out before she agreed to have sex! My idea too; sexual monogamy!

Now there's a case for having a long-term boyfriend or girlfriend, if I ever heard one!!

"I've never had sex I didn't like." - Dolly Parton

Shut Up And Lie Down

"I think men talk to women, so they can sleep with them and women sleep with men, so they can talk to them." - Jay McInerney

This may be truer than you might like to believe.

In over decades as a relationship therapist and sex educator I can tell you it is the case more often than not.

Males, as a rule, will say anything to get a female in bed. It doesn't matter the age or circumstances. The females, without much experience, believe what is said or whispered to them. It's all sweet and flattering.

Who doesn't like hearing those pretty complimentary words?

It's usually how beautiful you are, how sexy you are, or all the things I like about you.

Before she knows it she's in bed with him.

That's when the situation takes a turn. What do you know about one another? That depends on how much time and what questions were asked before the bed. Have you seen each other at your worst? Angriest? Under pressure? Is what was told to you the truth? How do you know?

What do you not like about one another? What then do you like?

How was affection and caring shown before the bed?

All part of the *package*.

Now it's put up or shut up; literally.

How is the kissing? What is the stamina? What about the body? Does he/she smell good? Is there pubic hair? Muscles? What about the seductive voice? How about the *lead up* to sex? Protection against STDs or birth control? Lots of areas to explore and react to. How about a massage before? Are you comfortable about your body in the light? Breast size, penis size; circumcised?

There's a lot going on in the beginning. It's the discovery phase.

Usually people are at their level best here. It is with time that the real you comes out and shows itself.

Sometimes a relationship is just for sex. Actually, it is good exercise!

That's fine for a lot of people and females use their sexuality to hold on to a guy. Today they are freer and want sex, but it is different from a male's need usually.

Males reach their prime at about age 18 and females about 35. Not fair, but a good idea to have a younger man as you get older.

Many males do not want an ongoing relationship or intimacy and play the field. Hookers are not paid for sex. They are paid to leave!

There is nothing *dirty* about sex so long as two or more people agree to it.

Outside of the bedroom is where the relationship is made. Sex itself takes little time but the consequences can be long lasting. The positions, unless you are involved, look ridiculous. It's like the saying, that kinky is using a feather and perverted is using the whole chicken!

Being uninhibited is a good thing in bed. Can you judge that before you get there? Sometimes. It depends on how people are when talking, eating, dancing and so on. Being constrained, too polite, reserved and sort of shy will give you a clue. Touching and fondling will let you know how your partner feels about you physically.

If you can't keep your hands off one another that's a good sign about what sex will be like.

Today for many young people it's sort of, "Okay I'll come in for a drink and sex, but that's it."

Jumping into bed before testing and knowing a person can work out but often it's not going to lead to a full or on-going real relationship. You should only do what feels comfortable to you. Females decide about when sex will take place. They should decide under what circumstances they will allow it. If alcohol or drugs are in the picture the decision may not be clear or a good one in the end.

There is nothing better than good sex coupled with love, but that takes time and testing.

We get no guarantees in this life and not much is forever, so it is in your best interest to think about these issues before they present themselves and not jump to a decision on the spot or before you are ready.

Many females believe that the guy they sleep with and who has said all those pretty words will be theirs for the long haul, only to discover it was his way of getting her to lie down and shut up!!

"Among men sex sometimes results in intimacy; among women, intimacy sometimes results in sex." - Barbara Cartland

Sex Yes…. Sex No

"A little theory makes sex more interesting, more comprehensible, and less scary----too much is a put- down, especially as you're likely to get it out of perspective and become a spectator of your own performance." - Dr. Alex Comfort

You can't escape it; sex! It is everywhere. We see it all over the place in many forms and today we hear about it all over the news.

The media, law, and women have changed and that has opened the door for all sorts of issues being brought up and out.

Two of the biggest these days, especially for young people, has to do with both consent and sexual satisfaction.

The problem with consent is that there is no real way to be sure that you have consent.

This is mostly true for females.

Many young men with hormones raging and the sexual *imperative* driven by their bodies often assume that a female wants to engage in sexual activity.

Now that can come about from a variety of sources. She can be attractive and obliging and giving out signals that tell him she likes him. She indeed may.

Her idea of being close or enjoying one another may be a different message from the one he is receiving.

Touching, fondling, kissing, and telling someone you like them may indeed be giving a green light for sex to a young male.

Has she implied that it is a *yes?*

Does he stop and ask that question? Well, maybe. Does that mean he will stop his advances and pursuit of sexual release? Not necessarily. Should it be in writing? Definitely not!

But how to not be considered a *tease?* How to give a clear, as opposed to an ambivalent message?

That is not easy, and many young women have given mixed messages and then when sex is inevitable, they are feeling guilty or embarrassed or angry. It's not so black and white and it is not rape in most cases.

There is no protocol and every case is unique but the bottom line is that females need to speak up and say what they want or what they do not want.

This is also true when there is a relationship or even a one-night hook-up. When it comes to real sex; communication is the key.

While we are conditioned from birth and within our culture and history today's females are expecting to have sexual fulfillment.

They are exploring their own bodies and know how to achieve orgasm.

When with a partner it then becomes what to say and how to be satisfied. This is usually not a big problem for the males but here too they can let their partner know what they enjoy.

For females they prepare for sex. They shower, dress, perfume themselves and so on when they expect to have a sexual encounter. Interestingly it is females who respond to fragrances more than males so he should be putting on the cologne. Men do not prepare much, if at all.

For females it is difficult for her to ask for what she wants. Does she have the right words? Does it make him feel less potent? Is she too pushy?

If it goes into too much detail does the *magic* vanish?

For a female, orgasm takes patience. She is slower than he is.

He needs education and there is no school teaching this vital information!

Actually cunnilingus is a good way for her to achieve orgasm. But it takes a lot of information for him. Cosmo, the internet, porn, and so on can help but that information is not the whole story for every individual.

I want to run the real school!!

In the end sex *yes* should be a shared mutually respectful experience with open communication. But that should also include fun and showing love in many forms.

All of this takes time and maybe many experiences. There is no rush.

While some experiences may not be pleasant or fulfilling each person has to figure out what works for them. Then they have to go about finding it.

How nice it would be if the messages were clear and both males and females could say what pleases them and then learn how to deliver the final supreme pleasure.

"Sex lies at the root of life, and we can never learn to reverence life until we know how to understand sex." - Havelock Ellis

Shut Your Mouth... OR Open It

"Good communication is as stimulating as black coffee, and just as hard to sleep after." - Anne Morrow Lindbergh

That word 'communication' is bantered around a lot. What does it really mean... or do?

We are sending out messages all the time; yes, verbal and non-verbal.

What we say is important and has meaning BUT what we DO is the real test.

Now our mouths are used for this *talk* and for so much more.

We have our first feeling of need gratification when we are nursed by a mother or given a bottle. The mouth is used to eat. That is also an area where we feel pleasant sensations.

Think of the memories of wonderful meals at home or out with people you care about. The thought of a favorite dish from childhood evokes feelings that are warm and sweet.

Think of all those foods that are supposed to be aphrodisiac. It starts in the mouth.

Think of oysters that trigger the production of sex hormones, chili peppers that release endorphins in the brain that mimic how you feel when aroused. Avocado to maintain vigor, chocolate to spike dopamine and feel pleasurable, and banana, (and don't forget the shape!), triggers testosterone production, honey regulates estrogen and testosterone.

There are other foods that are in this list. Coffee gets women in the mood for sex, and watermelon acts like Viagra and so on.

You get the picture; the mouth is the core of much in our lives. Just sounds make us respond in a variety of ways. Memories of sounds are there as well.

It is also used for sexual pleasure. Kissing, licking and biting are all included.

There are sexually transmitted diseases that can be gotten through the mouth. Herpes, gonorrhea, and syphilis, and hepatitis are in this list. Oral sex needs to be concerned about here.

Even in some religions bread and wine take on a special significance.

The mouth in all its ramifications is a real source of both pleasure and concern.

Now, back to the words that come out.

Words have meanings and they are never erased once out.

There are differences in the ways men and women connect through language.

Men, for the most part, are practical and think in broad terms. They are rational, and often withdrawn. They deal directly and are goal oriented. They use *love* to get sex.

Women, on the other hand, generally like to connect and share and nurture. They appreciate small gestures, and their moods go in waves. They often expect a response without having to ask. They want intimacy and use sex to get *love*.

They give a lot emotionally and want a relationship to be the core of their lives.

Men fear opening their hearts completely and women fear being abandoned.

They both have a difficult time, as a result, to say what the other wants to hear.

Often the automatic response may feel good but in the long run it may have been a bad message.

Now we can't be thinking of every word all the time, nor should we. But over time we should know what to expect and what our partner might like to hear.

If the messages are not getting across well, or there is misinterpretation only communication will solve the problem. So, more talk!

Romance and sweet words are necessary for women.

Valentine's day is just the day for your mouth to be open!!

"At a dinner party one should eat wisely but not too well and talk well but not too wisely." - W. Somerset Maugham

The Really Weaker Sex

"Once made equal to man, woman becomes his superior." - Socrates

Lynn Hubschman

In this year when it seems likely the United States may have its' first female president the question comes front and center ...can a woman do it? Is she a real woman if she wants this power? What is likely to change?

All good questions.

While I believe the biological differences that are inherent and genetic between the sexes, and the differences are significant, this notion of the weaker sex becomes paramount.

Being accused of being *sexist* often, I do not deny that the only areas I am *feminist* about are education and the workplace.

In all other realms I believe women hold a definite place by being *feminine* in the traditional sense of the word.

They should be the *softer* ones, and the gender that is seen as the non-aggressive one when it comes to men and love.

Women can be assertive and go after what they need but they usually do it in a different fashion than men.

Men are out there *slaying dragons* to be sure but today women also hold responsible positions and work hard for less money than men. This is true with even the best education. They are in colleges and graduate schools in record numbers. They are professionals in every field but they are still women.

They are the ones that allow sexual behavior, and they bear the children. They are the primary ones to raise children and run households.

True, men have brawn and are physically stronger, but women are stronger in other ways.

They can work through situations in easier ways than men without brute force. They can compromise and work through long-term solutions slowly. They are just plain, *different.*

The stress of just living is not easily handled. There are three to five times the number of suicides among men than with women. Talk about weak or strong!

Now when it comes to women doing a job traditionally seen as *man's work* the problems arise.

This is especially true in something like running a government or the free world. What would the world be if more women had positons of power and ran governments?

The common thinking goes something like, *she has too much testosterone* or the like.

She is not attractive therefore not feminine. She is power hungry, like a man and so on.

Maybe some of this is true. There is no one brand of man or woman. There are gradations.

Having worked professionally for decades with the transgendered community and patients I can tell you the differences are not in the genitals! It's all in the head and your perception and goals for self.

The true test of masculinity and femininity in many instances is in the bedroom. However, for some rare creatures that is not the case. Then we have to look beyond all that or the ability to have children.

So, what we are left with is a scale of many categories to look at and judge who is weak, strong, male or female.

The culture defines some of the parameters and our own education, experience, and early family imprinting all weigh in.

Whom do you see as your own ideal of man, or woman? Hollywood versions, people you know, or magazine pictures? Should she be thin and beautiful? What should he be?

What makes someone, *strong* in your eyes?

Women for the most part bear the greatest burden of emotional weight. For my money they are hardly the *weaker* sex!!

"Social science affirms that a woman's place in society marks the level of civilization." - Elizabeth Cady Stanton

Russian Roulette Sex

"When you meet a man, don't you always idly wonder what he'd be like in bed? I do." - Helen Gurley Brown

Now that's a lady after my own heart. And don't be surprised that males do the same, maybe more so. Sex rules the world and the intellect and mind are no match!

While it is true, we all want love, the sexual pull drives us, and we can maybe fall in love afterwards. Love takes time.

Monogamy is not a natural state. Only nine percent of the species are monogamous and a third of them are primates and 90 percent of birds are. We are not birds!

Females are picky as they need romance and someone to help rear children and support them. Males focus on youth and attractiveness and want to be sure any children are their own.

We don't want to be rejected or alone; most of us. Miss Havisham in Dicken's 'Great Expectations' lived out her life in a wedding dress and became embittered after being spurned. Most people are able to suffer lost love and move on. Sex drives us. Nature wants to reproduce itself.

These days we have multiple options and ways to meet one another. The more mature and insightful know who they are and what they need.

There is a lot of calculation and playing games until the *right* partner is found.

We cannot be totally self-sufficient unless, we love our vibrator!

Handling red flags and dealing with all that any relationship entails is one of the most difficult things in this life.

Making a relationship front and center takes a lot. Narcissistic people are disabled here.

Feeling secure with another person holding your heart, is not easy to obtain.

Trial and error and testing over time can make it happen.

The more you know the better.

NOW what happens when you lose your virginity or get pregnant by *chance*?

A wide variety of scenarios can be played out. Many times, losing virginity for females takes place when they are under the influence of alcohol or drugs.

Sometimes it's just part of the culture and *everybody's doing it.*

At times, it's curiosity and wanting to get that part of life over with.

It can also be a way of feeling loved or rebellion against parental wishes.

It can be a way of proving to oneself that you are wanted in that fashion.

Sometimes it just feels *right*.

After that, it is up to each individual to decide how they choose to use their bodies and sexuality.

When I was Director of Social Work at a large city hospital we had a government grant to help with all the young unwed mothers. We offered birth control counseling and supplies. We offered school opportunities to complete education and we helped with baby care and whatever a new mother needed.

The hope was that this would prevent further unplanned births. Guess what? It didn't.

The reasons were varied. Ranging from wanting to hold on to a guy, to wanting something of their very own. It made for an extremely difficult future. Big problems for the individual, the child, the family, and for society in general.

With unwanted pregnancies in an upper-class group, some of the dynamics may be the same but they are able to provide for themselves and their child. They may also have a partner involved for their needs; emotional and material.

What is a surprise today is the rather large numbers of educated bright young women who have sex and do not use any form of birth control even though they know all about it and it is available.

Russian Roulette Sex! Again, the reasons are varied.

A guy may force the issue, not wanting to wear a condom, and she wants to please and hold on to him.

A relationship includes sex, and often the hope for love. Alcohol, drugs, and the idea that it *won't happen to me* can take over. Surprise. I have had clients who became pregnant after the first sexual contact with someone. It can happen. Sometimes the topic is not broached, and the partner assumes that birth control has been taken care of. Surprise again.

Taking this kind of chance has huge consequences and also is not a responsible way to handle something so important in life. Is this how you plan your future? Your child's?

Thinking your partner will happily accept a pregnancy may open up areas about them that you never knew existed.

Not sharing the pregnancy is not a good option. What does that signify?

While there are choices for birth control and thank goodness, we live in a time when that is available, there is no wonderful option, usually. It makes sex a bit dicey, to say the least. But with all of it, have sex, enjoy it, learn about you and your partner and don't play with chance here.

If you like to gamble; go to Vegas!!

"One person's safe sex is another's abstinence." Alice Kahn

Take The Clothes And YOU Out Of The Closet

"Asking *Who's the man & who's the woman* in a same-sex relationship is like asking which chopstick is the fork." - Ellen DeGeneres

At the end of the year many people decide to make *resolutions* and attempt to correct something they don't like about themselves or their lives. All well and good. Problem is many cannot stick to them and others won't allow it.

The issue of being *gay* is a tough one.

Many young people are aware of their leanings at tender ages but attempt to ignore or push the feelings away. It is not easy to be *different* in our society; hypocritical though it may be.

Parents of children who show signs of preferring to be or be close to the same or opposite sex also do not want to automatically accept that their child may be gay.

And then there is the outside world who may see it, taunt it, or ignore it. That can include a plethora of people including relatives, teachers, friends, and strangers.

However, as with all strong feelings of attraction and passion, the feelings do not and cannot disappear. Being homosexual is NOT a choice.

Sometimes people experiment and then decide they are or are not homosexual. Then, of course, some are bi-sexual, but here I am talking primarily about those people who are basically gay.

While there have been all sorts of ridiculous people and a wide variety of ways to try to *change* an individual; nothing will work. It can't. It's part of who that person is and the drive to connect emotionally with another is strong, as with any other person; homosexual or not.

We all want to be loved and we all want to be close and intimate with another. It's the way of life.

It is never an easy course to find another. For gay people it is a bit scarier as they are taking a leap of faith finding another gay person to partner with. Many therefore choose to make sure the person is also gay by going on-line as opposed to meeting in person.

Like with all couples, it is a good idea to *audition* for a lover. It does not happen automatically, although sex can occur fast.

With gay guys there is a lot of experimentation. With gay females they seem to maintain relationships longer but not always. There are any number of gay men that have been committed to one another for long periods, or life. Some very famous ones.

While I have worked with and written a book about transgendered people I have also worked with many gay couples; both male and female.

The areas of distress are the same as with any couple.

Communication and keeping passion alive are big ones.

Coming *out* is a huge step. I recommend cleaning out the clothes in the closet and then coming *out* with who you really are.

Telling parents is frightening, no matter how educated and understanding and liberal they are. No parent says they prefer that they have a gay child. BUT they can understand that in order for their child to live a full and happy life this has to be the course.

If the parents absolutely cannot accept it there may be a breach in the relationship and sometimes that can be forever. If there are siblings that can also be a big problem. The sibling can accept or reject, and they can move to the favorite child position, if they were not there before.

For many siblings and parents, they feel shame. They feel they did something wrong to cause this to happen. Not so. It is a fact of nature. You came that way… period!

Being a full human being and having fun and doing some good in the world and being a responsible adult is what we all strive for. It is no different for someone who is homosexual.

Actually, there are any number of fabulously successful creative and artistic gay people.

Now if the gay person has to exaggerate it and flaunt it that can be a problem. Just like any obnoxious person; the behavior should not be in your face or offensive or belligerent.

Fighting for legal rights has been long and difficult, as they always are. We have made progress however and that was not easy for this group.

Having or adopting children has been a source of struggle, even though many children with their natural parents hardly have idyllic lives!

Being *mistaken* for gay or straight when it is not the case can be awkward or amusing; depending on the individual and the circumstances.

When they say someone is *straight* does that mean others are *crooked*? Just a question.

Love has no gender, and everyone searches for it; no matter what.

People who live their entire lives *in the closet* suffer and cannot be genuine and live a complete life. I have know a number of them. It is sad indeed. Conformity works for society but being true to oneself makes for a better society.

Clean out your closet but be sure to come out of it in the end!

"Either you are homophobic, or you are human—you cannot be both" - Abhijit Naskar

A Robot Brothel

A woman and her physician husband are having dinner in a fancy restaurant.

A shapely young lady comes by with a huge smile and greets the husband with a big kiss.

As she walks away the wife asks, *who was that?*

Oh, he says, *I know her professionally.*

After a quizzical pause the wife responds, *Whose, hers or yours?*

"The human condition is not perfect. We are not perfect specimens any of us. We're not robots." - Michael Orvitz

Are robots' perfect specimens, I ask you?

Well, get this; there is now a sex doll brothel opening in Toronto Canada, offering sexual services with silicone made dolls!! You heard that right... Not quite a full robot but close.

Don't write this off as nonsense or some off the wall idea. It may not be.

Just think what problems could have been avoided if such a facility was used and no one had to pay off a porn star!!

Just think how non-embarrassing a *failure* to perform would be.

Just think how cheaply one could get off breaking up a relationship? Just imagine a no nagging life! How about no demands?

All possible with a *doll*. A real *doll*!

The brothel will have a variety of types; colors, hair and eye color, shapes, and so on. It's your choice. We all have different ideas about beauty.

AND the best news; in time there may be male ones for females to use too. It is all about the stimulation of the body parts and what goes on in the mind after all.

Here there is no fighting over anything, no guesswork, and no control issues. Imagine.

Half an hour costs $80 and so on. They will be sanitized and no problem of disease as well.

They will be discrete and no shyness or awkwardness about coming or going to the facility.

That will be lawful and guess what? Most of the community is fine with it. Over 56% said, *Live and let live.*

Now the real benefit will be that people can perhaps open up sexually and be freer so that they can be better with real live partners in the flesh and blood. It can fulfill fantasies and can cross all sexual barriers such as gender and so on. Sexual S and M won't be a problem here either. Want two ladies? No problem! And people without partners or disabilities can be fulfilled.

AND I really don't think you can fall in love with a doll or robot... or can you?

In keeping with the new sex technology how about all the new apps that can deliver whatever you want when you want?

Sex toys delivered within the hour, meet people you've never known, right away. Toys like, G-spot vibes, and some that play the music you like at the same time! You name it; someone's working on it.

Sex is so personal and often not satisfying. These new ventures may open possibilities that could benefit many many people. Some apps offer instant help with talking to physicians or therapists and any of that can truly help couples willing to talk. Virtual experiences may indeed be the answer to enhancing relationships, not detracting from them.

In New York there are sex education groups for grown-ups. These offer open forums for groups to meet and talk. Since, even today, most young people receive limited education in the matters that they want to discuss and have to deal with; they become limited adults in these areas.

Most young people only want to hear about intimate life from peers, but adults are ready to deal with others in the same boat and people with professional experience.

As a sex educator for over 30 years I can tell you none of this is too soon and long overdue.

As a relationship therapist, I know sex is a highly emotionally charged subject and so very personal that people will tell you what's in their bank account sooner than reveal themselves *nakedly* where it really shows who they are.

If I ever want to quiet a room where I am speaking, to a halt, whether it's four or a thousand people, all I have to say is, *Let's have every other person stand up and tell us about their sex life*. Works every time!

"People are fascinated by robots because they're machines that can mimic life" - Colin Angle

Mucho Macho

"The basic problem is that our civilization, which is a civilization of machines, can teach man everything except how to be a man." - Andre' Malraux

So what makes a man a man? What do we mean by masculinity? How do boys learn to become men?

The theory is that fathers teach sons what it means to be a man. That is not always a good lesson. Many fathers are not comfortable in their *maleness.* Many abuse the privilege. Many in fact do just that, *abuse.*

Now, Judge Ruth Bader Ginsburg, not withstanding, women can do much that men can do BUT they are NOT men!!

After having worked with transgendered people for decades and writing a book about that issue, I have a few ideas about all of this.

What you are is determined by your brain, not necessarily by your body and your genitalia.

There are examples of women being like men and men being like traditional women. We all know what we have been taught is the norm for both of these. While the determinants have changed over the centuries we still have rather defined criteria of what a man should be and likewise what a woman should exemplify.

To be a real man means you are strong, independent, and able to get IT up!

When it comes to relationships between the sexes there is a wide variety of behaviors.

Men usually take the *lead.*

The female can tease, taunt, and tantalize but it is the male who makes the *moves.*

He has anticipation and can learn how to relax and enjoy the sexual act through *giving* of himself.

Since his organs work differently than a woman's he often has problems with knowing how to slow down and be versatile in foreplay and bringing her to orgasm.

With a loving relationship there should be discussion about what each one likes and what is not pleasurable.

Many people are shy about sex and that's okay. Not everything is for everybody. Whatever feels good is fine.

We set standards that are often unreal for many people; like the simultaneous orgasm. Who cares?

Are you having sex, or making love? That is the real question.

As people age, especially men, sex can become an aspect fraught with fear. All men experience *failure* at some point, and this can set the stage for future disappointment; for both parties.

I had a client who complained that it took too long for her to masturbate him to orgasm and all she kept thinking was, "This is taking too long, I am getting tired, and when will it be over?" Men can have orgasms and ejaculate without erections.

Another client complained that she had to drink a lot of wine before she was able to even get into the mood.

Men on the other hand, usually have a more immediate response. A young female told me *All he did was make a deposit and roll over.* He was a selfish lover and cared nothing about pleasuring her.

Interestingly, there is a theory that the tongue is mightier than the penis. It is the only muscle not attached at both ends. It can touch, taste, and lick!

If a male is *educated* about how to perform cunnilingus it can be rewarding for both his partner and himself. It takes education and practice. It also relieves him of fatigue and premature ejaculation if done correctly. Her orgasm through this method is said to be better than penile penetration.

The penis, by the way, is a miracle body part...

The length is not really important as most people believe. It is the width that makes the case. The clitoris is not deep inside the vagina either.

The female clitoris is there to be stroked in a wide variety of forms. It usually takes fifteen minutes or so to achieve orgasm with the right moves.

The skin is our largest sexual organ. Touching any body part that one likes, kissing, massaging and all that, will be a part of good love-making. There is never a rush to great sex.

Rhythm is not just good in music!!

In the end macho can be just *putty* in her hands... literally!

"Man is a brute, only more intelligent than the other brutes, a blind prey to impulses... victim to endless illusions, which make his mental existence a burden, and fills his life with barren toil and trouble." - H. G. Wells

Her Ears Will Open Her Legs

"Winning her would be like coaxing a butterfly to land on his hand. Patience, gentleness, and perhaps a prayer or two would be required." - Mary Jo Putney

Many of our senses are involved when it comes to attraction and loving someone. Much of it is the feeling of wanting to be joined sexually.

Today, females are using their sexuality much like men. Their drive is as strong, and they are open to all sorts of sexual behavior. Without the fear of unwanted pregnancy, it's a whole wide world. With the Internet it's the world at their finger-tips.

So, how's a guy going to get her to bed?

Through her ears!!

That's right; she will respond to what she hears. If she is smart she will test it out and see if the behavior matches the words. She will see if he is consistent and not just there for the short run.

Women are being themselves and seeking to be satisfied… in bed.

Sometimes it may mean having an affair. About fifty percent of married women are thought to have had an affair. Close to the figure for men. Lots of reasons for this. Boredom, partner's health problems, exploration, having a new and exciting experience, better sex; just some of the reasons. An affair is not marriage. It is the distillation of attraction and sexual desire without the day to day activity.

Being out in the workforce has certainly opened up more opportunities, to say nothing about using the cell phone for contact.

But if a guy is really smart he knows that saying sweet things, that he genuinely believes, accompanied by gestures that are loving will get her to want to not only be with him, but to truly care about him, their relationship, and sex!

If he is hopping from one bed to another; in the long run, he won't be satisfied emotionally.

If he wants a real relationship, he has to talk the talk and walk the walk.

He needs to listen, like her personality, and make her feel special. He has to be available and attentive to her. The sex drive cannot be the main driving force.

Learning the art of wooing women takes time. An atmosphere has to be created. He needs to be confident and not complaining all the time. He needs to be positive and fun. Money won't do it either.

She will love talking about anything, sharing ideas, and giving him not just her body but her heart.

She will not want to think of life without him. She will dream about and plan her future with him.

Just his *essence* will be a powerful force. Women as a matter of fact are more sensitive to smell than men, so perfume should be made more for men than women.

The last love is the best one; not the first one!!

Once her legs are open to you, you may want to explore further and plan.

Here is where the head comes in and there are areas to talk about.

How is money used? Are children part of the plan? How do differences get resolved? Are the sex drives similar? Do the families get along? How is love expressed?

It all begins with the eyes and what you are attracted to. Then the ears come into play. Then...

"There are many fish in the sea, but never let a good one swim away." - Matshona Dhliwayo

Harassment; Sexual and Otherwise

"Sexual pleasure, wisely used and not abused, may prove the stimulus and liberator of our finest and most exalted activities." - Havelock Ellis

No truer words have been spoken. But what is going on in today's world with all the accusations of sexual harassment; some of them decades old?

It is most disheartening to hear and find out long or recent bad activity from and about some of our most trusted leaders and personalities.

Just what is going on?

Now there may be a huge variety of responses to that question. Some you may like, while others may sicken you.

Many are indeed surprises.

The adage that rape and overt sexual advances are a form of power holds true in many instances. None of this is new business. It actually has been business as usual throughout history. Using sexuality to gain something from a man has been a woman's method for generations. Men using power and money to obtain sexual gratification is nothing new.

What is new is that the media can broadcast these activities immediately to a wide range of eager listeners and observers. The news can ruin a man for life. No more secrets. No more hidden behavior.

So, how come it continues? Do these men believe they are above it all and impervious to the outcomes?

Many do…and many have gone on to benefit themselves.

There are, of course, other forms of harassment. Verbal, and subtle acts of betrayal or subterfuge. It can be from someone who has power over some aspect of your life, or from total strangers who dislike something about you; real or imagined. Harassment is never easy to bear or even witness.

When it comes to sexual components that gets really tricky. Women dress and act in ways to entice and interest men in them as sexually desirable. When I see bare chested and bare bottoms all over the Internet and Facebook I wonder what they are sending as a message. What do they expect to happen from that behavior or 'advertising?'

That is not being a misogamist; it's just common observation and a question. By *stimulating* a vibrant male's reaction, the control may be gone!

Do not get me wrong. Forcing any sexual activity when it is not consensual or wanted is WRONG.

But look at the intelligent, educated, successful men that have succumbed to female wiles. The list is long.

In former years, women did not speak up and the laws were not favorable to such shenanigans, but today that has all changed. And true, some women have lied to pay back a man they had problems with and accused them of sexual misdoings, when they did not occur. It is not always a cut and dried situation.

What is indeed sad and a sorry reflection on today's society is the extent to which all this stuff is going on.

When a pat on the bottom was a form of *endearment* it has now become a grave offense.

The numbers that are involved is also alarming. Most *accused* men do not do this briefly and to one woman; it is a pattern. They, in the past, thought it was 'fine' and women didn't mind that kind of attention. Well, wrong! Today they have lawyers pointing fingers in courts.

So, what is okay?

Short of a greeting that is innocuous or a smile, many men now are scared to relate to women, letting them know they are interested in them sexually. That can bode badly for future possible relationships that can lead to love in the end. That would be too bad, but that's the way we're headed.

I doubt that Americans will opt for arranged marriages, chaperones or letters of introduction to connect with a person that they are attracted to. Quite the opposite; they hop in and out of bed rather frequently now after only brief meetings.

My worry is and has been that romance and the capacity for intimacy may be in decline. What will that future look like?

In the end, harassment comes in many forms and the interpretations can vary but like most things in this life; you know it when you experience it.

The known perverts; pedophiles, rapists, and sexual deviants are few and far between. It's all this middle ground that is now in question.

If all of this makes men think twice about their use of their sexuality; then good. If all of this makes women stronger to speak up about what they will tolerate; then good. If it then makes them learn to share feelings and passion in positive ways, then we as a society will have moved further up the human ladder and real love with great sex can be the goal.

Let's toast to that as a new year approaches.

"Taste is the mark of an educated man, imagination the sign of a productive man, and emotional balance the token of a mature man." - Philip N. Youtz

Fighting To Get 'IT' Back

"To be attached to what you don't want to be attached to is suffering, and to be detached from what you want to be attached to is suffering." - R.D. Laing

Yes, shall we talk about this aspect of life? You bet... because we all go through some form or many forms of this type of pain.

Because my topics always deal with relationships there will be no difference in this case. No matter what the relationship is, was, or can be, there will be times, maybe lots of them, where the thing just isn't *working*.

The needs change over time and the ways in which couples move away from one another is emotional and sexual.

If the bond has been there for a long time and the two-people involved truly love one another they can overcome any breach in the relationship and even move on in better ways.

There is no time limit to make that bond strong, but it does take time and working through a variety of differences. How they get resolved sets the stage and pattern for the future.

In the beginning of most connections the sexual coming together can make whatever else is going on, feel okay.

The sexual life is the *glue*. AND it works.

It works in many ways; certainly, the body responds if it is done *well*. The mind and heart go along, and the feeling is so damn good you want to keep repeating the experience.

It makes you want to be close.

Now, over time and certainly with aging, the body changes and that part of your life may not be what it was or what one of you may still desire.

What then?

The need for affection, desirability, and attractions do not just disappear.

There can be many different responses. If one partner is not willing to *substitute* the old ways of expressing themselves a partner can *wander*. There is no shortage of willing sexual partners out there. Maybe being fulfilled *elsewhere* even makes the basic relationship doable and pleasant. Dealing with the subversive behavior may cause guilt or maybe not. Some partners feel they have and still do deliver *enough* at home.

Then there is the issue of trust. That can be a big hole in the picture. Not telling in order to not cause anger or unhappiness is often the case.

Now, without the sexual component, there can be a breach by being emotionally *connected* to someone outside the primary partner, but sex is not a factor here.

Does that make it *better*? I think not.

Whatever takes your thoughts, time, and connection to another in any form can destroy any relationship. You are not there to meet the needs of your partner and give them yours*elf!*

In a primary relationship, you go through the mundane. You *weather* the storms. You see each other's gross parts of self, and you still stay together and enjoy one another.

Once there has been *another* to be appreciated and appreciate you… there's a problem.

Emotional needs are so strong that people will do anything to have them met. And I mean anything.

Once the *deception* comes out in any form; the fun begins.

First question; do you want to continue this relationship at home… or GO?

The *Go* part is easy.

The *Stay* part takes a heap of work.

How the anger or hurt comes out doesn't matter. It's there.

How long it takes, depends on the individuals and how they perceive being *wronged.*

What they then say and do to and for one another AND the relationship, is the next step.

Often hearing the reasons for betrayal and understanding them is step one. Next comes the fact that you don't have to accept the behavior just because you understand it. But you can work on a new commitment and look at how to survive and indeed make the relationship grow as a result.

You've GOT to talk, and talk, and talk some more!

Nothing in any relationship is to be taken for granted or seen as *forever* unless you do the regular housekeeping of sharing feelings and trying to work things out together. Love is expressed in many forms and two people who truly have love for one another will not let ANYTHING destroy their wish to remain together and enjoy their lives as a couple.

It is really YOU and ME against the world!

"Telling the truth is a pretty hard thing." - Thomas Wolfe

Comfy Sex As Opposed To...

"Good sex is like good bridge. If you don't have a good partner, you'd better have a good hand." - Mae West

Ha ha and true!

When a relationship gets too comfortable people react in ways that are definite turn- offs when it comes to the bedroom.

While being secure and knowing your relationship is stable and *safe* is a nice feeling, the manner in which you behave, and dress, and react may not be supportive of good sex. Comfy is all around us today. The way we appear, how we speak, the lack of politeness and manners, and so on.

When we let our bodily functions occur in front of our partner we can be viewed differently. How appealing are the sight and sounds that should only occur in a bathroom? Being slovenly and not smelling sweetly is not a come-on.

Knowing all the moves that will take place in the sexual repertoire is not exciting. Getting it *over with* and not continuing to connect doesn't help matters.

So, in the end what I am advocating is not comfy sex in many regards.

Young people today are actually starting their sex lives later and they are having less sex than previous generations. That's the facts!

Polyamory is common. Look it up.

Anal sex is also more practiced than ever before.

The percentage of high school students having sex has dropped from 54 to 40 percent.

Many GenX'ers report having no sex for periods of time.

About 60 percent of people under 35 live without a partner; one in three live with their parents!

Reasons for all of this may include the hook-up culture, economic conditions, anxiety, depression, use of opioids, technology use, and other issues.

Interestingly the use of digital porn, dating sites, dropping of testosterone levels due to the environment, careers, and sleep deprivation, are all possible contributors.

While there are hundreds of reasons for having sex, there now seem to be many for not having sex.

Today many younger people prefer not having to be really involved with another person over time, and they can live with alternative forms of sexual behavior; i.e. the vibrator and masturbation as examples.

There are web sites for everything; to help you do IT, and to help you NOT do IT!

Some research shows that erectile dysfunction and porn have often made females more desirous of sex than males.

Pornhub the most watched porn site had lesbian sex as the most watched site, by men and women. The second highest watched was animated porn. People described it as a diversion and a way of relieving tension.

Some of all of this may be the reason the teen birth rate is down and that's a good thing.

Only about half of college age students have hooked up or had a meaningful relationship. Most said they hoped for a long- term connection.

Many said their parents push for education and their extra-curricular activities took up a lot of their time and energy. Anxiety about a job also factored in here. Lots of pressure!

Love is not high on the list and many lack social skills. Flirting, dating, being romantic and knowing what love is all about is not easily come by.

All the apps for example, like, Tinder, Bumble, Match, OK Cupid, and Coffee Meets Bagel, take time and messaging is a lot of work. Most do not lead to dates. The photogenic also have an advantage here.

Sexual minorities prefer apps over meeting in public.

Meeting at a public place does not happen much anymore. People are not ready, and women are extremely cautious with the #Me Too movement scaring them.

The outcome of all this is that the sex toy industry is booming, and people are not having sex or bad sex if they don't want to. One area of interest is that anal sex has risen in popularity. Even though many females report pain or not liking it.

Good sex occurs over time with information and communication; especially with someone you love who loves you.

Millennials prefer privacy and talk about how they feel about their genitals.

Desire and arousal and all the helping products today can make sex really fabulous.

Good sex makes you happy!!

We need education in this vital area and certainly before having babies.

So be comfy, but comfy with love and passion that you tend to like a beautiful flower.

"...sex is the consolation you have when you can't have love." - Gabriel Garcia Marquez

Bare It… Then Bear It

"I knew I belonged to the public and to the world, not because I was talented or even beautiful, but because I had never belonged to anything or anyone else." - Marilyn Monroe

Lately I have been perusing Facebook, mainly for this blog and my book. While I am technologically *challenged,* I've found a slew of people requesting to be my *friend.* Now this is sort of fun and it's a big wide world out there.

What I rather quickly discovered was the way in which people *advertised* themselves.

So many young beautiful women are there showing their breasts in every imaginable fashion. Many are obviously enhanced by plastic surgery. It is amazing to me. Just what do these ladies think will happen? We know… men will respond.

Now the guys show their muscles and cars. Interesting: not other body parts.

These females bare a part of themselves that is there to attract and say they are a sex object.

Don't get me wrong; when I stop being a sex object, it's all over. I think being desired in a sexual fashion is what being alive is about. But let me tell you a secret.

Leaving a mystery and fantasy and wish to explore more is far sexier than showing it up front.

What happens after the guy takes the *bait*?

A fairly recent book: *Testosterone Rex* by Cordelia Fine examined the ideas that men are more risk takers than women. They are more lustful, aggressive and competitive than women. She dispelled all of this. She gave two fascinating non-human examples. The male macaque monkeys often carry and groom their babies and female sandpipers are promiscuous. Cute.

Anyway, I just think that showing breasts and often 'bottoms' or figures in seductive ways does not enhance your sexuality or make you more desirable, and certainly says nothing about what comes next.

In another article in Philadelphia Magazine there was a huge spread about what goes on in the city. Headings included;

'I'm a cheating newlywed' followed by 'I'm 77 and having the best sex of my life.' (That one was encouraging!), and then there were, 'I'm a secret dominatrix.' (This was from a smart college senior and made me a bit sad). Another was 'I have to shave, what?' There were other parts of what goes on behind closed doors that probably made many local people shocked.

Because of my decades professionally as a counselor in this field I was not shocked. What I was, was sorry that people have become commodities and romance, longing and intimacy over time may be out the window in many situations.

Sex gets the ball rolling to be sure. No pun intended. But what is included in the flesh on flesh part afterwards?

Who says what, and what kind of relationship ensues?

Anyone who follows my blog knows that I deal with whole relationships and that means the ups and downs. When love enters the picture, there is much to *bear*.

What usually happens is that after a period of time sex alone can't hold two people together.

I much prefer couples to 'tease' and get to like one another along with the sexual component. If IT is right out there in your face what is there to wait for or offer?

The most famous love stories include sex to be sure, but they also have many other elements involved in the relationship; including the agony that real love involves.

The *bearing* of a relationship is not easy or learned. By being *bare* there may be a big hindrance to opening up other areas that would do the relationship a better service.

From my perspective, you should always be *marketable* and attractive. You should be looked at, admired, and sought after. If you are not *beautiful* in the movie star version that doesn't mean you cannot be desirable. And it's not just having a *good personality*. There are so many facets to being attracted that there are people for every type and every look. Just look around.

What happens is that after about seven years couples get itchy and begin to feel a partner is too well known, familiar and boring. They may begin to regard other people as potential partners for whatever. That's dangerous.

In time, I think we will have relationships that are contracts that we review and decide if we want to continue together; for three, five, or whatever number of years. It's beginning to happen.

It certainly won't be your breasts that make the contract renewable in the end!!

Develop as an interesting fun human being and that will hold up when time and the breasts sag. Plastic surgery can't be done in those areas... yet!

"When we consider the significant cultural shifts of the past few years, the removal of Pamela Anderson's breast implants must rank right up there at the top." - Suzanne Moore

The Real Perverts

"How lonely and unnatural man is and how deep and well concealed are his confusions." - John Cheever

Sex makes the world go around... and thank goodness because it is the primary drive and source of pleasure. It supplies both the mind and body with joy and the wish to keep repeating the experience.

We have all sorts of statistics and research about the subject, for decades. What we don't have is the ways in which perversion is viewed in a variety of instances and outside the realm of sexuality.

Let me explain.

Anyone who uses people for their own purposes when the person or people are unaware or incapable of being a willing partner may be a pervert.

True, we all *use* people for our own personal needs and purposes but usually it is for a mutually beneficial outcome. We both enjoy the experience or relationship.

Some relationships can be parasitic, sort of like the old-fashioned marriage where the wife *took* what the husband offered; monetarily and otherwise.

In other instances, there are trade-offs; beauty and youth for money, brawn for brain, protection for lack of control or ability and so on. Is any of this perversion? Could be... depends on the willingness or lack of it by the partner or group of people involved. This is only true if they are able to know what they are involved with.

If an individual cannot see or truly understand the circumstances they are being victimized. Life experience and education are important aspects here.

Just look around this world. How many millions of people are living miserable unhappy lives because of who is in power; mainly politically.

Most of humanity just wants to get by and have a pleasant life for themselves and their loved ones. Most of their time and attention is to survive or live well. And then how many *leaders* have caused wars and conflict and the poor choices they made for their own needs and sacrificed people in the process? Is this perversion? In my book, it is the worst sort of perversion.

Maybe if these decision makers were satisfied emotionally in their own lives and beds the world would be different!

I would require an EQ (emotional quotient) for every politician. Maybe that would help.

At any rate, back to perversion of the sexual nature.

In our world, today the second fastest criminal business in the world, after drugs, is sexual exploitation.

From 600,000 to 800,000 people are involuntarily involved in human trafficking annually!

The estimate is that there are 21 million people in the world in some form of human slavery!! Can you believe that? It is unreal to even think about. There are few countries that escape this.

Poverty and lack of education and ability to survive cause much, if not all of it.

Can it be changed? You bet!

Get rid of the real perverts who cause and allow it to continue.

As a sex educator for decades and therapist I have heard and seen it all.

When kids in school ask, "Am I normal if I...." it's usually some silly matter. Whatever two or more, people wish to do as consenting adults, is fine. As we develop and learn we put our experiences to good or better use. We have control over what we do as individuals. The rules set by society should be there to help and protect us. Sometimes they are not working for all of us. Sometimes money changes outcomes and sometimes power rules with a heavy hand.

In the US, there was a recent study that showed that high school students were having less sex, with fewer partners, and using contraceptives. That's good information.

By the same token, we can see *perverts* using unsuspecting young people through the Internet for sexual purposes. This is a problem. Kids are lonely, finding themselves, testing their sexuality and so they can be taken advantage of.

We can all have fantasies, especially when it comes to sex. Many can be acted out if we choose and agree with a partner to do... whatever. That's' all fine.

It is when it is one person's fantasy and the partner is coerced that it is perversion.

The issue is knowledge and control.

By controlling ourselves in the way we desire and by having a *voice* in our shared destiny, we can enjoy a perversion free life together. It would certainly make a better world!

Think about that when you vote!!

"So long as society is founded on injustice, the function of the laws will be to defend injustice. And the more unjust they are the more respectable they will seem." - Anatole France

Love Is Always Agony

"Who will tell whether one happy moment of love, or the joy of breathing or walking on a bright morning and smelling the fresh air, is not worth all the suffering and effort life implies?" - Erich Fromm

We all suffer in this life. Some more than others, but no one escapes.

The pain that might be physical is one area of distress. The mental anguish is another.

The problem is that all people have experiences, ideas, thoughts, and times when life seems unbearable.

The daily needs of living take a lot of time and attention, to say nothing of money. Any part of this can be a huge problem and cause anxiety, worry, or breakdown.

If you look at the numbers of Americans that take drugs, legal or otherwise, and drink to excess you know there is a problem.

When materialism reigns, there is never enough for many people, and the quest for what money can buy is powerful. That puts a terrible burden on individuals. The media sets it up so everyone can see what is available and then the race to obtain more is on.

Now there is a need and necessity for living, and we all have our standards, and that's fine. It is when the joy of living and loving is not paramount that there is an emptiness, no matter what is obtained otherwise.

In order to love we also have standards. How we and a partner look, what we wear, where we go, how we live, and so on. But in the end love will rule no matter what.

With love comes disappointment, anger, frustration, and yes, agony.

After that first *high* when all is so very wonderful reality will set in. It can be overlooked, excused, compromised or even ignored at first. But again, at some point there will be negative vibes.

If the bond is strong and tested over time and the *pull* to be together is there emotionally and physically, all bets are off.

Love in its' highest form is what it's all about.

Now, not everyone is up for this challenge, if you will. That's fine too. To be happy with someone and not be one hundred percent vulnerable and connected is dandy for maybe most of the world. Life can be pleasant and full.

However, when the connection is so strong that you cannot conceive of life without this person you are talking another story.

Going through the lows here become agonizing.

We really should teach young people that love is not Cinderella and what it seems at first. We need them to be prepared for true love and life. What most people will say if asked, is that they wish they had known ... fill in the blank. It's about relationships and what they entail.

Experience and learning take time in this instance, and no one goes to *Love* school. That's the school I would run!!

The other point in all of this is that if and when the relationship ends there is the pure hurt that feels like death or the wish for death.

Read history and novels where the partner left does indeed kill themselves as opposed to a life without the lover.

One of the classic stories is about the artist Dora Carrington. It's a love affair she had with a gay writer Lytton Strachey. Their relationship was platonic but so deep she ended her life when he died. Tragic.

To go on or even to imagine being with another is almost impossible.

I have had clients who talked about what they missed when a partner was no longer there.

One I shall never forget responded to my question about what she missed most, with, "His penis!"

She was honest.

No matter what the answer it is usually a compilation of things; the sound of the voice, the attention, the smells, the words, and a million-other small and large gestures. A person includes all of what attracts you to them. The routine of the relationship is gone. There is an emptiness, and that is a physical hole in the pit of the stomach and an ache in the heart. Life seems joyless and futile. The agony of love!!

Do you want to risk it? Is it worth it in the end? Do you have a choice?

Just know, there is NO connection that is the real thing that will not at some point include pain that will be unbearable.

To go on and live life going through the motions comes first. What happens later after the mortal sting remains to be seen.

"If you suffer, thank God---it is a sure sign that you are alive." - Elbert Hubbard

Is Love Really Worth it

"Love doesn't make the world go *round*. Love is what makes the ride worthwhile." - Franklin P. Jones

You can believe it or not.

Only those who have experienced the kind of love I write about can know this to be true. So, is love worth it?

There are all kinds of love to be sure, but that love shared with passion between true lovers is the epitome and what people all strive to achieve.

Those fortunate enough to have risked their hearts completely, no matter the circumstances, have the best and at times the worst of what a heart sustains.

To be flattered, desired, special, in this unique way makes us whole, happy, and fulfilled emotionally and physically.

This in turn makes us loving all the way around and content.

Searching for this and finding it can occur in all sorts of situations and most of the time, unexpectedly.

If it *happens* under circumstances that make it difficult, there are issues to work through. If it happens at the right moment in time and age it can just blossom.

No matter the reasons, and there are always reasons, why we fall for one person over others, the feelings of passion and wanting to connect will not go away.

We 'connect' in all sorts of ways; by sight, thoughts, talking, touching, sexually, and dreaming! Being 'connected' seems perfect, at least for a while; maybe even a long while.

The reality is that there will be differences, of all sorts, as we are not clones. There will be disagreements and even battles. There will be surprises and many unwanted, but the coming back to one another because we WANT to will be the sign of real love.

You cannot fight love, so don't even try!

We want that love to supply us with what we need or what was missing before. Love causes indiscretion at times, and sometimes even danger. So be it.

Is it worth it?

While we all experience loss in some form or another; a job, money, body changes, our looks, and so on, it is only the loss of true love that will cause the pain in the heart that will not go away; maybe forever.

There are many injustices in this life, and many *play it safe* in a variety of ways. However, the playing it safe with your heart is a big mistake in my book.

You will avoid heartache or heartbreak; but you will not have LIVED!!

For some the deal is the wanting of someone but the *having* doesn't hold up. That's too bad, because then it is the chase or early *high,* they require, not the intense intimacy that only grows deeper and stronger when handled well.

Those people who complain and find fault, shouldn't, because you can't blame another for what you have *allowed.* Some of the *bad* stuff can get calcified and just becomes a bad habit and the norm if you let it.

There is no big secret to happiness. It is learning to give yourself over completely to love. Nothing else comes close. Other areas are poor substitutes.

Humor, forgiveness, understanding and acceptance of a lover is not always easy. Being tenacious and believing in your love will get you through. Sex will glue it!!

It's okay to be a romantic pessimist but believing in love will work. All it takes is knowing you have the capacity for love and someone will find it!

"Sail away from the safe harbour. Catch the trade winds in your sails. Explore. Dream. Discover." - Mark Twain

First Date… First Test

"Every day is a new beginning and a chance to blow it" - Cathy Guisewite

Remember when you were in school and had to take a test to see what you knew?

There was anxiety. So too with first dates.

Recently a young eligible man said I should write about all of this… so here goes!

Today many people use the dating sites and look for people to *connect* with. Great. It's a whole big world out there.

Getting your profile to tell about you; having a *good* picture and doing a lot of searching is the norm.

It takes effort. It takes time. And most of all it takes honesty; hopefully.

Now there are a lot of not so honest people who *fudge* things. The main things here are height, weight, and finances. Some use pictures that are not recent and some tell *stories* about their education or life style. There may be no way to check these things except by trying to check these things. I have known wealthy women who hired private detectives to check things out!!

Sometimes educational background or employment can be easily obtained. Sometimes you can find someone who knows the person.

But let's say you go at it cold turkey just liking what you found on the site. The picture appeals to you and the background seems good and fitting.

So, on to that scary first test.

There is anxiety and you want to be at your best; look good, smell good, and be pleasant.

My idea is that you should go for a short time to a place that has lots of people and bring your cell phone and money to get home. You should not be alone with a stranger… ever!!

If you feel attracted to the person that's a good sign. If not, you may want to have another appointment or a headache or a sick mother to see.

Let's move on; you like what you see.

Sit and talk over coffee, wine, or food. Up to the guy usually.

What to talk about? No problem; NOT YOU right away. Ask questions about them, compliment something about them and then move slowly to talk about you. Any kind of talking is good; what you do, where you went to school, your family, friends, interests, travel… whatever. It doesn't matter. Let the *date* move it along and then you chime in. Whatever you disclose is fine. This will not impact the outcome. You are in the process of discovery. It takes time; no rush. Most of the time it's usually positive talk and no discussion about your weaknesses, faults, bad experiences. You don't want to talk about other dates!!

You will know if this person *fits* into your world and values. You will observe how they relate to you, waiters, and so on. You will know if their ideas mesh with yours but above all you will instinctively know if you really like them and want to see them again.

After that first date if you want to go on you can text or better yet call them and that goes for both males and females these days. You can say you enjoyed your time together and would like to have an encore, so to speak.

If you have a negative response or no response that's the message. Do not take it personally and get down on yourself or try to analyze why. You won't know and you have to move on. If it happens ALL the time you may want to take a good look at you! By and large people like people who are positive and interested in them.

If you are so inclined, you can hold a hand or touch a face or do what feels comfortable.

I have counseled young women who tell me they have gone to *bed* on first dates. Some have worked out just fine and others have regretted it. Only you can decide what works for you. You will get all the cues you need as to how the *other* person wants to be with you.

In situations that end I always ask what might you have known or done differently. The answers are always in the realm of, 'I should have trusted my instincts because the clues were there right away.'

You don't fall in love instantly, but you do feel you want to be with someone or be close to someone fairly… right away!

The problem sometimes is that the attraction is there and strong, but the head is telling you to run the other way You then have you decide what risk you are willing to take for what gain. Sex for sex is fine in many instances. Being a friend and doing fun things with someone is fine too. Being in love is a whole other ball game. That takes time, and many tests.

First dates are just that… firsts.

It then becomes like a see-saw. You share and your partner shares and you move along and over time it has depth.

There is no rule book, and no guaranteed outcomes. The best anyone can do is get in the game and risk it. There is someone out there for you who will appreciate you. Be you and be honest and it will happen. I promise!

"You can be sincere and still be stupid." - Charles F. Kettering

You Plus Me Equals US

"If I were pressed to say why I love him, I feel that my only reply could be: Because it was he, because it was I" - Michel De Montaigne

When any two people are together over time, several changes take place. They can be gradual or quick. The relationship will not stay stagnant or the same. It has to change.

There is no way on earth that any two people; man and woman, or same sex couples, can remain the same as time wears on.

Each person comes from a different life experience, and is a unique combination of feelings, thoughts and behaviors. Each one experiences themselves and their relationships to others, in their own worlds.

Feeling confident, insecure, fearful, successful, attractive, or desirable are all special and individual.

How anger, anxiety, and conflicts are handled, is a part of the puzzle as well.

Who we trust, and how we use our bodies, is again our very own experience.

We all have insecurities, needs, feelings, and opinions.

There is no GPS for how to maneuver or which road to travel. We are on our own for the most part. We struggle through; some better than others. Some gain insight and work on areas to improve their lives, while others flounder around, make mistakes, repeat them or learn from them. Each of us travels the road of life, basically alone in many realms.

Most of us like to be in control, as that protects us from utter emotional destruction.

HOWEVER, the search for love; which means loving and being loved can only happen when we give ourselves over to complete vulnerability.

Sometimes we fake love just to make believe we have it. Sometimes we fight it off, and there are a myriad of other patterns to get what we need emotionally; or try to.

At times we are all awkward, self-conscious, or at a low ebb. We all have rejection at some point. We all have self-doubt at times. The question is; in the end are we feeling we are deserving of love?

So, here we are, two people together, hopefully for the right reason; love.

We become intimate and share our *selves*. We talk, and have joint experiences, and plan our lives.

Things get in the way; time, jobs, money, children, in-laws, and many other areas where we can differ. Sometimes violently.

Maybe one or both have fantasies not expressed. Maybe one or both have ventured outside of the monogamy bond; and not just in the physical way.

Maybe we have drifted apart and into our own world; having trips, plans and dinners that keep us together in a sense.

Men seem to have the need to spread their *seed* more than women. That is changing a bit. Women want security and especially if children are in the picture. Children, by the way, make the duo a whole different ball game, and change the model of being a loving couple in significant ways.

Men, it turns out, need a deep and meaningful loving relationship to feel their lives are well lived. They fall in love faster than women and will say *I love you* earlier than women in relationships. Men suffer when they lose a love, make no bones about it. Yes, they are generally more pragmatic, strong, and commitment avoidant, but when *in love* they want that closeness. Widowers, by the way, marry more and quicker than widows.

Now when there is a long-term relationship the feeling of being too familiar can take away the desire to be erotic or sexual. That is where the *you* and *me* need to work on the US.

Being touchy and physically close can include sex, or not. It is a feeling that is expressed with the body, words, and deeds.

Taking life together too much for granted, and not keeping passion alive is what is missing. Females use words; males use their bodies. Many females miss this point.

We all fear loss and there is only one way to conquer it; with true love expressed.

There are indeed times to be and feel alone, but a relationship that has been there, and tested, and loving will be the best. Being *alone* can't match it.

Coming together to US, after bad times, can make a renewed beginning that can be exciting as well as, comfortable and loving. Being erotic takes time, and imagination. Adult intimacy is not simple. The body is more than genitals. Fantasies, and any enjoyed behavior, is fine. Be uninhibited. Lose control and give in. Then you will be truly joined and a happy US.

"Personally, I think that if a woman hasn't met the right man by the time she's twenty-four, she may be lucky." - Deborah Kerr

Why Are You With HIM

"Accept unhappiness of the deepest love as the price of feeling fully alive." - Unknown

Nice quote, isn't it? The reality is it's true and anyone who has ever know deep love knows it to the core. If you honestly answer the question of why you are with him you may know the truth... and then again you may not!

We do not choose whom we love. It chooses us.

When you are in that kind of a relationship there is no one who can replace him. There is no one you long for. There is no one else you want to touch and give all of yourself to; emotionally and physically. It is a hell on earth when he doesn't do what you need from him.

The theory that is probably true is that you are a part of his life and he is ALL of yours I don't care what they say; men and women are different!!

When you bring each other happiness all is wonderful. When there is a thorn in between you it is pure misery.

While no one is happy all the time the scale has to be tilted in the favor of pleasure over pain for it to be a good connection.

There are always problems. Always misunderstandings. Always unmet needs at times. There are any number of obstacles to love. Anyone who thinks love is easy knows nothing about love.

A recent book, 'The Highly Sensitive Person In Love' by Elaine N. Aron is about just that.

There are people who are extremely sensitive; both men and women, and their love lives are less happy because they pick up all sorts of subtleties and reflect on them. They also demand more depth in their personal relationships in order to be satisfied and none of that is easy.

They see threatening consequences in their partner's behavior and they worry about how things are going with the flaws they observe.

Many of these people are also sensation seekers with a curiosity and need to explore.

Partners with different temperaments really do not understand what the other person is feeling or how they experience life. That causes big problems.

Many men are also sensitive but they are not thought to be *real* men if they are.

Women like to be with sensitive men but they prefer to marry those that are not.

A goal is to make that situation change and have sensitive men and women love one another.

Intimacy is approached cautiously with sensitive people. They really don't want to be hurt. They also don't wish the other sensitive person to overwhelm them with their needs.

The sensation seekers fear boredom and a lack of variety so they don't like commitment.

Initial attraction can fade fast with familiarity so the trick is to make life exciting and not dull, with surprises!

When it comes to sex sensitive people like to find sex mysterious, and powerful. They are turned on by subtle cues not explicit ones and can be easily distracted. They find it difficult to go right back to *normal* afterwards.

Sensation seeking men and women tend to enjoy sex more, want more partners, and have had more, and feel they can enjoy sex without love. Interesting but not really news.

We all know how sensitive we are and how our partners address love and sex.

When you are with your chosen one you know what that feels like. When he is not meeting your needs, you can be extremely sensitive and still want him in the worst way.

When you are hurt, you may think the most awful things about him and never want to see him again. You are hurt and you want to hurt him; or play the victim.

There is no getting around it; love is PAIN!!

The best way to solve any of this is to communicate and SAY what you feel. Maybe he can change and maybe he can't. If the love is strong, and the sex makes up for a lot of hurt, it will go on and on and... on.

"To find oneself lonely with the creature one loves is to plumb the full depths of desolation."- Radcliffe Hall

When A Child Divorces

"When love is strong, a man and a woman can make their bed on a sword's blade.

When love grows weak, a bed of 60 cubits is not large enough." - Talmud

One of the difficult moments in life occurs when your child says they are going to divorce.

As parents, we all hope for a good life for our children.

When they marry, we hope the choice is a good one. It may be for them, but often we are not pleased with the choice and have to accept it.

Some families have not spoken to one another because of just that reason; they really cannot accept the partner their child has chosen.

That is too bad and even when the in-law is not someone we can like or even 'stand'; for the sake of the child we go along.

If time does not make things better there can be really bad feelings and they will show themselves in one form or another, mark my words.

The reasons can vary and don't truly matter. The partner may be of a different background, religion, class, or just not what you would have chosen.

The old saying that if at the wedding the groom's parents say she isn't good enough for him, and the bride's parents say the same; the marriage will work!

That may or may not be the case.

Sometimes a child picks someone very different from their parent of the opposite sex because they really do not respect or like what they have seen growing up. That is a big problem because in the end that is what they learned a marriage partner was supposed to be like and they were used to that pattern of marital relationship.

If, over time the couple are not enjoying what should be a *good* relationship and if there are children it can be a heartache BUT it can also be an opportunity for change, growth, and a better life.

The parent has to be there in whatever form the child wants; just to listen, to give a hand, offer money, or whatever will be needed. The child needs support and understanding and kindness.

Perhaps professional counselling can be offered to see if the relationship is salvageable.

Whatever the final answer if divorce is inevitable there will be pain, and some regrets and suffering in some fashion. That can be short if the new freedom is feeling better, or bitterness if there was much hurt.

The thing to keep in mind is that your child needs good legal advice and financial protection.

If they ask for advice give it, and your opinions, but they have to be independent and stand on their own two feet from now on.

If small children are involved that area needs careful attention and planning. The hope is always that parents although they do not wish to continue together can act in the child's best interest. Often one or the other is angry or hurt and wants to *pay back* the other partner by using the child. That's playing *dirty* and is hurting the child more than the ex-partner.

Children, even very young ones know what goes on emotionally in their homes. Just ask any kid in kindergarten about his or her family.

Older children can take sides based on what they feel for each of their parents.

Hopefully the parents can address the concerns and answer the basic questions. Children need to know they did not cause this and that they will be loved and provided for.

As grandparents, a lot can be offered unless the children are withheld from you. That is a disaster and true heartache.

In the end, most children keep close in some form to the people they feel love them. They know.

Often grandparents have problems with their adult children not liking the manner in which the grandchildren are being brought up. This can cause any sort of disruption in families.

They are not your children and if you have done a decent job raising your child you need to trust they will be able to do a good job raising their own children.

As a counselor, the best are those that can move on, accept reality, and make progress in their own personal development. Life moves forward not backward.

Experience, both good and bad, painful, and joyful is all good learning.

Children will have issues around divorcing parents but they too can learn in a beneficial way.

They will choose their mates one day and remember the things to watch out for!

No one has a rose garden for life, and everything is finite. When it is a marriage and divorce it is not easy but today it seems to be a common way to learn about mature love.

"Love, the quest; marriage the conquest; divorce, the inquest." - Helen Rowland

The Bitch Factor

"A bitch loves being born. It's her first experience of making another woman scream and cry." -Pamela Stephenson

We've all heard it, or said it, *She's a bitch*!

The word has definite connotations and we know what it means when we say or hear it.

It's that definable something that means a woman is behaving in a manner that we do not like.

She is often demanding, inconsiderate, self-serving, narcissistic, and not what we view as positive.

Now there are times when any of us can be like that. Maybe we had a bad day, the hair doesn't look good, someone did something we did not like, and so on. We then turn on that aspect of ourselves. The question becomes; how often does this behavior occur, or is it a part of the personality all the time?

Being *bitchy* can be a factor in a relationship that makes it exciting. Many men have been raised by mothers who were bitches and that is what they know and expect from a woman.

There are a whole group of men that like this type of woman as she keeps them on their toes. Some like having a demanding woman to lead them and tell them what to do, and even think.

I once had a client couple that exemplifies this whole pattern.

He was very well educated, and wealthy. She was fairly attractive and bright.

They were married for a number of years and it was his second marriage.

They had children together, and he was a docile, kind, wanting to please, husband.

The relationship was one where he did her bidding all the time. They came to see me after they had planned a vacation and he planned golf days, and she took a fit.

Once in counseling he saw the pattern.

She thought it was just a fine regular marriage.

The history showed her mother had been dominated by her overbearing father and she hated seeing that.

His father had been the busy money maker who was rarely home.

They both had reasons for who they turned out to be in the marriage. With one failed one he certainly tried his damnest not to end this one. The children also factored in.

She was referred for psychiatric evaluation as I felt her pattern was so ingrained, it needed dynamite to change it.

He was helped to see what type of life he was leading and realized he had not been happy for a long time. His needs were brushed aside and not given the slightest attention… until he wanted to play golf.

They ended up in a messy divorce.

Often my work is helping people to come to terms with making a difficult decision and ending a relationship in a constructive manner. The hope is that they will have learned enough to go on in a happier fashion, with better relationships.

Often however, the patterns persist as the individual has not changed and the needs and habits stay the same. It is not unusual to see a man go from one bitch to another.

As bitches lose their looks and the body changes, they control with different hooks. They become more demanding and intolerable.

Have you ever seen an older couple where the husband is so down trodden and beaten down, that he is a mere shadow of a person? They are all around us. Look outside any mall and see the older men sitting on benches while their wives spend their money. They sit with vapid stares. There is no personality or energy left. They become like puppets with their wives pulling the strings.

They gave up long ago. It was easier than battling. The sad part is that many of these men were successful in careers, but after retirement they lost it.

Some escape with things like golf, for instance. They get out.

There is a difference if a man calls a woman a *bitch*, as opposed to a woman. With men, it's usually about her being demanding of him. With women it's usually about her being nasty. It sometimes is a form of competition. What is especially amusing is when one *bitch* calls another one a *bitch*. Then who is the REAL bitch?

Any of us can be bitchy at times and that's okay. It's all a matter of degree.

"A bitch is more memorable than a sweet housewife." - Bette Davis

We All Use Each Other

"If we all said to people's faces what we say behind one another's backs, society would be impossible." - Honore' de Balzac

Truth in its' pure form is maybe not a good idea in all human relationships. We need to *use* one another.

Does that mean we are all liars, two-faced, or hypocrites?

In part perhaps so.

There are no angels walking this earth and no perfect or full-time wonderful people.

The fact of the matter is that at times the truth may not be what is the best or even the kindest way to engage with someone.

Is there real empathy in people? Does anyone truly act unselfishly?

My own feeling is that we are all in this life to mainly satisfy our own needs emotionally.

What we do in the guise of charity or kindness gestures serves us in some fashion. It makes us feel good, important, or worthwhile. It gives us a pleasurable feeling. That is a good thing.

In intimate relationships we do use one another all the time; knowingly or more often, unknowingly.

With family members, parents can *use* their children for their own purposes to make them look successful. They can use children in harmful ways sacrificing the child's welfare for their own usually angry or immature needs. This can be extremely harmful and a very poor use of another person; especially vulnerable children. At times parents use their children to live vicariously through them or to make up for what they did not have or achieve. Again, a poor choice, and this behavior doesn't allow the child to become their own person unless they are strong enough to eventually fight off the parent's influence.

With siblings, there can be other uses; to share or help one another or to go the other way and sabotage one or another for a competitive advantage... for whatever reason.

Adult children can use parents for all sorts of reasons; time, money, favoritism, you name it.

We all want to be thought well of and appreciated and will go to many lengths to achieve that goal.

We use people at work for our own purposes. We use friends for all sorts of things; time, company, listening, complaining, going out, decision making and again the list goes on.

There is no guide line or rule book for how to best use people. Generally, we know when it is for good or evil. Often we overuse some and others are underused. Some are outgrown and others are cultivated as new *prospects*.

We and life are not static, and if we only want what we know and are accustomed to we may not grow and our lives are merely repeated boring habits.

Using each other means that we run the risk of being unappreciated or misunderstood at times and that's all normal. Then only communication will solve the dilemma. Some relationships may have to be salvaged and some of it can be painful or cause us to examine the situation and our part in it.

With intimacy we use one another in all the ways possible. The problem is that no one person can meet all our needs all the time. We have to learn to compromise; that nasty business.

Then it becomes what values are most important. What can we give up, loosen up, or change?

If we use one another well enough and love one another truly we can use each other well.

Even with maturation and changes the love that we share will let us use each other in the most important ways.

Daily life, sharing decisions and plans, enjoying different activities and people, physically connecting including sex, and what we do with money and how we live are all ways we use one another.

The bottom line is it's fine as long as we really love and care about the *other*. My pleasure comes from loving you!!

It's only when I use you for solely my pleasure and care little or nothing about yours that there can be a problem.

So, don't be afraid of that word *use* in any of these aspects. If we didn't *use* one another what do we need you for??

"Love makes bitter things sweet; love converts base copper to gold. By love dregs become clear; by love pains become healing. By love the dead are brought to life; by love a king is made a slave." - Jalal Al-Din Rumi

Compliments And Criticism

"If you can't say anything good about someone, sit right here by me." - Alice Roosevelt Longworth

We all really like to hear nice things said about and to us. It's natural. Nothing wrong with it.

The question becomes; is it the truth?

An older man I knew who said his lover constantly told him how *gorgeous* he was, questioned it. He was nice looking he thought, but gorgeous? After time and many years, he finally said he heard it so often he now believed it!

Now that's a nice outcome and it is true we can believe positive things about ourselves when we hear them said often. How many children grew up in families where parents doted on them; made them feel beautiful, smart, or talented? Many. If you look around at all the people who have huge egos and think they are God's gift to the world, when in fact you may see them in reality as homely, rather stupid and certainly not talented, you know they heard a message growing up.

Is it a good thing to have that kind of an ego, when it is not based in fact? Well, maybe. It makes that individual feel good about themselves. However, if it is too strong it may not allow for compassion or caring genuinely and completely in another. It becomes a matter of degree.

When as adults, we hear compliments we USUALLY know whether they are justified. We have lived long enough to have a realistic opinion of ourselves.

If we are putting up a *front* and trying to impress, that job may not hold water forever. The *real* you will become apparent. Maybe with a scratch of the surface, or when things are not the way you would like, the real self comes forward.

The motivation for giving compliments needs to be addressed. Was it given in the beginning of a relationship when you couldn't have bared your true self yet? Was it given when the party offering it wanted something in return, now or down the road? Was it given under the influence of alcohol, drugs, or pressure from someone else? All important considerations to be aware of. Many times, compliments are given to curry favor or have someone *like them*. There are also people who cannot abide negativity, or who are doing *holy* work in their belief system. Some individuals are too damn competitive to tolerate complimenting another.

People can be 'strange' and not always predictable. We also need to know that relationships and opinions can change over time due to a whole plethora of reasons.

We need to look at the compliments we give, and to whom, and under what circumstances. It is a two-way street as are issues in all relationships.

Now when it comes to criticism that's a whole other ball of wax.

Many people are critiquing others all the time. How they look, how they behave, what they do with their time and money and so on. Usually when it is excessive it is because they themselves feel inferior and that is a way to feel better. There is no PERFECT person, and no one has all the answers, and no one is all knowing…. so.

Someone is always prettier, smarter, and richer, and more talented. Look up not down!

It is very easy to criticize, especially when you yourself are not *so hot*. There are also a lot of dissatisfied, unhappy and angry people out there. Life today is frustrating and can be overwhelming for many.

Sometimes people will compliment and then take it away at some point with criticism. So, what to believe; the positive or the negative? Can be quite confusing. The real message will out over time. The words *always* and *never* should not be used in any of this context. No one is *always* anything. No one is *never* anything. We are a big bundle of plusses and minuses. In a relationship that is caring the positive should certainly outweigh the negative. If the ego is strong, criticism will be appreciated and may offer a hope for some changes. If the ego is weak criticism will pile up in the head and the person may feel quite worthless. Dredging up old negatives will also not be helpful. It *stacks the deck*.

Some of this also depends on the point in life it all occurs. There are times, and with aging or illness things change, and people become more sensitive; especially to criticism.

In the end, your own head should decide what to believe. If you allow negative thoughts or unhelpful rumination to go on and on, it will make your life rather or very unpleasant and unhappy. Only you can think what you think!

If some words or phrases are used constantly, they may be just tossed off as habit and have little meaning behind them. The rule is to trust the behavior; not the words. Teach this to every young child!!

"People ask you for criticism, but they only want praise." - Somerset Maugham

When Spouse Means Enemy

"We continue to see one another like two people that are resolved to hate with civility." - Lady Mary Wortley Montagu

There is not a marriage on earth that at some point doesn't have MAJOR differences. Some are never resolved, and most are dealt with in a variety of fashions, short of leaving.

When two people come together as partners they bring along what they learned at home growing up; therefore, the parents are right there in the marriage. How men relate to women and how women feel about men is there before they hit the alter.

That's why the best insurance is to look at the parents' marriage, and if it is a good one you are way ahead of the game. Most people however, have seen and been witness to relationships that are a lot less than loving.

Over time any relationship changes. Once passion has gone, it becomes much harder to find comfortable and loving ground.

Then the pair can drift into the dutiful mundane era and live out their lives. Others can be cordial and share daily activities, children, and the business of life, but there is no really warm, caring connection. It is like two roommates, or good friends, sharing their lives together. Many, many couples EXIST just like that for decades.

Then there is the mate who is not happy with their spouse and seeks solace from another; and that can be fully or sexually or emotionally. To keep their self-esteem and have a *friend* to confide in and complain to works for some.

When that happens, the spouse does indeed become an ENEMY! They are the *outsider* and the one that is resented. They are treated in a fashion that spells out in living color, *I really do not like you, or want to be close emotionally to you.*

In a good and working mature relationship the grievances are addressed directly and with the spouse. In an unequal relationship a partner seeks reassurance elsewhere.

This can occur in any number of situations, and at any point.

The partner will certainly be aware that something is different, and when one drifts emotionally the other one usually knows it. If they don't, they are not really there together emotionally. Hence the reason to look elsewhere.

When it becomes 'felt' it is then up to either one to bring it to the fore and see where they go next.

What is especially common is that women, because by nature they are nurturers, they will often tolerate being *badly* treated. If their self-esteem is high, they will deal with it and not be diminished.

You need only to look around to see many women living in *awful* relationships, because they do not feel they can go elsewhere, or because they do not feel good about themselves.

In a situation where a female has high self-esteem, and is independent, which many are today, the male partner may find a less than equal person to cling to. There, they are not judged, and they feel important and needed. Talk about unequal.

When the situation is brought to the fore the couple can get into it, and then the relationship may move to a deeper level. Love and caring will always win out. The ENEMY can again be the *best* friend.

It is not an easy or pleasant road, but it happens frequently.

The true ENEMY will be found out and removed.

This can happen with outsiders or even within families. When family members are the confidant and are party to making a spouse an ENEMY there can be a big adjustment within the immediate family. It will change all the dynamics.

All sorts of machinations can have been a part of this theatrical production. It can include secret calls, texts, meetings, money involvement, gifts, and so on. The deeper the involvement the more difficult to untangle. The longer it went on the more difficult to get through.

The only way OUT is to clean it out; like an infection. It will sting but once healed the scab will come off.

The length and depth of the primary relationship will be sorely tested, and it may fail, or again it may be a new beginning, new awareness and new sensitivity to one another.

"I have my bitchy side, but I don't think I'm really nasty. I think that a lot of other people probably think that I am. Fuck them." - Debbie Harry

What's In It For You

"Work out your own salvation. Do not depend on others." - Buddha

So, what's the story here? It's a hard one to live by; depending on yourself for fulfillment. That takes a heap of work, insight, and behavior.

We ALL behave in ways that we believe will bring us happiness, and contentment. We often fail in the end, or for periods of time. We all, in one form or another, think about what's in it for us.

That can be a mantra and a lifelong goal. Do you achieve it?

Most of us have moments, or long periods of being fulfilled and happy. Most of us suffer periods, or long periods, of not being so happy. That's life!

When we examine what's in it for us it can be about our job, our relationships, and whatever we engage in.

We look at situations and decide if we think they will *work* in our behalf. We choose. We choose our education, career, and friends. And indeed, at the root is that question; will it satisfy us and our needs?

Some friends are there because they are thought to benefit us in some manner.

BUT the big issue here is when we engage in romantic relationships and think, *What's in this for me?*

Close relationships offer us something we need; emotionally, and or physically.

We want to be desired. We want to feel we *matter* to someone. We want to be seen as attractive, sexual, and important.

Now, it is true some people choose a partner to be *taken care of,* psychologically or financially. Some choose partners to be seen as youthful, and vibrant. Some choose partners to move up the social scale. Some choose partners so they won't be alone. Some choose partners…. fill in the blank.

So, back to the question; what is in it for you?

There are martyrs, but even those people get something, *out of it* for their emotional benefit.

No act is without a base for self-fulfillment!

Because of my background, I am most concerned about what goes on in intimate, or not so intimate relationships.

To *connect* with someone, there can be a number of patterns and reasons that get you together. The big one here is, of course, sexual need. Today with dating sites and the Internet and Facebook, finding people is easy. Knowing about them is risky and takes time. Being *fooled* happens a lot. And when the sexual drive is strong, it can lead you into territory that is not so good for you. You can get what you were after but in the end, you may be paying a big price for it, emotionally. Many people today have lost a bit of pride over bad connections here.

That *learned* journal, Cosmopolitan magazine, did a survey not too long ago and found that thirty-five percent of women are having sex on first dates. Sixty percent are having it by the fifth date. Seventy-three percent of men have sex by the fifth date.

Both men and women say their main goal in dating is to find a serious relationship.

What does that consist of?

They want to love and be loved and that means getting something out of it; beyond sex.

How do people go about that these days?

Is wooing and romance dead? I wonder.

Can a relationship lose its' power? You bet.

How many are willing to put up with the 'stuff' that goes on in every relationship; hurt feelings, lack of open communication, needs not met… and so on.

Who learns how to develop a good and sexy pattern together? How do people learn how to resolve differences?

All my good questions. What do couples need to know beyond the *me first* attitude?

Can you put *another* and their wishes and needs ahead of your own?

Are you open, honest, and assertive about what you would like? How do you relate with a partner, with the friends, and family members? Are you able to be loose, spontaneous, and playful? Are the values compatible? We could go on and on.

And there is no real love without real pain, off and on. Who prepares you for that and what can you not compromise?

All of this is against *What's in it for me*.

We don't learn that *giving* is the true source of happiness.

By *giving* one usually, *gets*.

It should not be a one-way street. It is never fifty-fifty either.

What are your goals and how do you go about getting them met? Are your current means working for you?

Can you examine them honestly and change what may need changing?

If your happiness can come from pleasing *another* and loving them, you are on the right track. If it still is, *what's in it for me*, you had better work on you!

"The physical union of the sexes... only intensifies man's sense of solitude." - Nicolas Berdyaev

With All Your Faults...

"I don't think men and women were meant to live together. They are totally different animals." - Diana Dors

Do you agree? I kinda do.

We choose mates, not by accident. They appeal to us viscerally and we are drawn to one another for basically mating purposes. What do we do with and to one another?

Turns out society has set up rules to live by, and rules regarding responsibilities to partners and children born from our relationships. However, laws are usually a generation behind the behavior.

When Gus Kahn, in 1924, wrote the lyrics to, *It Had To Be You*, he started it out with the words, *With all your faults, I love you still*.

Do you? Do you really love him or her with all their faults?

It's a nice wish, and for some it is true, but for many, the faults override the love, and then the relationship slowly or quickly erodes.

The qualities that were so *cute* and endearing in the beginning later become annoying and at times intolerable.

What are the behaviors that get to you?

Usually it has to do with a woman trying to control a husband or vice-versa. Or it can be just those little behaviors that are repetitive that finally add up and get to you.

Have you ever been in a car and not heard a wife complain about her mate's driving?

The other issue is that what one partner considers a fault, is just a way of behaving or reacting that is now a pattern.

Over time the *fault* looms large and is not what one bargained for.

We do change and some of the habits get worse, and what may have started out as a minor annoyance now has become Mount Vesuvius.

You can get set off over any part of the pattern.

At times it seems irrational, and indeed it may very well be. It can be the last straw.

Maybe there were other factors weighing in that led up to it.

A bad day at work, not feeling well, a headache, problems with friends or family. You can think of any number of examples that will take away that, *I love you still.*

Over time it will shake out, and the relationship will sink or swim based on a myriad of situations.

Overcoming difficulties is a test of real love.

Can the love grow and survive?

That depends on what the faults are and how the partner reacts to them. How often is there a problem?

Is the same issue a disaster time and time again?

Can you tolerate it, move on, or do you give up?

If it really *had to be you*, then you will survive.

Recently I had a couple who had been married several decades come for counseling, because she was *not happy*.

Their communication was not good, and their sex life was poor.

She announced she was not leaving even though he *annoyed* her over and over again with his habits because, *Where was she going to go?*

That's not a good enough reason to stay.

With time they were able to move on to a better relationship, because at the bottom, they did love one another and were good to each other. It is not easy to change and especially when the patterns have been long-standing; but it is not impossible if you work at it.

Overlooking and forgiveness are great qualities in a relationship.

Yes, men and women are different animals and they are also different people with varied backgrounds and ideas. Can they adjust and accept each other's differences? You bet they can!

It works in and out of bed!!

Are you perfect?

Let's ask your partner!

"Most women set out to try to change a man, and when they have changed him they do not like him." - Marlene Dietrich

Who's In Control

"You can tie my hands, govern my actions; you are the strongest, and society adds to your power; but with my will, sir, you can do nothing." - George Sand

When it comes to relationships, it's all about power and control; who has it, how is it expressed, and what is the end result?

The infant screams and that gets he or she what they want, usually.

The toddler yells, bites, and says, *No!*

If the parent needs to be in control they can exercise it in a number of ways, including force. The child has to fight harder or give in. This sets a pattern for later life.

Adolescence is particularly tenuous, and the teen can do a whole mess of things to get their way and infuriate their parents.

As adults, rebellion can continue, and the young adult can proverbially *slap the parents in the face* with a whole ream of things. The ultimate is when a child chooses values diametrically opposed to their parents, as in marrying someone that the parents really disapprove of.

There is no winning with a child in the end, and in the real end, the parents have a role- reversal and need the child more than the child needs them. In some cases, the parent holds on to control with money, or other means including withholding approval and love.

Many times, the parent has a need for control and power that keeps the child, even as an adult, in a childlike position, and the child is not strong enough to risk being a grown- up with the parent.

It can be a tragic situation.

When these people get into love relationships they are ready to give up control usually as that is what their role has been in life. OR some go to the other extreme, and finally have a chance to be the *boss*. They can then wield power in many forms, including bad ways.

There is always the matter of control in life; from real bosses at work, boards of directors, and then, of course, laws, and government rules.

No one is completely free, and to be a free-spirit takes a lot of doing.

Within close romantic relationships the idea of power is certainly a factor.

As a counselor, I get to see who sets the rules in any relationship.

It can never be fifty-fifty. In mature relationships couples discuss things and arrive at a mutually agreeable decision. In some, there are categories and lines drawn. He takes care of the finances, while she decides how they are spent. She takes on the responsibility for most of child- rearing practices, while he takes care of the cars etc.

How time and money is spent are the usual big areas for control. Some couples however, argue, or even have huge fights, over what might be considered minor decisions or ways of behaving.

The choice of friends, how relatives are included or not, and so on can be major areas of disagreement and tussle over who's in control, and who gets, *their way.*

The patterns are usually set early on and continue for the life of the relationship, but they can sometimes change when an individual decides to take a stand. Then it's up to the two of them to see where the path leads.

What is especially interesting these days is the shift with women having leadership roles outside of the home, and then continuing that at home, or reverting to being *taken care of.*

Changing and shifting gears is not easy.

Being the *strong* one and having the loudest voice, or the ability to not *give in* takes energy.

Now when it comes to the bedroom, control is also seen here.

Who makes the first move? What happens next?

Basically, women decide when and for whom they will open their legs. They have that control; notwithstanding rape of course.

Men are *subjected* to the females lead here and they are also sort of at the mercy of what the woman knows and will enjoy, or tolerate, or want to experiment with. Interestingly many women feel that when they have total control over a man they lose a certain respect, if you will, and do not feel the same toward them. On the other hand, many powerful men, outside the home, really like to be the *weak* one in bed, and like their woman to take the lead and let them relax in that way.

Power can be used for good or not so good. The abuse of any power is not a goal. At the crux of it all; the giving up totally, with the orgasmic response tells the entire story. Being satisfied physically also includes being satisfied emotionally. How many really accomplished men are there that are fearful, almost petrified, of displeasing their partner? They have the fear of God in them.

How did that happen, I wonder?

"I have never been able to conceive how any rational being could propose happiness to himself from the exercise of power over others." - Thomas Jefferson

Who Are You… Really

"We don't create a fantasy world to escape reality. We create it to be able to stay." - Lynda Barry

All of us have three lives; the public, the private, and the fantasy life.

In our public lives we share what we want others to know and think about us. Those in the real public purview have a difficult time hiding anything, especially these days.

Shy or introverted people keep to themselves, while outgoing extroverted types are *out there*.

What the world or people close to us thinks; matters. We put on a *show*, so to speak. For some, it is easy and for many, having others know us at all is not comfortable.

How many times have you heard he was not who I thought he was? The public persona is often a real myth. Sometimes we expose aspects of who we are without giving a *hoot*. Other times we are very careful. It may depend on with whom we are. A boss, a new love, an in-law…

What we are as a compilation may be a great mystery to the outside world.

Privately we are and should be somewhat different. What goes on behind those *closed* doors is indeed private.

No one knows what happens there except the people who are there living it.

As a therapist I get to hear those stories, and many are shocking, and often unbelievable.

The rational everyday lives of people are difficult. I often think of women's lives in the past, that were made up of all day and night shopping and preparing food, cleaning, and doing laundry. It left little time for any other reality.

Today, of course, women still are the primary keepers of home and hearth and child-rearing, but there is much help; dishwashers, washing machines, take-out food and so on.

Privately people take out their frustrations and hurts and anger at home where it is thought to be private and safe.

When the truth comes out, as it often does, everyone is shocked. Who could have guessed?

All of the scandals, especially of celebrities and well-known people is overwhelming.

It can include abuses at home with spouse or children, dishonest dealing having to do with money, drugs, sex acts, and any number of things that you can think about. The public face and the real face privately, are two different faces.

At times it can just be a release of inhibition or free spiritedness that is *allowed* at home. It can feel safe there.

Now the fantasy self is another story. A guy walking down the beach kicking stones sees a genie pop up. The genie says you can have three wishes. He says; I would like peace between the Israelis and the Palestinians.

And the second wish?

Everyone in the world to have all the food they need. How about for you, personally.

Well, I'd like my wife to do whatever I like sexually, oral sex, in particular.

The first two; no problem. That third one… impossible; except for fantasy.

Fantasy. We all need it and use it in a variety of areas. Kids want to be *cops*. Teens want to be the most popular. Adults want any number of things; money is a big one.

Movies and TV and the Internet offer help to stoke this fire.

Fantasy can play a huge part in the creative juices. BUT it is in the area of horizontal versus vertical life that fantasy plays its' largest role. Who do you think about besides your partner in bed? What do you wish they would do? What do you imagine yourself doing?

Can your fantasy ever become a reality? It has for some. And then again, it has cost many a big price. How many people in the public eye have been exposed with their pants down? Answer; lots. Can the three YOUS be merged into a complete whole person?

The answer is a resounding, yes!

It happens when you are *comfortable* in who you are and you bring out the you, you choose, when you wish. Some people share all of themselves with others or a significant other. How nice is that? Talk about freedom!!

"I have a private life in which I do not permit interference. It must be respected." - Vladimir Putin

Should You Lower Your Expectations

"Do not go gentle into that good night, Old age should burn and rave at close of day, Rage, rage against the dying of the light." - Dylan Thomas

A look at how some people have lived and died gives us a clue about what this life is all about. Many of them did rage at the *dying of the light*.

What interests me is how much they compromised and were their expectations ever lowered?

Maybe people become unhappy because they do expect too much... from themselves, and from others, and from life in general. Who sets the standards? Society? Family? The media? Celebrities?

A look at some people and how they died may give us some insight...

John Jacob Astor, a very rich man, spent his life, not in the family business but, tinkering with mechanical devices and writing fiction. When he divorced his wife of eighteen years and at age forty-seven married an eighteen-year-old, he was open to severe criticism. To escape, he took her on a long voyage... on the Titanic.

As a famous and chivalrous man, he had an opportunity to go into a life boat; instead he sent his pregnant wife and he went down with the ship!

Cleopatra... need I say more?

President Warren Harding had led a full life and at his death there was much scandal surrounding him. He was involved in a problem with the Veterans Bureau and his people selling illegal government supplies. The Teapot Dome where his men sold oil leases for bribes, and he served liquor in the White House during Prohibition, were two of his problems.

Another big story was a woman who claimed to be the mother of his illegitimate child. She said her affair lasted well into his years in the White House. His wife refused an autopsy, so no one ever knew what killed him and many rumors abounded including one that said she poisoned him! After his death there were letters found to a second mistress!

Nelson Rockefeller led an interesting number of years that included two marriages. When he died, a twenty-five-year-old woman was found with him, dressed in a robe. There was food and wine on a table and in his will he forgave a forty-five-thousand-dollar loan he had made to her to buy an apartment. How nice!

Catherine the Great led a most fulfilling life. She had her husband murdered and proceeded to have flings with many, many men. When she died the sixty-seven-year-old ruler had earlier dismissed her twenty-seven-year-old lover and collapsed. From age sixty she had no teeth and such varicose veins that she was in a wheel chair. Her former beauty was gone.

Interestingly, her only child, Paul, who was never close to her, bitter about his father's death, had her buried next to him; the man she slept with the least!

So, what do you expect out of this life? Take a look because as Socrates said, "The unexamined life is not worth living for a human being." That doesn't mean you need to ask how you feel about every little thing or analyze all details in your life, BUT it does mean it's a good idea to sometimes take a look and step back. When things are not going the way, you want is usually a good time, but even better, is to do so occasionally just to see where you are going and what your goals are. Emotionally we have a hard time and it is not easy to be objective about ourselves... that's why we have therapists. It can be helpful, if you cannot do it alone. Often our friends or family, especially children, cause us to reflect and really look inside ourselves, not just in the mirror. Each decade also causes changes. The movie, 'This is Forty' is a good peek at what I'm talking about here.

Anyway, today we want everything fast, and trade sensation for emotion all too often.

I don't suggest lowering expectations; I suggest taking a realistic look and tailoring them to obtain what you need. Descartes said, "I think therefore I am."- Cogito ergo sum.

What I really like is, "The secret of life is in opening up your heart." - From that wonderful philosopher, Chita Rivera!!

Too Many Choices

"The surest way to corrupt a youth is to instruct him to hold in higher esteem those who think alike than those who think differently." - Friedrich Nietzsche

A recent article in the New York Times by Gabrielle Zevin entitled,' Why Don't You Just Get Married? Let Me Explain' deals with an aspect of this issue today.

In essence she has been with a man for twenty-two years and they have never married. As she is turning forty, she is looking at the choices. And it is a choice today; not like years ago when women were not independent, educated, or able to stand on their own two feet. As a matter of fact, about forty percent of the babies born in America today are to single women!

Her point is that she had no need to marry and choosing on a daily basis to remain in the relationship perhaps made her relationship work better than her married friends.

I kind of agree with that. It means not taking one another for granted. Either party can leave at will, and there is an element of being on your best behavior in a sense. It means maybe not doing *gross* things in front of one another and not being so familiar and *safe* that you are not boring or too *relaxed* about the behavior.

There are some benefits to being married however, as one gets older. She points out that getting, sick, and being in a hospital may be easier for partners to share if they are legally bound. There is also the issue of finances and Social Security benefits, for example. Travel and sharing a place to live becomes easier for married people. All that notwithstanding, many couples choose to be together without the walk down the aisle and piece of paper.

The choices today are there.

Recently I was at a dinner and seated next to a divorcee about forty-five. She naturally told me her story. She was married for about twenty years and had no children. She had a career and her husband was a *free spirit* and liked camping out and not being confined in a job too long. That finally got to her, so that she had to end it. Now she is alone, and not seeing anyone, and scared of all the choices out there.

We talked about on-line dating sites and they frighten her. She doesn't meet too many *eligible* men. While she is young- looking, and bright, and quite *dateable,* she is lonely.

Interestingly when I speak to men they talk about too many choices. There is always someone *better* that could come along. They don't even have to be attractive or successful. They just have to exist. It is a different ball game.

With all the women looking for men, it becomes as though they are merely a *commodity.*

Now don't get me wrong; I still believe both men and women want to love and be loved. They just go about it differently. Most males are the initiator still.

I think lots of experience is good. It helps in final selections.

I also think that, when married, we should have to re-choose one another every so often; maybe every five years. That would put us on a different track and behavior.

We might do as the penguins; get together to have offspring, and then when they are not totally dependent on us move on to a new partner. Without wanting children marriage takes on a whole new perspective.

I saw a TV interview with Ivana Trump when she said she prefers younger men now; after two divorces after Donald. She would rather be a *babysitter* than a *caretaker,* is the way she put it, I think. Again; choice.

Whom we choose to share our lives and love and bodies with is entirely up to us. We do not have arranged marriages here. We choose. How we choose is related to many factors and how we come to our conclusions has many predetermined factors. Who we are; how we became who we are; and what our society tells us, all factor in.

To choose to be a non-conformist about something so traditional and time-honored is not an easy path. Explaining our choices is not always easy.

However, only we can make the choices and only we live them. So, choose wisely as the price and consequences for poor choices can be quite high. But you can also learn from bad choices if you take the time and effort to.

"A good marriage would be between a blind wife and a deaf husband." - Michel de Montaigne

Tough Love Isn't

"It is ominous for the future of a child when the discipline he receives is based on the emotional needs of the disciplinarian rather than on any consideration of the child's own needs." - Gordon W. Allport

How true this is. And unfortunately, how often it is the case that it is the parent's problem, not the child's.

Children basically are *victims* of their parents.

When young, they learn how to behave in order to have the parent's approval. This can be shown in many forms; with nice compliments, a showing of affection, gifts, and privileges.

In short order every child learns how to please.

In time however, children want to assert their own will and thus begins the chain of events that can lead to years of problems.

Parents want children who are *well behaved* and compliant. They try to teach their children to avoid danger; whether with a hot oven, or cars in the street.

More subtle are the values that parents hold that they wish to instill in their children. They want to be *listened* to and obeyed.

How often have you seen a child being hit by a parent? It happens. Often it is so that they will not be seen as having *bad* children in front of others.

Of course, parents are bigger and stronger and until a child has developed and grown they are no match for brute force.

I once had a client with an adolescent who wanted to be a musician. As he became of college age his parents wanted him to apply to schools to become a doctor or lawyer. He refused and only wanted to go to a music school.

They were wealthy and withheld support and would not pay for a music school. Eventually they told him to leave home and *make it* on his own.

Being a sensitive young man who was not worldly-wise, he left and lived on the streets with no family contact. The parents were very upset, but told me in counseling they were applying, *tough love* to teach him what he needed to learn.

Well, in my book there is no love in *tough love.*

This young man eventually became prey to drug dealers and ultimately died.

So much for teaching a lesson!

Often the world will teach what parents can't. Sometimes for the better and often for a big wake up call.

To try to force your influence with what we deem *tough love* can ruin a child for life.

To accept and see a child as different from you, or wanting something different for their lives, is not easy for parents, but tough love? Never!

When you really love, you love someone with all their differences and with the ups and downs.

Parents usually want the *best* for their children. They want them to have better lives than maybe they had. They have experience true, but it is THEIR experience and their generation.

When I read about these, *tiger moms* and what they do to very young children, I cringe.

You may get what you are after, but you ruin the person that child should become.

Yes, I believe in discipline and correcting children and wanting children to behave in a civilized manner, but how to get it, and how far, to impose your wishes.

Many parents dream about their children making them proud. That's fine, and they can express their desires. Children know what parents hope for.

Going against that is a problem, not only for the parent, but the child has to be strong to buck the messages. Guilt is not a good thing.

If there is only one parent that makes it even more difficult. If the child is the parent's primary source of happiness and success that also makes it a *loaded* issue.

It is the fair balance of making your wishes known, protecting small children from harm, and sharing your life experience that is best. Beyond that it can be a crap shoot.

Most people follow the values they have seen lived in their family of origin. Parents have to trust that in the end their children will do the same. If not, you can only hope their children will give them the same run for the money that they gave you!!

"The scars left from the child's defeat in the fight against irrational authority are to be found at the bottom of every neurosis." - Eric Fromm

Uniquely YOU

"It's pretty damn hard to bring your uniqueness into actual being if you're always doing the same things as a lot of other people." - Brendan Francis

What is it that truly makes you, YOU?

Looking around it is amazing to observe that so many billions of people have the same features; eyes, a nose, and a mouth, and head shape... but we are all different! Even identical twins have some difference. It is amazing, isn't it?

Dealing with how we look can be a major source of making a person stand out.

Have you seen the people with tattoos?

Have you observed many hair styles today?

Have you seen the pierced parts of people?

Have you seen the way some people dress?

Have you looked at the make-up and nail treatments some wear?

We could go on and on.

These readily observed differences can and do make individuals unique. The question is what does any of that say about such an individual?

Do they just want to be looked at, talked about, noticed?

Who hooks up with these people? Why?

Then there are the other areas for difference. These have to do with what a person does.

How do they behave in the world?

Are they talented in a specific area; art, music, writing, intellect?

What do they do as far as work is concerned?

What do they do in their leisure time?

How do they behave socially?

What is their life experience?

The last area for difference has to do with personality.

Being an introvert, or extrovert says a lot.

Do they relate easily and openly to others?

Are they needing attention all the time?

Are they caring or selfish?

It all adds up to a unique package.

Now when it come to love, that uniqueness is a total person that you either respond to and want to be close to or not.

There is the theory that pheromones play a part here and you in a sense, *sniff out* the person who turns you on.

Be that as it may, we all know when someone attracts us. We all know who we want to climb into bed with.

Our bodies set off by our eyes and ears lead us.

When someone I know was asked why they were in love with their partner and chose to stay with them they replied, *It's his youness.*

It is a condition that no one else holds for you. Whatever the factors are and whatever the combination of those factors is; you are unable to have it with anyone else on this earth at that time. And let us not forget there are about seven billion people on this planet!

The problem becomes a huge one when that person is no longer there or available for whatever reason, because their uniqueness and combination of what they alone are, cannot be duplicated.

How often do people talk about a quality or set of qualities that their loved one possesses or possessed that cannot be found again in any other person?

Sometimes I hear that they *settle* for some of the beloved's attributes or looks but cannot fulfill the total package.

We are all unique and the thing about it is that, you want to be happy about who you really are. Then and only then can you offer yourself for love to another and be appreciated.

Then and only then you will not be able to be replicated by anyone else in their life!!

"If I'm such a legend, then why am I so lonely?" - Judy Garland

She Makes More Than He Does

"Money, if it does not bring you happiness, will at least help you be miserable in comfort." - Helen Gurley Brown

Right. Many people are not happy, and it is true money won't do it BUT, it will allow you to substitute happiness from other sources... and that, could make you happy.

Happiness is a relative term and it certainly is not a given or static. It comes and goes and is different for all of us.

If you were asked, *what gives you your most pleasure?* My hunch is it would not be money or things. Most individual pleasure comes from relationships, and after decades of counseling people, I know that to be true. That's the reason for this whole exercise; writing a book to help people achieve good relationships and thereby be happier.

In 2015, 38% of married women earned more than their husbands. By now that figure has risen quite a bit.

Now, it is also true many women are not paid as they should be, and often are paid less than men in similar or the same job. Unfair! This is getting attention and hopefully changed in time.

The old adage about the Golden Rule; *He who has the gold rules*, is still pretty much true. If you bring in the money you get to decide how it is spent or used.

That was formerly the domain of men; husbands and fathers. Today the pendulum is swinging.

It has caused a number of significant issues in the relationship between men and women both in and out of the bedroom.

There can be a variety of responses emotionally to the whole issue.

Women may become *bossy* and want to be in charge.

Men may be angry and try to assert themselves in other ways. They may feel emasculated.

Woman may be demanding and irrational in expectations.

Women may be downright tired. They still do most of the housework.

Who bears the real responsibility with children?

Partners can feel ashamed of the roles they now play. They may not tell the truth about it all to neighbors, friends, or family members.

Women may feel guilty about their situation, or resentful. Men can feel left out of their wives' lives.

What then happens to love? Sex?

Quite a lot, and it depends on a number of factors.

What were the reasons for the partnership to begin with? How was caring, and love displayed? Was there mutual respect? Can they find reasons to admire one another besides the wage thing? Is the situation temporary?

It doesn't matter; if they have that bond as tight as steel. Maybe he is creative and can't earn a lot. Maybe she is better at things that he can admire.

If they don't make it a big deal the pair can have a loving, sexy, long time together.

If not, divorce may be likely.

It depends on your values and how you see a man's or woman's role.

If they come together to decide how the money is spent that can be an equalizer. If not... problem!

Whoever holds the power in the relationship may or may not be related to who brings in the most money. Sometimes money is there from family and no work is needed. That can be both a blessing as well as a handicap; causing a lack of ambition. In truth there are some people who are just plain lazy. And there are people who, for one reason or another cannot work; alcoholics, drug addicts, mentally ill, and physically ill people cannot be good wage earners usually. Some just have down times.

There may be gamblers, illegal means, or risk takers; again, who tolerates what is the question.

We all need money to live the lifestyle we choose. It is unique for each of us. How we get it is the question.

Today many families have two wage earners, and the way they negotiate the time and money tells the story about how they really feel about and relate to one another. None of it matters if it suits them and relating through technology works for the relationship. If you want to see the truth out there look at the checkbook!!

"There are people who have money and people who are rich." - Coco Chanel

Sacrifice For... Love

"Without sacrifice there is no resurrection. Nothing grows and blooms save by giving. All you try to save in yourself wastes and perishes." - Andre' Gide

Sacrifice is one of those words that makes you sound almost like a martyr. It can be that way in a relationship if only one does the sacrificing. The idea is that both parties sacrifice for the sake of the 'other.' When true love is the base, it can still seem, or feel like a *sacrifice*. It is also the degree or type of *sacrifice* that is involved, that counts.

Now the combination of say, bacon and eggs, is a good duo. However, while the chicken makes a contribution, the pig really sacrifices! Think of the last thing you did to be or show *caring* for someone you love. Then think of anything that you consider a sacrifice that you did for that person. Are they one and the same?

Did you receive pleasure from pleasing your partner? Did you resent what you did for them? Do you repeat the action? Do you grit your teeth and clench your fist emotionally to do what you do for them?

Is it a REAL sacrifice?

Now doing something against your judgment or nature can truly be a sacrifice. Making someone you care about happy as a result may guide you and get you through. If, however, you grow to resent your actions more and more, you may turn out to be the proverbial 'sacrificial lamb' and you can be taken advantage of easily. That won't allow the love to blossom; it will thwart it.

What may be a *sacrifice* for one may be a duty for another, a bad habit, or just the nature of the relationship.

The story of the 'Gift of the Magi' is a good one to illustrate the point.

He sells his watch to buy her a comb for her hair and she cuts and sells her hair to buy him a chain for his watch. How fabulous is that??? What we do for one another is usually out of pure love and wanting to do whatever.

Now, I have had clients tell me all sorts of things they have done; usually with a lot of embarrassment over whatever. One older couple gingerly told me they were asked to leave a restaurant for behaving in an *inappropriate* manner! Great! He was pleased with himself while she wanted to die of shame. She couldn't even bear to ride by the place for years after that.

Sacrifice?

There can be any sort of sacrifice made in behalf of another. We think of parents sacrificing much for the benefit of their children. It comes easily in most of these situations. We think of sacrifices people have made for the pride of country or freedom.

That comes without much emotional pain.

We think of any number of such instances where the *sacrifice* is willingly and even joyfully given.

The problem occurs when a partnership feels one-sided.

If you are the one always doing the giving, even when it rubs you the wrong way, then it is an area that needs talking about, and hopefully adjusting.

If the pattern has been deeply ingrained over time, it may be extremely difficult to give up. Even if one relationship ends it can be repeated with a new face.

Sometimes in an extreme form it may be almost like giving up *yourself* in the service of another. That is certainly not a good thing. It has to do with your sense of self-worth too.

Sometimes a partner is so controlling that the other one feels like it is a demand, or that they may lose the partner if they don't comply. Then they are definitely taken advantage of.

So, when we talk about sacrifice it should be a joint effort and yes, one may do more of it than the other but the other one joins in the effort.

When it all works well, and love is strong it may not even seem like a sacrifice and it becomes a way of giving that works well for both parties.

My pleasure then is from pleasing you!

A good relationship doesn't keep *score* as it just IS.

"Giving is the highest expression of potency. In the very act of giving, I experience my strength, my wealth, my power... I experience myself as overflowing, spending, alive, hence as joyous." - Erich Fromm

Show Off... And On

"There is many a lonely heart beating beneath a diamond parure." - Mary Dunn

Being a *show-off* can be fun. Truly, it can be. I think we all do some of it. We can be hypocrites about it too. The fact is we all like to be *on top* in some fashion from time to time.

It is just human nature, as we are competitive.

You can see it all around you at all ages.

Young people like to look good, be fit, and show off in a variety of ways.

Young men like muscles. Young girls like fashion and so on.

As we get older, we show off in the areas of how we look, and what we do, and what we have.

There are *intellectual snobs*. They have to show off their intelligence and thoughts to make sure you know they are smarter than you.

There are people who have to show how trim they are or how thin they are. Many young women look like they eat from recipes from the 'Anorecic Cookbook!'

Indeed, many do have eating disorders in the effort to be thin. Their self-image is distorted and they see themselves as *fat*, even when they are painfully thin. Where do they get these ideas? Probably from the movie stars or fashion magazines. I have seen many young women who have bodies like twelve-year-old boys. It is not a pretty, or feminine sight.

Even older women fall prey to this malady. That is really unpleasant to observe. And watch them in restaurants and see what they order and eat.

Men work out and that can be an obsession. How much bulk and muscle are attractive?

Being strong is fine, but at an extreme it can be off putting, just to look at. Many exercise as though they would die, if they missed a day. While exercise is good for you in moderation and makes you feel good, it can be destructive if it takes over your life.

Competition with money is a biggy.

What can I have or do to prove I have a lot of money?

Just look at all the foolish people wearing or carrying something with a well-known brand name on it. You have to recognize what it is right away or they are not happy.

Why would you want to wear something or carry something that has someone else's insignia or name on it? Isn't your name or initials good enough? Apparently not.

And let's not talk about the car you drive. Or let's talk about the car you drive.

How many have gone into debt for this reason? They are showing the whole outside world what they think they are... rich!

Jewelry? We could spend pages on this one. The diamond industry has really sold people a bill of goods here. It is a waste of money EXCEPT for those who need it!

Women and handbags and shoes... another fun group.

Thousands of dollars for two leather straps that are called designer shoes. And they hurt when you wear them too!!

Houses and their contents. Now here you do live in them, and you do have nice surroundings, and your family enjoys the amenities, BUT here again; how much is really used?

Earlier in my life I was at an affair with one of the Rockefellers. I was all *dolled* up and had on my 'best' jewelry. When I was introduced to the wife of one of them, I was shocked to see her in a dress that looked like it came out of J.C. Penney's and she had on costume jewelry!! She had NOTHING to prove!!

I learned then and there that if you have IT you don't have to flaunt it.

However, it is fun to outshine sometimes. Women especially like to impress other women with their figures and style and what they have. Men are competitive in sports and jobs and success with money earned, but women want to impress other women.

Men really don't care how your nails look or what you are wearing or whose shoes are on your feet. They care how you present yourself and if they are attracted to you. That doesn't come from clothes. They care if they think you are *beddable*.

Women notice what you look like in different ways. So, your being *better* in these areas is for them, not men.

With women being educated and earning money, they are moving into the realm of men and competitive there. However, in order to be fulfilled emotionally they must return to being WOMAN with a man.

A book, 'Beyond Mars and Venus,' by John Gray is really good, explaining our differences hormonally as men and women, and how to achieve the best balance in these areas.

So, what should we do?

Well, show off if it makes you feel superior in some way, from time to time. Nothing really wrong with it.

But, being emotionally content is the best thing to show the world, because then you are really happy and can relate in a truly 'superior' fashion. The packaging can look good; nothing wrong with that but it is not what will really make you the 'winner' in the arena that counts!

"I'm tired of all this nonsense about beauty being only skin deep. That's deep enough. What do you want ----an adorable pancreas?" - Jean Kerr

Relating Through Technology

"Planned obsolescence is another word for progress."- James Jeffrey Roche

If you look at the history of people relating to one another, you will find that what is going on today seems rather sterile.

We have come from living with families, to living near one another, to barely connecting in person for any period of time.

Our wonderful technology now allows us to see one another, talk to each other, and write instantly to whomever we wish.

It is a wonder to be sure and the ability to relate in this variety and fashion is the stuff of science and new ideas.

Now, what does it all mean?

What has or has not improved and gotten better?

For my money, it is both great and awful depending on who is connecting with whom and what is really going on.

When I go out, everyone has a phone in their ear or on their lap. Everybody is *talking* to... who?

I suspect much of the *jibber-jabber* is about nonsense. I also have a suspicion that many are calling the weather, or their mothers, just to look busy and important. How much conversation can go on that is so valuable?

Yes, it is good for emergencies, for appointments, and getting information. But constantly??

It is most interesting to me that some *emotional* conversation does happen.

I have even heard of a partner announcing they wanted a divorce through social media!

The dating scene is great, as it opens up the world for meeting and getting to know new people. However, it has also been fraught with weird people masquerading as someone they are not, or people who plan to take advantage of someone they plan to meet.

It also provides the opportunity to keep on searching for *someone better*. That search may never end.

The relationships can be short- term and rather superficial. This prevents true intimacy.

That is a big problem down the road.

While companies, politicians, entertainment, and news can be widely and quickly spread, the difficulty is who to believe and what are the sources of information? Who decides what is real?

Another issue is that most people only follow those individuals who agree with their own philosophy and never get to hear a new or different point of view. That reinforcement does not cause people to grow and learn. Not a good thing.

There is a new form of technology every other minute it seems, and everyone wants the newest gadget. Is that progress? Is it all necessary?

We all have to decide what we want and more importantly, what we feel we really need in our lives.

Seeing four-year old's playing video games at a family dinner is not my idea of connecting with one another for long term memories of *family*.

Watching young adults at a restaurant looking at their phones and texting is not my idea of the road to romance.

Having a robot for all sorts of purposes, including, sex, is not my preference either!

It is all a bit much.

Cars that drive themselves; what next?

We seem to all be isolated in our own little worlds; not emotionally with each other, not talking together about what is important; feelings, and heart to heart.

Do we even know our neighbors anymore? Their names, their lives, their needs and ideas?

As we become more independent and isolated it can only get worse.

When we lived with family or nearby, with friendly relations with neighbors and with diversity, we were able to be both independent and socially joined. It was a good feeling, most of the time. We also learned how to get along and negotiate and deal with problems.

How is that learned today? With a gun?

Technology is wonderful for all the good it does; helping with the things that took up time like housework, or travel, or communication, but we really need to examine how much we need and how it all affects our daily lives and intercourse together.

Being able to see and talk to a grandchild far away is lovely and fun, but it will never replace holding them and giggling in your arms!

Use technology as you wish; just make sure you are not sacrificing the real deal; being close and joined in the significant ways that make us human.

"In their worship of the machine, many Americans have settled for something less than a full life, something that is hardly even a tenth of life, or a hundredth of a life. They have confused progress with mechanization." - Lewis Mumford

Ready Or Not

"Jealousy would be far less torturous if we understood that love is a passion entirely unrelated to our merits." - Paul Eldridge

We have all known a period when someone *bothers* us in a way that makes us feel competitive.

Now it can be about anything.

How we look, what we have achieved, what we possess, our family, or whatever. Sometimes it is about very superficial things, and I am brought to mind of a woman who said other women were *jealous* of her because of her jewelry. Did she know how shallow or superficial she sounded? Probably not, as that was her value. That business about, *you can't be too rich or thin* will take you just so far.

Being jealous of someone's looks may be futile as you are who you are; make peace with it!

Being jealous of someone's talents or accomplishments may push you to do more; not a bad incentive. You do have to realistically know what you can accomplish however, and this can sometimes be a problem.

The trick is to accept who you are and keep trying to be the best that you can be in whatever area. Now when it comes to love it may be a different story, as we all look for that *special* someone. When you are with someone and dating, it can be a bit of a problem if someone else who appeals to you, crosses your path. Ready or not, it just happens.

What to do then?

Today females can take the initiative and talk or let the guy know they are interested. Guys can make sure they connect or have a way to reach females that interest them.

It is a smorgasbord out there and sampling is necessary in the long run. We do compete for attention, and for love. Some males especially, love the chase and conquest… the long haul, not so much.

Some people let pride get in the way of going on with a relationship that may have some bumps in the road; which all relationships have. All we can control is ourselves.

We can control our thoughts and our actions. It is up to us. And ambivalence is part of life. Nothing is totally pure; positive or negative. The adventure that is called, *life* is a bundle of feelings that go up and down. Who we are and our self-esteem is determined by how others relate to us from day one.

This message gets reinforced on a continuing basis. Sorrowfully, many get a negative message that is very difficult to shake. But it is not impossible.

If one area is weak buttress up in another domain! It doesn't have to be that song of Bonnie Raitt's," Nothing Seems To Matter." There was a line a recent college graduate gave me when the situation presented itself of a guy wanting to take out a girl he saw with another guy. It was, 'Just because there is a goalie, it doesn't mean you can't score.' I really like that attitude.

Some people give up easily and some fight to the death… emotionally or at times realistically.

To keep pushing on is the message of getting through this life. There will always be challenges and we must decide if we wish to take them on, or not. Sometimes jealousy will rear its' ugly head when we are unaware and then we are caught by surprise and have to evaluate all sorts of things; ready or not. That can be a good thing… or maybe not.

Whatever we decide to do will show us who we are, what we value, and how we compete.

Most males compete in careers while most females compete in the arena of looks. Again, we are basically different. No matter how unisex this generation thinks they are, some ingrained differences cannot be erased. I say, *Hooray.* While getting over rejection is never a fast or easy process, it is a learning experience and should be seen as such.

Taking life day by day may have to be de rigueur for the immediate present, but in time, it should get easier and put into perspective, and provide an opportunity for emotional growth.

Not a bad outcome.

There is no one who has it all. There are always prettier, richer, smarter people. Your job is to be the person you can admire and then no one can upset that inner peace and contentment... no one!!

"He that falls in love with himself will have no rivals." - Benjamin Franklin

Revenge.... Is So So Sweet

"The woman who cannot hate like a bitch afire, and express it, cannot love like a tigress, or a kitten." - Brendan Francis

That's right!

Show me a person who can *hate* and wants revenge, and I will show you a passionate person.

When we feel, we have been *wronged*, no matter the reason, the natural response is, *pay them back,* and seek REVENGE!

There are many, many reasons to feel *done to* or for any of us to be furious.

Sometimes it is justified and sometimes it is our own thoughts that may or may not be correct. No matter the cause, if we feel it, we are entitled to our feelings. At times, the person we want to 'hurt' in return is not the real person that we should be angry at.

Many times, a partner feels their partner has done something they find awful or stupid or really despicable. They want revenge, BUT they choose to hurt the party the partner was involved with, as opposed to the real source of their anger; the partner!

Sometimes it is infuriating and you want revenge on everyone involved and maybe even the world, as a result.

Now, how to get revenge?

There are any number of ways; let your imagination run wild.

Screaming and cursing, physical attacks, withholding sex, money or children. Cutting up clothes, burning letters, not cooking, cleaning or paying bills, works. Calling or sending nasty messages is a style for some. Telling *secrets* is another ploy. Calling the IRS and reporting a person, spreading the tale to others and so on. Finding a private detective, telling government agencies someone has done something illegal or that they are a rapist, child molester, bad parent, on drugs and so on goes on all the time.

Now when the revenge is acted out it just feels good; it does. There is a satisfaction that the debt has been paid and there is a smile that accompanies it. Just thinking about doing harm in some fashion to another may be all it takes.

But I am here to tell you that hate should not linger as it will get you in the end.

Be done with the issue and move on.

Know that this life will dish out enough grief and bad times to everyone, including the one on whom you wish to take revenge. We all get a dose of bad times. Some more than others.

It is usually the case that people who are not doing or have not acted in the ways they should, get a BIG dose of payback, in one form or another. They do!

Stay tuned and you will hear about their hard times or see it in living color.

Trust me, no one gets out of this life fancy-free, and everyone has rotten times and some have really rough roads. The *bad* people know what they are, and usually at some point, they get what you wish for them.

No one escapes.

You don't have to waste much of your own precious time thinking about it… will happen!

While it does feel good to have retribution and settling the score, you do not want to emotionally keep it up as then you are the one paying a price.

Get on with it, and make your life pleasant and happy, and that is as they say, the best revenge.

Let the world and the one you hate see YOU happy!!

"I don't agree that love gives the best insight. Hate gives a much better, I think, when hate keeps its head." - Maarten Maartens

Politics and Love

"Politics, and the fate of mankind, are shaped by men without ideals and without greatness. Men who have greatness within them don't go in for politics." - Albert Camus

This is true not only for men, but for women as well today.

When it comes to politics and love anything is game as this recent election shows us.

What a person is, comes through on television; you see the real deal.

Television is an X-ray into the heart and soul of who this person really and truly is.

You can learn about a person from any variety of sources. What you learn from their opponents is another window.

The media has flooded us with information; some true, some not so true, about each of the people who have wanted, (God knows why), to be our president.

Just think of the ego and narcissism that it takes to want this dangerous job!

I can think of no other reason that would drive anyone to seek the position.

Just think of the time and effort, the money that running for office, any office, let alone President of the United States requires.

Think of the power sought. Think of the adulation from others involved. Think of the temptations available.

All of it is not conducive to an intimate caring one on one relationship that spells... L 0 V E! Love requires intimacy, time, attention. Real love means that person is the one that turns you on. That person makes the world alive for you. That person is your core being.

Now let's see where politicians are with that as background.

Usually out in left field. There is the adoring spouse standing on the platform nodding at everything the political animal says.

The spouse who is silent and is just THERE.

You've seen it time and time again.

How many politicians have had sexual scandals? Hard to find one who hasn't.

How much does anyone know about what goes on behind those proverbial closed doors?

We all need *heroes* and we all want them to be examples to strive for. We want people who are 'better' than us to look up to. When was the last time any politician filled that role?

What happens is, many start out altruistically but the money they need to run or stay in office puts them into another camp. They become corrupted; whores if you will. It's part of the landscape.

Sad.

When anyone wants to *do good* for *the people*, it usually becomes a losing game.

Power is indeed an aphrodisiac. They become above the law and omnipotent.

Being a partner to someone with that kind of ego and power takes more than most partners are able to give.

What happens then?

You got it... another partner.

Many try to keep face and keep up a front, or even a relationship, when it is truly DEAD... just for the sake of staying or gaining power. Who is fooling whom?

The people involved know the truth, and sometimes it shows to the outside world, like it or not.

Looking at our current election, it is fun to watch the machinations going on and trying to envision the bedroom scenes. Amusing, to say the least.

What do they talk about? The campaigns? The opponents? The next step? The money needed or how to spend it?

It's anyone's guess. My hunch is it's not about how they love one another. With all of this my suggestions for the vice-presidential picks... are, Hillary can have Bill.

AND Trump can have Monica Lewinsky!!

"Politicians, like prostitutes, are held in contempt, but what man does not run to them when he requires their services?" - Brendan Francis

Promises, Promises

"From the promise to the deed is a day's journey." - Bulgarian Proverb

How true is that!

At this wonderful time of the year with a brand-new year approaching, the proverbial *resolution* comes into play.

How many make resolutions and what are they about, and how many are kept?

A new year means a new beginning in many senses and making promises is a natural process.

Children make them all the time. They promise *to be good* and to clean up their rooms and so on.

Adults make promises to themselves and others about several categories; their bodies, their living conditions, and their goals.

Some people make promises when they are angry, or when others are angry about something with them.

Some make promises when they are happy and want to improve some aspect of their lives.

Some are small and rather inconsequential, while others are important, and some are life- changing.

Yes, there are promises to lose weight, to drink less, to fix something in the house, to not spend money frivolously, to go back to school, get a better job, and so on.

Can anyone trust the promises made?

That depends on the past experiences.

That is also the reason we have lawyers and written agreements!

The big issue that I want to address here is the area of promises about relationships.

There is huge group of people who made promises in one form or another, but who were not about to stick to them or carry them out.

How many parents and children are estranged?

The *agreement* was the promise to protect and love one another for life.

Life however made a change in that plan.

Parents and children become enemies, so to speak.

A variety of reasons may have caused this and led to this outcome.

Parents may not like the partner a child has chosen. There may be a payback for earlier perceived wrongdoing. Values may differ. Stresses such as divorce and on and on, may have led to the fallout. Many parents scapegoat a child or their partner, if they feel disrespected, or do not like the way a partner treats their child. There may be *secrets* that cause the communication to cease. Whatever the reason, it takes time to get to that unfortunate end.

There can be siblings that do not connect with one another.

Again, the reasons can be varied.

What is sad from my perspective, is that families miss out a great deal and people feel badly or guilty about such actions.

I do not deny that some estrangements are good and can be beneficial, even necessary in some cases… if the relationship is too toxic or debilitating.

Estrangements can be for any period of time and some last a lifetime. Holidays, family occasions such as weddings and funerals, are especially poignant. There is a *hole* if you will, that is there.

When it comes to that really big promise; *I will be here and love you forever,* in marriage or a long-term relationship, it can get really dicey.

That promise needs addressing; especially these days.

I don't care how many New Year's you have shared, that promise should be reevaluated and looked at every so often.

That is the one promise that I believe should be meaningful and given breathing room for free choice every so many years; maybe every five years.

Then it has a chance of being fulfilled and trusted.

In any relationship, communication; open, and honest, is the key.

There can be things withheld, to be sure, in order to protect a partner, but by and large sharing ideas and feelings is crucial to keeping the promise to be there and loving you forever, alive!!

This New Year make those promises to yourself first, and then to whomever you choose… and then let's *talk* next year!

"We promise according to our hopes and perform according to our fears." - La Rochefoucauld

The Perfect Wife

"She should be beautiful, sexy, intelligent, fun, kind, caring, AND… A deaf mute who owns a distillery." - Anonymous

Nice, huh?

Many men would agree with this definition, and in the past a number of women sort of filled the bill.

Women were there to *serve* their men. They did not have educations or careers and were in a sense totally dependent on their husbands. The ways in which they *earned* their keep was to do for him.

They cleaned, cooked, and had their children.

Keeping him happy was the goal.

Is this still true today?

Let's look at it.

While many women work and raise children at the same time, they have become independent and do not need a man to support them or give them a place in society. HOWEVER, the old traditional roles still hold water even in the best-case scenario.

What do women and wives need from a man these days?

Maybe the same old stuff… and it is attached to a penis!

Yes, sex, is an important part of a marriage or relationship. Maybe that's all some modern women need from their guy. Of course, they can buy vibrators and dispense with a man altogether, if they so desire.

Lynn Hubschman

What do men want from a wife today?

Many do want equal partners. They appreciate a wife who is educated and successful and enjoying a career. In fact, today many wives are the primary breadwinners. In many instances the roles that were traditional have been reversed.

What do we think about that? How do families work it all out?

There is no one answer today.

With the advent of birth control, women were free to express their sexuality. They learned about how to enjoy their sexuality. With feminism many became demanding in the bedroom. In some cases, this made their men retreat and feel less a man.

For my money the old roles are not there by happenstance; they have been ingrained as a result of our biology and long history. Not everyone agrees with this, I know.

By and large the old traditions still hold water.

Maybe some of the behavior has changed, both for good and bad, but the basics are the same.

Yes, there is a continuum and there is no one pattern for all, but the words, *feminine* and *masculine* still mean the same as they always did.

The softening around the edges has occurred and that may be a good thing. The movement too far to the *other* side may not be so good.

Men still want beautiful, caring wives, and women still want strong, successful husbands. These things were not created out of thin air. The attitudes were based on who would make good parents.

There is a book out called, 'The Fortune Hunters' which is about the dazzling women and the men they married. The author is Charlotte Hays.

She gives the histories of many famous women and what they did to rope in their wealthy husbands.

The traits that they had or cultivated were across the board. The lengths they went to in order to become married to these men are amazing.

Included are the Duchess of Windsor, Jackie O, Pamela Harriman, Arianna Huffington, and many more.

True men want a wife who turns them on, and that is first and foremost in most cases. Being a housekeeper and running a home is important for many. Cooking well can help, and so on. BUT it is the care and emotional nurturing of HIM that they really respond to and want. How each wife holds on to her husband over time varies, and many lose their partner to another.

In these cases, he is the primary decider. He rules through his position or money.

There are cases where she finds another man and decides to leave.

I once had a client who was talking about being enthralled with Mayor John Lindsey and would like to be his wife.

When I asked what she had to offer him and what she might do with her life she said, 'I just want to take care of and love him.'

That's a life for some women but what of their talents and ambitions?

Today many women are not just appendages doing his bidding. They are out there doing their thing and coming home to be a loving wife as well. It is not always easy. The needs of both parties have changed.

So, who is the perfect wife today?

ME, of course!

"My mother said it was simple to keep a man, you must be a maid in the living room, a cook in the kitchen, and a whore in the bedroom. I said I'd hire the other two and take care of the bedroom bit." - Jerry Hall

Notice Me...Notice Me

"Whatever you may be sure of, be sure of this.... that you are dreadfully like other people." - James Russell Lowell

Okay, so is that a good thing or a bad or discouraging thing? You decide.

In a sense, it is a human condition that unites all people. However, and this is a big however, we all search for a way to be unique and appreciated for that uniqueness.

This happens as adults when most of us have outgrown the need to be accepted and like our adolescent peers. There are many who do want to stand out and do just about anything to be different during those adolescent years. Here it takes some funny forms.

Most teens want to look like and do what their peers do. They need that camaraderie and sense of belonging. The ones who are not in that group find another group that is *weird* in its' own way. They dress a certain way; like all in black. They wear their hair in unusual fashions, and they drink or take drugs along with their particular set of friends. Then there are the ones that get pierced in every possible body part. And, there are the tattoo people. Have you seen them? Are you one of them?

Recently, I have seen many with so many tattoos that you cannot tell if they are wearing clothes or if the entire arm or leg are full of tattoos. Have you even been waited on in a restaurant with one of them that took your appetite away?

Some of these tattoos cost a fortune and some are done by well-known *artists*.

In any event, it is a way of being different and unique and yes, noticed!

What happens when they reach sixty years old, I wonder?

Now being noticed is a good thing.

Standing out in a crowd is not bad. Being *special* is a good feeling. We are all individuals to be sure. Some people need to be VERY special.

It then depends on your talents and qualities that make people remember you, want to be near you, be your friend, or emulate you. Even for posterity it becomes an issue.

Today being *politically correct* is a big concern for many people. Even legally we have to address this.

But aside from that, how do we get noticed?

When it comes to romance and finding or attracting a partner, we use different approaches.

We can look the way we think we should, to attract such and such a type person. We can use our intellect, and personality to attract attention. We can extend ourselves and become chameleons to be what we think a particular type of person wants. But if we are not GENUINE it won't last, and we will be found out. What we truly are cannot be denied and not for long, certainly.

So, the trick is to know yourself and what you have to offer and develop that part of you that makes you truly unique and special.

Yes, we are all special in our own way, and hopefully, to at least someone else, or a lot of someone *elses*.

It does begin from birth and being wanted and really special to parents. If that didn't happen it can be dealt with, and other people can fill the void, but it is harder.

We can learn from rejection and failure how to be resilient. We can matter. We can become stronger and more insightful, which will give us strength to have control over our lives in the long run.

If we try TOO hard, we can lose our true selves, and that will not serve us well, forever.

Many times, people feel inferior because of the values and standards we have, in the case of physical appearance, for example. Remember Jimmy Durante? Most people with his large nose would hide in a closet. But he did the opposite, and was not just noticed, but loved as a result of his personality and talent, which he developed. It is up to the individual.

While we do not live in a vacuum, we can isolate ourselves enough to take stock of who we are and what we deliver to others and the world. It is up to YOU!!

Want to be affectionately noticed? Do something nice for someone!

"Be yourself is the worst advice you can give to some people." - Tom Masson

Marry Him... Please Don't

"It is hardly possible to estimate how many marriages fail to prosper or are actually ruined because the man lacks any inkling of the art of love." - Count Hermann Keyserling

Some of you may know or have recently read in The Atlantic magazine the article by Lori Gottlieb, *Marry Him*.

I, for one, disagree with what she has as a premise; get married just to marry, or to have children; especially, if you have reached age thirty and have not found, *Mr. Right*.

That would make you marrying Mr. Right Now! DON'T do it!!

I don't care what she thinks. I have lived long enough and been in this business long enough to tell you it is a huge mistake.

True, being alone, wanting children and getting older is not easy, for the best of women.

Makes no difference how beautiful, sexy, intelligent, rich, or interesting you are; finding love is NEVER easy.

HOWEVER, to live without it, you might as well be dead. Having children, which attaches you for life to someone is a BIG mistake. What do you think you are demonstrating to those children?

What kind of choices do you want them to make? I know all the rationalizations. I know all the arguments, and I also know human nature. Whatever your emotional needs are, they will not be buried forever.

You can read the lives of many fabulous, and some not so fabulous, females, who chose not to marry and then fell in love at some point, and indeed married.

And yes, marriage may not be forever or without its' anguish, but being in love, and being together is worth whatever the price.

My theory is also that people who have the capacity for love, and feel good about themselves, usually do have *others* find them and connect.

I truly wonder about those females who can't be themselves and accept a man for who he is and let love blossom. You CAN teach people, and partners in particular, how to love.

The first step is that one we all know; physical attraction. From there, everything else flows.

You can see him without the rose-colored glasses in time, and you can see ALL the warts, however the physical pull should get you back and through it.

I also am sexist, and believe males are more easily satisfied, while women are picky and find all sorts of fault.

If you are a real woman, in my book, his attraction and turn- on to you is all that matters to get the whole shebang going!

Those females who are alone, and complain, aren't doing what they need to; looking at themselves and working on their ideas and values.

If your feet aren't next to someone you really care about in bed, you are wasting your life.

You can lie to the world and even to your mother, but not to yourself.

Again, I don't care what anyone says, we need to love and be loved.

Substitutes can assist, and maybe that's all there is in your lifetime, and maybe you're okay with that. That's fine… it's your life, but this is not a dress rehearsal!

Romance is not taught; it is learned, and it has to go through fire and brimstone to endure.

Who decides what is right for you?

Fairy tales are read from childhood, but real life is not a fairy tale. Often, it's a nightmare. Okay, that's life. That's marriage, and that's love.

Some have many trials and never get it right; some have one that is good forever; and most have a couple that make the grade.

I know love is possible. I know love can last. I know love and passion make this life what it should be.

What I also know is that it takes a leap of faith to follow your instincts, and then lots of work to keep a flame alive.

So, if you are *making do*, or *settling* be aware... you may be unsettling yourself for the rest of your life.

DO NOT DO IT!!!

Having *anyone* is not a necessity. Having a baby alone is a really tough road, and being with someone who doesn't excite you, (no matter the age), is just not worth it.

This is a big wide world, so don't tell me finding someone to love is impossible... I don't buy it!

For the New Year; Find somebody to love!!!

"A husband is what is left of a man after the nerve has been extracted." - Helen Rowland

Monogamy Is For The Birds

"Love has been in perpetual strife with monogamy." - Ellen Key

This is not a new issue.

The Chinese and Indian cultures have been around for about 7000 years.

The Jews are here for around 5000 years.

The Mayans about 4000,

The Romans about 2500.

All have had relations between males and females governed by rules.

The rules included being together for periods of time, raising children, and dealing with disintegration of relationships.

To be sure, they have all evolved and changed, and the roles have moved in a variety of directions.

Humans started out as polygamous, and the transition to monogamy began about 0. 5 million to 2 million years ago. We are still in transition, I believe.

The reasons for monogamy strongly include the care of the vulnerable infant. Two parents can do a better job as opposed to one parent handling it all. This is a strong reason for males remaining with their partner.

They also want to be sure of their paternity. The drive to have the species continue is strong and the *best specimens* are selected.

There are other reasons as well.

The need for resources and protection is important in many cases.

Societies need order, and partners want to make good *investments*.

If we look at all the species inhabiting planet earth what do we find?

First of all, we know that ninety percent of birds are monogamous. Some are monogamous only for mating and rearing of the young.

There are some that do mate for life. These include: Swans, Eagles, some Owls, some Parrots, Albatrosses, Doves, and some think that Pigeons may not choose another mate if theirs dies!

Most fish are not monogamous.

Now when it comes to mammals guess what? Only three percent are monogamous!!

That's a message.

These include; some species of Wolves, some species of Fox, and some Apes, like the Gibbon.

The Prairie Vole is most interesting, as he mates for life and will go to the extreme by fighting off any other female that approaches him.

Try that on your guy!!

With we humans, living longer, and females being independent, the task for being monogamous for life is a rough journey.

It is true, many do love and enjoy being together for life, and have figured out how to do that well.

But for very many, serial monogamy seems to be the case. For others, a fling may suffice.

If you want children, it is usually a good idea to have a partner that is loyal and caring and helpful in providing and looking after the child's and your welfare.

Without children, or when they are on their own, it is easier for a male to be promiscuous. He has less usually to lose. However today that may be in the flux of change, as women are the breadwinners in many households.

Attractiveness is a lifelong issue for both males and females.

One fact that was surprising to learn is that when competition for females is strong for the male his testicles and fertility increase. How about that!

When conflicts occur it usually is around the tradeoffs of investment and/or attractiveness.

We all yearn to love and be loved. How to get there and for how long are questions for every individual since the beginning of time.

Passion and the continuation of the species forces us to CONNECT!

"God, for two people to be able to live together for the rest of their lives is almost unnatural." - Jane Fonda

Marriage Gives You License To...

"When a husband and wife have got each other, the devil only knows which has got the other." Honore' de Balzac

While I write a great deal about many aspects of marriage, the overall situation is often neglected. That being the case, let me address it here.

Marriage as an institution has its' roots in property rights and authenticity of children being the father's. Arranged marriages protected these rights and assured families that the new couple were of equal rank.

Today however, that is all changed in most cultures. Witness the recent wedding of Prince Harry!

The beginning of most relationships that are fueled by desire and love have a glow that surrounds them. You can see it in the eyes and in the body language. It is indeed magical. It is wonderful and consuming.

The beloved can do no wrong. Whatever the problems are, they are masked or overlooked and excused. Passion covers it all and makes the relationship positive. Any idiosyncrasies or even downright annoyances are brushed aside.

How long this phase lasts can vary.

How much time is spent together is important. Under what circumstances the couple see one another is another factor. How any differences are brought up or solved or swept under the rug is vital.

So, let's say they get along just dandy, and the passion is there, and they decide to marry.

Big decision. Now they have to include family and make plans.

Step number one on the road to …

Maybe they get through all the planning, picking out china, and deciding where to live. The pull to be a couple is still strong.

Then they are on their own in that home and by themselves to live it out.

Here is the tricky part. Once married, there is a license to be whoever you really are, and to interact together as you wish.

That license says in small print;

Now I can be a slob.

Now I can say whatever I feel like saying.

Now I can be as demanding as I wish.

Now I can decide what I want to do with money.

Now I can be the boss.

Now I can have sex, or not have sex.

Now I can tell others what I choose about my life.

Now I can…

This is the rest of your life, or not.

It is really up to each partner to be as courteous and caring as they might have been before that license was issued.

The passion will wane, as having a readily available sex partner changes the dynamic.

You no longer have to woo and win someone. They are yours. It is easy. Maybe too easy.

There is no mystery, no conquest, no longing.

Being romantic after the license takes thought and work. Yes, work. It does not occur automatically. My own bias is that it is the female that keeps the fire burning; adds a bit of mystery. She keeps him interested.

Today it is very easy to see, work with, or find, other partners for whatever reason. That means the bond at home is not strong enough to resist outside influences. Or perhaps the needs have changed. Maybe those cute habits before the license are now just plain annoying. Maybe you now make issues and argue or even fight about all sorts of things.

When I see couples heading for divorce I always ask if they had any clue about the things that now want them to be apart; they all say *yes,* and can enumerate them.

To be sure there can be crisis, ill health, death, and certainly having a baby that cause huge changes. But if a couple is really bound together, they can become tighter.

There is nothing like marriage but marriage. My idea is to have that license expire every so often, like five years, and have a couple have to renew it!!

"Today he admits, he gave his sons one piece of advice: Never confuse I love you with I want to marry you." - Cleveland Amory

Love... Less Love... More

"Women are meant to be loved, not to be understood." - Oscar Wilde

"Men are a luxury. Not a necessity." - Cher

Two good ideas. One by a homosexual man, and the other by a sexy lady.

There are many schools of thought when it comes to love, and certainly when it comes to the question about is love necessary, or is sex alone just fine.

From my experience, which is vast, and I have heard it all, both can be the case.

There are times, and indeed people, who just enjoy sex and may never have experienced or risked being totally in love. Who is to judge?

There are issues surrounding all of this. Lately there are groups, mainly in New York, that have people coming together for discussions about it all. Finally!

Some people like to feel, *sad.* They complain all the time, and get into situations, or allow things to continue, knowing they are not happy. Some people are *needy* and look for closeness by having sex.

Many get invested too early. Some are out there to prove themselves. Some offer all sorts of *favors* to be close.

Men want to be dominant and strong. They want to have sex.

Women want romance and commitment.

Love means you want to be with that person no matter what, and don't want to live without them. Now that doesn't mean being a masochist or an enabler or a caretaker, although many fall into those categories.

It is good to need someone to love. It is torture not to have that, if you are capable of it.

There are *users* and there are *losers.*

If you jump in too fast with no background information or testing of what you need in a relationship; you ask for trouble.

There are some *rules* put out by therapists that include: no sex until after two months. No oral sex, except with someone you really love.

Attraction is not a choice. It is in us, and we physically respond.

Men choose females that are attractive and that are healthy to bear children and carry on their genes. Even in the animal kingdom.

Women choose strong men to protect them and their children and provide for them. Does the term *alpha male,* ring a bell?

How you are treated depends on your values and what you think you are *worth.*

If you are treated poorly it's because you don't think you deserve better and allow that behavior.

Men actually need females more than females need men, in most cases. Sex is not the same drive for each of them, usually.

Females like *bad* boys who are ambitious and can have other pretty girls if they wanted.

Men are not as emotional as women. They like secure *ladies.* If a female is too *easy,* they miss the chase and conquest, flirtation and playfulness.

For females there are qualities to look for in a man if you want him for the future.

How does he treat his mother? How is he to people who cannot fight back; waiters, cab drivers, secretaries? Is he considerate of your wishes? Is he too controlling?

You set your standards, but not with demands.

Guys look at you as well. Is she a nag? Is she sensitive to your needs? Is she too *clingy*? How does she handle money?

All the questions you can imagine play out over time for any couple.

There is no need to review your sexual histories with one another, but many do.

Sharing what is erotic, and what you each enjoy when it comes to sex, is a way to be close and to communicate something really important. None of us run on *radar*. At least not yet!

In the final analysis, we are all different and have our own unique needs. The goal is to find what suits us and that can be sex… less or sex… more. With or without LOVE!!

"I know I am in love with you because my reality is finally better than my dreams." - Dr. Seuss

Married And Alone

We have all heard of the brothels for men to visit and have their *needs* taken care of. They are everywhere.

Finally, a *house* for women was opened in Las Vegas. They had a variety of services available.

For one-hundred dollars you could be fondled.

For two-hundred dollars you could be hugged and kissed.

For three-hundred dollars sex was available, AND,

For five-hundred dollars he would LISTEN to you, when you talked!

Ha, ha… and not so ha, ha.

Many women, and I think some men, feel they are married, (or in a long-term relationship), and yet they feel very much alone. Having someone there in the presence is not enough.

Going through daily activities and just talking about stuff, does not have intimacy, caring, loving, or real connection emotionally.

A partner who doesn't touch you, laugh with you, enjoy special moments with you, or let you know what you mean to them, is what I am referring to here.

You can very definitely be ALONE in the relationship. You might as well not be there, as anyone could be taking your place. The YOU is not appreciated.

You can be respected, and you can share activities and niceties, BUT you are alone. You feel it.

Sometimes it can be a brief period, or it can go on for a very long time. Even if sex is still viable it can just be a matter of, *doing it* but with no real warmth.

Recently I had a conversation with a male friend, who had been married a long time. He spoke about never wanting to be touched. When I questioned him about what was missing and knowing something was not right, his response was, 'I never thought about it.'

That is too bad, and we need to be thinking about our needs and feelings in an honest manner.

Then the task is to share them with our partner.

Now, if age, mental problems, life's stresses, or physical issues, get in the way that too can be discussed. Maybe the focus has to be altered but there are ways around those problems as well. If things can't be improved then you have to decide whether you want the relationship and manage, or if you need another outlet.

Memories may suffice. Other family, friends, hobbies, interests, or pets fill the bill for many. If you need another person, you are ripe and ready to share love that has disappeared or may never have been there in the first place.

Time does strange things and relationships are never static forever. Needs can change.

Being alone in a partnership is a very lonely unhappy feeling. Sometimes it can turn into real resentment or anger.

Today with dating sites and Facebook, there are any number of ways to meet and connect with people. Some short-term and superficial, and maybe dangerous. Some can be positive.

The thing about loneliness in a long-term relationship is that it feels stale and brittle when you are together.

The only way to really solve it is... you know it... talk and talk some more.

Get the feelings out.

If the capacity to change is there that should do it. If not, at least you tried.

At times it can feel like you are talking to a stranger who doesn't speak your language. Indeed, some couples where there are basic differences, can be in that mode for a long time. Sometimes the capacity to even understand the hurt is not there. Then you are up a tree and have to determine if there is enough to keep you in that relationship.

Connection is through caring and expressing that caring in many ways on a regular basis.

There are many lonely people who are NOT living alone.

"I could never be lonely without a husband." - Lillian Russell

Love Minus IN

"Never underestimate the power of passion." - Eve Sawyer

Hopefully you have all been there or hopefully, again, will get there one day; having love with passion.

In all my decades of counseling I have met any number of people who regrettably have never known and experienced that unbelievable feeling of total abandon; real true love. That means the mind, body, and soul are turned over and out of your control. You give up your SELF!

That is always sad to me, but I certainly understand the fear, and inability to love that deeply; it is a frightening manner in which to live. And that's okay. It can still be a fine, productive and happy life for many. Happiness is relative, (name of a former blog, by the way). We all have limits in every area, and love may be one of the most precious qualities we cannot share completely. Again, that's fine. Whatever works.

We have many varieties of love. Hopefully, we are *loved* in return.

We love parents, siblings, friends, colleagues, pets, and even strangers. We share parts of ourselves in any fashion we are comfortable with.

Now with a partner we can share a history, and we can go through the days in a comfortable, mundane style. We have disappointments and anger, and all the ups and downs that life offers. We may have had a passion, but time and familiarity have worn it away. There is no challenge. There are few surprises. There is no resistance and nothing to *fight* for. He or she is *mine.*

We settle down to a simple daily caring and that is NICE. Nice but flat and predictable.

Sometimes crises can shake it up. Then there can be growth after the trauma. Often this type of situation will cause a readjustment, if you will, that makes people change and evaluate their lives. They can gain appreciation for life and their partner in a new and deeper way. It opens up new possibilities and behaviors. It's Nietzsche's," What does not kill me makes me stronger." That, of course, implies it has not killed you! Some relationships do a complete turnaround as the individuals are now on a different level themselves. Sometimes the relationship may end or become' *brittle* as one has changed while the other has not.

At any rate, the going through the motions of life will go on ad infinitum.

Now let's talk about the IN part.

When you are IN love the world is technicolor. You are divinely happy, even at hard times, and you are emotionally hooked. You see the partner as turned on by you, and you are excited by him, or her. You want to be close, touch, hold, hug, kiss, and have sex… as much as possible. You only light up when they are there. You wait for their call or text. You melt at their voice. You dress for them. You are happy. You enjoy everything. Romantic movies have a different meaning; you relate to them and see yourself in them. Music is a way of being happy. Everything has a rainbow around it. You are nicer to everyone. The difference is noticeable. Love with passion is the height of it all. Being IN love is a way of life, and once experienced there is no other way to live.

If, for whatever reason, *it* is ended there is grieving. If you ended it for *good* reasons, there is learning to be gained for the *next* time. Whatever the length of time, and whatever the circumstances, being IN love is always *worth it*!

We don't teach people how to get there, or what is involved, so it is a chance that we have happen to us; we either grab it or live without it. Much learning takes place by trial and error and what we thought was *love* may turn out to be a form of love, but we are not IN love. Some people experience it once or twice in a lifetime. Some people never think about it or care to explore the issue at all. Many live *adequate* lives with *fair* sex, and others just plain settle for comfort and routine.

To be and stay IN love takes knowledge, insight, and risk, coupled with a lot of overlooking, communication, and forgiveness. Being creative and playful and offering surprises also helps. A sense of humor and self-deprecation can do wonders.

And best of all, there is no age limit on any of this. Learning how to share oneself totally is possible at any point in life. It is always sweet and wonderful.

Whatever your pleasure, go for it!!

"It is my misfortune that my heart cannot be content, even for one hour, without love." - Catherine the Great

Keep The Mate… Divorce The Children

"I think the passion many people affect for children is merely a fashionable pose. I have a notion that children are all the better for not being burdened with too much parental love." - W. Somerset Maugham

Someone needs to let out the secret… children are a pain in the ass… a lot!!

We have them, those that choose to, for a variety of reasons. Some of them good and a number of them for our benefit, not theirs.

When a child is brought into this world by mature loving parents there is a great beginning. No guarantees about the future for anyone, but it is a solid start.

The child is seen as an extension of self and someone to *give to.*

If the child is there to fulfill you and your life, make the relationship stick, or be there as *cute display*, be careful. That may turn out to slap you in the face.

As babies, parents dote on their children. They have hopes and dreams for them. They enjoy their growth and development. It's all pleasant. Extended family share in the process. Doing for the child as they become more independent lessens and parents teach what they want their children to learn. The values the parents live are what their children see and follow when they are under parental control.

As teenagers, the normal process is for the child to rebel. This can take many forms from mild disagreement to acting out violently. At times they can damage their lives for a long period of time, or forever. Dangerous territory.

Now as adults, there is a whole plethora of impending problems.

Some can come as the adult child discards the values from childhood. In some families this can cause a wide fissure in the relationship.

As adults, a child may marry someone the parents truly do not like and that will make the relationship very strained or non-existent.

There may be old wounds that never heal and keep being thrown in the parent's face.

There can be sibling competition. If each child, feels the parent favors another child, you are doing great. As long as they all get a turn!

No family is without its' issues, and no family is beyond help if they choose to work on it and take responsibility for their part in the drama.

It takes a grown-up to be responsible and talk through their hurts, misunderstandings, and unloving behavior.

Problem is emotions get in the way and being grown- up is not always possible.

Sometimes the parents take sides. If that happens the adult child knows who is *on their side.*

That can cause friction or even outright marital discord in a marriage.

When it comes down to the wire in family disputes the rule should be that we all care and try our best to resolve the problem and heal.

If it gets too out-of-hand, or the feelings are too deep or reoccur with no resolution, the situation will deteriorate.

Finally, the parents need to be together and care, and yet live their own lives no matter what.

In the face of a child's or children's misunderstandings or arguments or rejection the parents need to hold tight and help all parties move on.

It is always painful to go through all of the family upheaval but there is no escape as we are all individuals with our own interests and emotional needs. When it *works* family can be a fun time together and when it *works* the tough times are shared and made easier. At times the really tough times can force a family to join hands and pull together and show their love. It is too bad when that is what it takes, but for some that's the way it is.

A really hard role is the in-law role when you have to bite your tongue a lot. You may have to do that as a parent as well, but it is not the same. The deep roots and history are not there with in-laws. It also makes the emotions stronger for good and not so good.

The real bottom line is your life is lived with a partner, and not with a child, so nourish that and it will pay off! If the marriage is not good the child will be the substitute and that is really not good!!

"A child has a way of extracting from each parent precisely those elements he most needs; and this usually comes about best in their special moments of solitary companionship; it is then that he has a chance to break into the special twoness of the parents." - Lewis Mumford.

I Hate Everybody

"I don't agree that love gives the best insight. Hate gives a much better, I think, when hate keeps its head." - Maarten Maartens

Do you agree? I'm not sure, but there are times and before a New Year is a good time to take stock. There are days, and maybe many of them when this is exactly what you feel. No matter who you are; no matter how intelligent; no matter what you have accomplished, there are those days.

Now hate is a strong word and maybe it's not always hate. Maybe it's disappointment. Maybe it's a bad choice. Maybe it's a change in someone or you. Maybe it's a pile up of things. Whatever the reason or reasons, getting rid of toxins is good both for your body and for your emotional well-being.

Lately it seems people just don't give a damn. They don't care about how they do their job. They have *attitudes* and little is done to expectation, or god forbid, excellence.

The world is hostile and unfriendly, and people are stressed and not really happy.

That's a generalization, I know, but that's what I observe.

You can have a very displeasing experience and the person will end with. *Have a nice day.*

I, for one, want to choke them!

You can spend inordinate time trying to get something done and when you think it's fixed… guess what? It ain't!

Infuriating!!

Now when it comes to relationships it's another story.

No parent or child EVER does what you would like all the time. Maybe they are even deleterious to your development or growth, let alone pleasure.

What to do about all that stuff? Siblings? Any relative. You are *stuck* with these people for life… UNLESS you wiggle free. See them for what they are and if they are not conducive to your feeling good the majority of the time, cut yourself loose. Adults rarely change what they basically are without some major event or insight. Now this doesn't imply that you are always the reasonable and *right* one, but it does mean you should not be bound to anyone that you feel that kind of anger or even *hate* for.

With friends, they can come and go. We have them for different purposes. Some very few are really good friends and close and have your interests and well-being at heart. They're there for you and put themselves out for you. That happens when you are a good friend in return. If it is transitory or occasional or just for short spurts take it for that. If it has stood the test of time it can be worked on if a bad period occurs. What you share is a two-way street. If it's a one-sided affair maybe you'll tire of that. Brutus wasn't the only *friend* Caesar needed to worry about! Beware of the person who has no friends. That's a message.

Sometimes people show their true colors after a bit of time. If you are wary at first; stay tuned. You may want to run.

When we get in these hateful moods they are usually overcome in a bit of time by being and doing things you enjoy with others. With a spouse or long term love it's a process and we learn how to compromise and *get over it*.

There is a sour taste in the mouth when these occurrences happen. How long they last may be in your control and you should try to move along.

You can stay *mad* even hateful and then look at it. Make sure you are not unreasonable and then get on with positive stuff. Your happiness is up to you!!

If the situation is not redeemable or worth it to you get rid of it, or the person, and have people you enjoy around you. You needn't have anyone's *baggage* unless you choose it.

So, for the New Year, or any year, cleanse yourself and get a Voodoo doll!

"The woman who cannot hate like a bitch afire, and express it, cannot love like a tigress, or a kitten." - Brendan Francis

I Love Everybody

"To love deeply in one direction makes us more loving in all others." - Madame Swetchine

You knew after the year's end and the 'I Hate Everyone' piece this had to follow on the first day of the new year. It had to. Once cleansed of the bad feelings and people, we are then, and only then, free to go ahead and seek the positive.

Love is a word tossed around constantly but what does it mean to the people who say it, let alone the people who hear it? It can be a huge variety of things. The real deal is sort of like pornography; you know it when you see it, or in this case, feel it.

What actually happens is that to be in real love you have to then love the world and the people in it. It is like a catalyst for letting out good and positive vibrations. You are happy, contented, and fulfilled so you can radiate that out and you do.

You can always find the people who are in this realm. They stand out and like that pebble in the brook the circle goes on and on.

What is especially difficult is how to achieve that and then to hold on to it.

Looking at the world one is reminded that there is evil. Are people basically good or evil?

It was only about seventy years ago, the world watched as millions were put into ovens and killed. How does that happen? How does the stuff that goes on all over this world today get tolerated?

My own theory is that we are composed of many facets. Most people want to have a *good* life and take care of the ones they care about. It's the leaders of places that need to control and have power that cause the problems. They get power in a variety of ways and then the people suffer. Look around this world… it's not a loving sight!

True, individuals cannot control themselves and many situations, and do become hateful, nasty, and certainly not loving. All relationships are a mixture of plusses and minuses.

Life is full of dichotomies. Living with ambivalence is part of the human condition.

Life is trial and error. Life is full of *mistakes* and *should haves* and that's par for the course.

Life is painful. We need to teach children what life is really about. Fairy tales for children are fine for a while but real life is not a fairy tale.

Religion sells a hope and keeps people in line. Guilt and fear help too.

When Pandora was told not to open her box as all the evil in the world would escape, she disobeyed and opened it. All the evil flew out and she slammed it shut with only one thing remaining inside. Do you know what that was?

It was HOPE!

We have hope and that keeps many of us going and then in time we can learn to love. Life offers challenges and promise.

Is it possible to love everyone?

Well maybe not EVERYONE… but perhaps the majority in our lives.

Just imagine a world where the leaders were loving and kind.

Just imagine a world where most people did not have to act out their anger or frustration on others.

Does the sun shine every day? NO… but we can get through the storms knowing there will be sun again.

We can live in moments and retain the joy and yes, love, for as long as we can. OR, we can be non-loving and get used to that uncomfortable feeling.

We make our patterns and we get into *habits* of living.

It is true if we have not received love, we don't know what that's supposed to be like, feel like, or express. It is only by risking ourselves that we can connect in a loving way to someone.

Can we *love* everyone? Absolutely not. Do we have to test people out before we connect?

Absolutely. However, if we have not been able to have that closeness at least with one other person in our lives, for a period of time, we need to examine why.

Barring mental illness, I believe we can love or learn to love. Let's open that school and give diplomas!!

"Unfortunately, it is easy to imagine that anyone hates you, and hard to think anyone loves you. But you must be bold to believe in love if you would be happy." - Dr. Frank Crane

Independent Women... Get A Dog

"It's funny about men and women. Men pay in cash to get them and to get rid of them. Women, on the other hand, pay emotionally coming and going. Neither has it easy." - Hedy Lamare

Independence	**Love**
Competitive	Vulnerable,
Accomplished	Compromising,
Opinionated	Empathetic
Rational	Prurient
Demanding	Dependent
Mature	Silly
Analyzing	Tolerant
Proud	Forgiving
Appropriate	Spontaneous
Judgmental	Trusting

Here are some words that describe being an independent woman and being a woman in love. Look at them. They are very different.

What it takes to be a *successful* woman in America, or the world today, is quite different from the qualities a woman in love possesses.

Can one person combine the two aspects? Maybe. It is not an easy task.

You are one person; not a divided self. You cannot be one way to the outside world and another at home or with a partner.

In a relationship with a man it is not easily accomplished.

When a man sees you as *independent* and not *needy,* he feels you can take care of yourself. He doesn't equate your self-reliance differently when it comes to your emotional needs, and in fact, you may not display much need in these areas.

As a result, he will not be especially kind or loving in many ways. He lets you control the situation. You don't show or communicate what you might really want from him emotionally. You are not the soft, sweet feminine partner. You can stand alone and do what you want.

Too bad, because the bottom line is most females want to be adored and loved and sexually desired.

Men may benefit in a variety of ways from her independence, but not when it comes to wanting to be a MAN, especially when it comes to showing love.

Smart independent woman have learned what they need to do to get ahead in the world. They may attract a man, but then their heads get in the way. They see they may have to survive financial problems, boredom, and they see the guy's weaknesses and habits they don't like.

They are aware that if they get really involved it may lead to emotional problems, pain, divorce if they marry, or just personal survival.

Independent women don't want to risk it.

So, as a result, they are very cautious, and test the partner before getting involved.

They, just like men, don't want to give their heart away to be hurt. Both deny themselves the ultimate; true love.

Many, similar to men, like the chase, and find relationships exciting in the short- term. Having a lasting relationship with love and a working partnership is difficult to say the least. Most people long for close relationships and finding a love for the long-term.

Close relationships are always difficult to obtain and take time and effort, and yes, thinking. BUT, at some point the thinking part and control has to give way to what true love demands; vulnerability and a lot of forgiveness. Not easy to come by, and especially for the independent woman.

None of us wants a damaged or broken heart, however, there's no way around it when you know how to love.

We all have *baggage* and habits that are not *wonderful* to another person. The trick is to be human and accept another and get beyond the things that stand in the way of connection. Communication helps.

If, in the end, you are too much the perfectionist and too picky, and too independent; GET A DOG!!

"I am a woman meant for a man, but I never found a man who could compete." - Bette Davis

He's A Person Not A Puppet

"Love doesn't attempt to bind, ensnare, capture. It is light, free of the burden of attachments. Love asks nothing, is fulfilled in itself. When love is there, nothing remains to be done." - Vimala Thakar

There you have it. We engage with people; not puppets!

Now there are any number of men who want to control their women. They do it in a variety of ways. Some include being nasty, strong, bullying, withholding or supervising money, threatening any sort of behavior and so on.

What this is about is when females try to control, or attempt to change their partner.

This is usually performed in less heavy-handed manners, and with different controls.

In any relationship, there are areas and attitudes and ways of acting that displease a partner. No one can meet all your needs all the time. And you too are no angel doing what your partner needs all the time!

There can be things said, acting in ways that displease, and all sorts of things that get you, *mad*.

Females spend a lot of time over minutia and *hurt* feelings. It can sound sexist but in all my decades of counseling and observing, that's what I see.

Everyone is fragile and flawed.

Love includes loss; of some independence, and a lot of misunderstanding. We communicate on many levels. Often, we conjecture up ideas or misinterpret words or behavior. All based on our backgrounds, and no two people are identical in these areas.

We want completeness, and understanding and total acceptance. We are all vulnerable to things like flattery and hurt by neglect.

If we love and are loved then we need to ALLOW the partner to be who they are.

We fell in love with that person. If we ever thought we were capable of changing them or indeed wanted to change them; lots of luck!

True, there can be some aspects that can be enhanced or diminished, but the basic core will be there.

If you cannot control what you don't like you really need to realize that the PERSON is who you chose!

If you need control have children or a dog. Even here they move on their own at some point.

If the relationship becomes loveless as a result of your disappointment then you decide whether you want to continue.

The old Pygmalion story only works if the partner NEVER grows up and becomes a person in their own right.

How can you RESPECT someone who allows you to pull the strings?

While there are relationships of long-standing that are like a controlled puppet, the *puppet* may rebel, or worse, get sick.

None of us is happy all the time, and there are many obstacles to lasting-love with passion, but control will not work in a mature relationship that has true love.

If you are on guard a lot and hear the *wrong* word or endure the behavior that upsets you a good bit of the time, you should examine the core of what you share.

Being 'normal' includes some of the things we don't like. It's the percentage that counts.

We all usually change with time, and disillusion sets in. Arguments take two, and we do not learn about love in any school. We are on our own, usually with poor examples from the homes we grew up in.

The bottom line is to acknowledge that he brings you your main happiness and you don't want to live without him. You probably kissed a number of *frogs* before choosing him, so now learn to forgive, accept and show caring. It'll make you happier in the end!

"My happiness grows in direct proportion to my acceptance and in inverse proportion to my expectations." - Michael J. Fox

Go On… Make A Mistake

"A man who has committed a mistake and doesn't correct it is committing another mistake." - Confucius

We all make them, maybe a lot. There are a variety of *mistakes*. Some large affecting many people and some tiny affecting maybe only ourselves.

Lately it seems the world is full of them. The ones that are acted on, involving whole groups of people are the worst. They cause misery, and even large loss of lives. They are the crimes against humanity.

Most of the time they are based on bad thoughts that become ingrained from childhood.

Then there are the ordinary every day mistakes that we are all subjected to. Misinformation and lack of caring or judgment. These mistakes cause problems in our daily lives and are really a pain to deal with on a regular basis. People just don't *care.*

But the mistakes that I want to talk about are the ones involving people who are emotionally connected to one another and who care about each other.

These can include any family member or friend or colleague. Often it is because of faulty ideas or bad information that is not correct that causes these mistakes.

The real deal is between two people who love one another.

These mistakes can take a big toll if not dealt with well or handled honestly.

That old line about never having to say you're sorry is not so, in my book. Apologies can help get things on the right track again. It may take a heap of work to get it better, but it can only happen when two people recognize the problem and acknowledge the *mistake* and want to *fix* it.

Sometimes it is faulty thinking that causes the problem in the first place. Sometimes it is finding out something that a partner was hiding, or sometimes it is a real flat out knowing hurt that is inflicted.

We cannot always be happy and males and females are different in what bothers or hurts them.

If she feels overwhelmed, he makes a big mistake thinking she can put her job, the kids, or house etc. aside to give him what he wants. Her stress has to be dealt with.

If she nags and complains he thinks she is trying to control him and that is something he will fight. It is a mistake to think that he will just move on.

If really nasty things are said the mistake there will not disappear in your head.

However, if *requests* are made in a civil fashion each partner may hear what the other is asking.

We need to express what we need from one another and then test it to see if we can deliver.

It is a trial and error process and takes time for new patterns to become natural. We need to help one another understand what happened and why and what we will try to do to correct the *mistake.*

If the mistake was a deception, trust will become paramount. That will take time, lots of it in many cases.

No one can play *cop* twenty-four hours a day and no one should want to live that way.

It is usually the case that when a partner knows the other one will not *approve* of the behavior that causes deviance. The tighter the control the more deceptive they will become. A bad cycle.

When the truth comes out there will be a lot of drama and emotion and anger and hurt. All normal. The wronged one will lash out, and the other one may feel real guilt and remorse. Again, all normal.

Then the work begins to heal; and then the result if successful, may lead to a better connection, better communication, and better all the way around. Good outcome and good learning.

The old line that the person who keeps repeating behavior that doesn't work and expecting a different outcome fools themselves. They are just plain STUPID!

The final analysis is that we all *tolerate* different things in our relationships and only you can decide what works for you. Since we all make bad decisions from time to time and yes, mistakes, we need to be aware that our partners too are only human.

The challenge is to make your life the best it can be with all the *junk* that life hands out!

"If we do not always see our own mistakes and omissions, we can always see those of our neighbors." - Kathleen Norris

Guys… Flattery Pays Off

"The best way to turn a woman's head is to tell her she has a nice profile."- Martin Block

You guys need to pay attention.

This business of flattery really works.

Now men like to be flattered too. The areas they want to hear about have to deal with their sexual prowess, their strength and body, and their money. They like to hear these things about themselves from women in particular.

BUT women thrive on flattery in a different way; they need it to connect with a man.

The things they want to hear deal with mainly their looks. They want to be seen as beautiful. Their faces and bodies cry out for adoring words. If they hear them, they are YOURS!

Now the question becomes; is it the truth?

Some people are very good at sweet talking. Others outright lie to get what they want. The person being told those sweet words may, in fact, come to believe them even if they formerly felt differently. Tell someone often enough something and they may get to actually believe it. That can be a good ego booster. Even if only one person thinks so, it helps.

We all know how we *rate;* because we have experiences from day one telling us. We are beautiful, we are smart, we are talented, et cetera. If the message is reinforced it becomes how we really feel and perceive ourselves. If the ego then becomes strong, any adverse message is not effective and tossed aside. If the image we have of ourselves is not so secure it can be shaken with any small contrary message. Who does the *messaging* also counts. If someone we respect, who has experience tells us something about ourselves it matters. If any *fool* mouths off, we can discard it right away.

What gets *put in* early in life is hard to shake. Parents can do damage here and many do; most unwittingly. Often, we judge ourselves as compared to a sibling, for example. That can be good or bad and makes us competitive. Peers later give out messages, as do teachers and so on. The early imprint is hard to change but not impossible. Also, if we feel shaky in one area, we can *bone up* in others to compensate for our not feeling great.

Now flattery is well described by Aesop in his fable, 'The Fox and The Crow.'

A fox is walking in the woods and looking for food, as he is hungry. He comes across a crow with a piece of cheese in her mouth, on a limb of a tree.

He says, "Good morning, beautiful creature." The crow listened but kept the cheese in her beak.

The fox continued about how charming she was, how her feathers shone, and her lovely wings. She kept her beak closed.

Then the fox said that he knew she had a very lovely voice and should be the Queen of Birds.

Listening to his words she lost her suspicion and let out her voice. The cheese dropped right into the fox's mouth! "Thank you," he said and to himself, "Though it is cracked you have a voice sure enough but where are your wits?"

Get the message?

Of course, you do.

We all want to be flattered and we all want to believe the flatterer. It is so even if we are secure and know what is said is true. It is an acceptance and appreciation that it is not for naught that we are... beautiful, smart, talented... whatever.

Some people are genuinely modest and have a difficult time with flattery and that's just their nature. They are not used to or comfortable with it. Okay, so be it.

The thing is that in a relationship, men can use flattery to get what they want from a woman. She is indeed the crow and loves to hear what he is saying. Her ears are a great preamble to foreplay. Trust me guys; it works!!

There are men who excel at this and have honed it to a science. Be careful...

By and large, we all like to hear nice things about ourselves, and especially when we ourselves know them to be honest reactions. It makes us feel good and loving and wanting to *give* in some form to the flatterer. No problem!!

"I can live for two months on a good compliment." - Mark Twain

The Grass IS Greener

"And I'd like to give my love to everybody and let them know that the grass may look greener on the other side but believe me it's just as hard to cut." - Little Richard

Yes, just as hard to cut BUT it may in fact be greener for a variety of reasons. Perhaps it is cared for better. Maybe it's owner knows things you don't. And then again it may be luck and where the sun shines.

There is this thing called competition and comparing ourselves to others. It is human nature.

We do it in a variety of forms.

It isn't just the grass that we look at.

How about the house?

How about the wife?

How about the children?

It all comes back to us and how content we are with who we are and what we have accomplished and achieved in this life.

Material things are important and are the measure in many respects.

What have we done with our careers and talents? What have we produced in our children? How does our partner reflect on us?

I am here to say that indeed sometimes the grass is greener in any aspect you choose to measure. We can be envious and become angry and bitter, or we can work harder to achieve higher goals.

In some respects, looking at the greener grass may spur us on.

In my area of expertise; marriage and all relationships, I have helped many people who have moved on to greener grass.

Some have been very happy they did, while others learned over time that their own old grass was just fine and green enough!

With relationships, NO ONE knows what goes on behind closed doors except the people who live there. From the 'outside' everything may look perfect and wonderful. However, on the inside it may be quite a different story and far from *perfect*.

If you are considering moving on to greener grass, you had better do some homework first.

Start with you.

What is it about you that wants to make a change?

Have you matured or changed?

Have your values changed?

Do you see your partner differently?

Are you just bored?

All of these questions should be examined before you leap onto a new ship, so to speak.

While it is true, many second marriages also end in divorce, many have offered a better way of life and emotional fulfillment not possible before.

Even without the benefit of marriage, the more experience the better.

If the new partner is a sheep in wolf's clothing or a repeat of what you left, it will mean that you have not changed. Your emotional needs are the same and you will keep repeating the same pattern. It's YOU, not them!

Today there are a myriad of ways to meet people and thus compare what you have. Many choices do not necessarily make the task easier. For some it is the constant chase and looking to see what can come along better. There is no inner contentment or peace with a partner under these circumstances. The grass is ALWAYS greener elsewhere!

The parts of any relationship that are romantic and fueled by passion in the beginning will change with time. There will be droughts, and earth problems, and maybe a lack of sun, or bugs, or too much rain. All part of greener grass issues and people problems too.

So, before you leap, take stock of YOU, your relationship, the other person, and do diligence so that your lawn will be the one others envy!!

"Get busy watering your own grass so as not to notice whether it's greener elsewhere." - Karon Waddell

Compared to…

"Whatever your age a man can leave you for another woman or die (of the two, I think dying is preferable)." - Helen Gurley Brown

It may be preferable and today there are any number of people not wanting to be committed or in a relationship with intense intimacy for too long.

How come?

There may be a variety of reasons.

We get our ideas from society, our own personal history and our genes.

Today society gives a plethora of messages about relationships and mainly that there is a whole world of people out there to be explored and maybe, just maybe, someone *better* will come along so why settle or get *nailed down*?

Just look at the Internet and dating sites, or Facebook. You can compare and pick and choose people all day and night. You can meet them and compare them. Comparisons on every level; how they look, act, and relate to you. All important to be sure but when to really get involved or stay involved over a period of time?

As a therapist, dealing with relationships, sex, and love, for decades, this is a whole new world.

Major changes in this world have caused women, in particular, to be freer and independent. Antibiotics, computers, and feminism have drastically caused women to behave differently from past generations.

It is no longer just men that can compare and act as they wish within a relationship.

Old relationships can be brought up silently or even verbally for comparison with a current lover. This does not make for a good feeling usually; even if the comparison is not positive. It means someone else is lurking in the background.

There can certainly be comparisons with more than one partner in the present. Again, both men and women have a variety of experiences and comparison is normal. When it is comparison with the body and sexual life; that is crucial and if the partner doesn't *measure up* that can be the end.

Sometimes the comparisons are fantasy or people that are not known in reality, ie: movie stars et cetera. Then it becomes just unrealistic.

Men actually like women who are demanding respect and they fall in love with strong people today. Absence also helps; not the clinging vine any more.

Women fall in love in the present and judge a man as they are with them.

The list of substances used in relationships often tell a story and often it is a result of comparisons. This is also true when a loved partner has died or moved out of your life.

Alcohol is taken to forget. Pot to feel peaceful. Cocaine to feel sharp and confident. Ecstasy for ecstatic sensations. LSD to meet 'Lucy with diamonds in the sky.'

These may *work* for a while but at some point, reality will set in and then the real work has to begin.

Saying 'That was then; this is now' can get the ball rolling. Maybe it has to be said a thousand times a day in the beginning. If you stay with constant comparing and no one measures up, you are *stuck*. You may stay that way for life. Up to you.

If you know the comparisons are there and real BUT you want to move on you HAVE to live in the present and maybe compromise and deal with the situation really objectively. There are NO angels walking the earth and the one that your barometer uses for comparison had *bad* parts as well as *good* ones. Concentrate on them!

Take every person's good and bad points and maybe make a list to see them in black and white.

Remember, you too are being compared… with…

"A girl can wait for the right man to come along but in the meantime, that still doesn't mean she can't have a wonderful time with all the wrong men."- Cher

FIRST… Love Thyself

"To fall in love with yourself is the first secret to happiness" - Robert Morely

Not so fast… or easy.

The message is there from day one.

You are or not pleasing to the eye. You are or not a *good* child. You are or are not the sex child the parent might have preferred.

You do or do not remind parents of someone they like.

Acceptance of YOU or lack of it has begun.

Because we are 'victims' of our parents we have no choice but to incorporate what they say and do into who we become, and what is valued.

Too bad we don't license people BEFORE they become parents and test them; we do it for a myriad of other things, but neglect this most important task.

There is not a person alive that at some point, and unhappily for some, have a lifetime of dealing with something or things they really do not like about themselves.

That being said how do we get to self-love?

And also there are those who say it is not a good thing… they are WRONG!

If I asked, *What is the worst thing about you?* What would your answer be?

Following that, of course, is name the best thing about you.

While some of who we are is just 'there' and most can't be altered; namely a lot of how we look, there are ways to deal with anything these days.

How often do we hear, *I hate my hair, I hate my nose. I wish I was taller/ shorter. My breast size… my penis size…* and on and on.

It is not meaningless or trivial. People see you as a physical BEING.

To get love Mother Teresa with her looks found a way.

Bill Cosby, no Gregory Peck, also found a way to connect and be close.

I am acknowledging how we look affects the way we are responded to.

BUT and a great BIG BUT; it ain't enough.

We need to learn how to accept us in total with all our faults, flaws, hurts, and bad experiences.

Arrogant people are not people who really like themselves and have to put on attitudes to make themselves feel better.

It is always a struggle especially if you have had horrible things happen. You feel embarrassed, betrayed, or even the cause.

You may harbor the feelings and have them fester inside. You may lash out at others or you may be self-destructive to relieve the anguish.

We all try to *save face*.

We have to deal with ingratitude, rejection, indifference and so on. All of us.

What to do?

Number one we need to acknowledge what we feel. Then we can share it. Doing so often opens others up to share significant things about themselves.

Next step is to find and do things you enjoy and be with people who make you feel good.

There are always others who are prettier, smarter, richer, more creative and so on.

There are also a whole bunch with less than you in every category.

You can choose to be unhappy, or content. That does not mean not striving to be better in whatever area you choose.

This does not mean narcissism or only loving oneself either.

Do not keep the toxicity from anytime or anyone going. Move toward what works for you.

In the end your happiness is solely dependent on you!

Yes, yes, I know some people have traumatic or very serious issues that have happened. It is a sad list.

And true some never recover, but there are any number of examples of people who have gotten through and then help others as a result.

My hope is that everyone can free themselves from those *chains* and love who they are.

BECAUSE you cannot love anyone if it doesn't start with you!

"Self-love often seems to be unrequited" - Anthony Powell

From Red Flag To White Flag

"Who has time for toxic relationships? If someone isn't honoring your feeling it's not a real relationship. If you feel drained after spending time with someone, that's a red flag!" - Doreen Virtue

Now here's an area where you should basically trust your instincts. Red flags are everywhere, and you need to be aware and not dismiss them. The beginnings of relationships should be full of desire and wanting to be with someone and be physically close.

If passion does not pull you that is a big red flag. It doesn't come with time. It's either there or it's not. Once you are *hooked* in that way a great deal can be overlooked, denied, or ignored. Rose colored glasses won't make it better over time. When the passion wanes, the things you were not liking come into full focus. Even with passion, over time, the red flags may wave harder.

What are some of them? They can be anything from small annoyances, silly behaviors, or large insurmountable issues that will more than likely, only get worse with time.

Lynn Hubschman

Things like drinking to excess, drugs, nasty attitudes to inferiors, bad temper, physical acting out and just plain insensitivity.

Trust me he or she will not change!!

Trust the behavior NOT the words.

If she is suspicious of your every move, talks all day and night, nags, or spends money foolishly she will continue to do so after you are together for any amount of time.

Some people try to hide what they know are *bad habits,* but the truth will out.

It is a good idea to check with people who have known the person you are wary about and get their opinions, especially if they have known the person for a while.

Get a history. Sort of like having a questionnaire to have filled out. The more history the better.

Watch them closely when you are together whether out or in.

There is always choice and one of the best red flags to be aware of is when your family and or friends do not like the person and do not think they are *good* for you.

They see things you may not; those rose-colored glasses. Thinking they will *change* for you is a big mistake. While some change may occur, the basics will not be very different.

Interestingly the changes that are positive may come out as a result of love and being happy.

It really is; is there enough positive to outweigh the negative? Only you can decide that.

People have done all sorts of things as a result of good sex, or real love.

Life will dish out a variety of ups and downs and hard times. That's when the real tests will arise.

You can adore someone, love every inch of them, and show it, but what do you receive in return?

If, in fact, they are everything you ever wanted then you have the best that life offers.

Women and mainly men have a difficult time with the other issue; surrender.

They may try to *escape* and not be bound by their feelings but that doesn't work.

Many couples have tried to let go and have found it was a useless exercise, only to come back to the relationship.

Sometimes when the *chase* is over, and the relationship gets too *comfy* there is no challenge and one or the other may think the relationship should end.

Once the surrender takes place there is a change.

The white flag is hoisted.

It can all start with that drive, the kiss, the touch, and the connection; emotional, intellectual, and physical.

No, nothing is ever perfect, and it probably will only be in short spurts and mostly in the beginning. The red flags may be minor or occasional or huge and intrusive. Do not ignore them!!

The white flag is necessary on both sides. That feeling of not wanting to be without this person will guide you. In a sense you give up a part of yourself for the sake of the relationship and what it offers you, emotionally. Sex plays a role here and at times may cloud the whole business and you need to be honest and acknowledge that. It is not a bad thing, but it cannot sustain a relationship over time without more than that. It can keep you in a relationship for a long time and that may be all you want.

See the red flags, embrace the white one, and maybe there is another color called *wait and see* that will mean caution. Sort of like the red, green, and yellow car signs! Stop, wait, and then GO!!

"Reason lost the battle, and all I could do was surrender and accept I was in love." - Paulo Coelho

Cinderella After The Ball

"And what, for instance, would have happened had Romeo and Juliet lived to middle age, their silhouettes broadened by pasta? "- Anita Loos

Interesting question. And one to explore with the Cinderella story, as well.

We really like fairy tales. They are comforting BUT guess what… a lot of people believe they are true!

They set the stage for a hope, a dream, and an unlikely outcome.

Does anyone teach you that? Absolutely not.

There are any number of documentaries and real-life stories we read about or see in the movies but Cinderella stays with us as we heard it as children and it got embedded in our memories.

As a relationship and marriage counselor for decades I can tell you people really do think marriage will solve all their problems and they will live, *happily ever after*. HA ha ha! Ain't necessarily so.

While to be honest there are many really good relationships and marriages over long periods of time there are many more not so great ones. The divorce rate is one statistic; half of all marriages end there, and second marriages are even higher.

Look at the facts.

Cinderella was not loved by a stepmother. She was made to do drudgery housework and did not get to look pretty. In addition, she was surrounded by *sisters* who made her look and feel awful.

Try playing that on your piano and see how good you feel about yourself!

Then the *magic* night and she goes to the Prince's ball and he is smitten. That does happen in real life. Look at real princes like William and now Harry.

Fortune and luck play a role.

She loses her glass slipper, and he goes on the hunt.

That happens too. We have Facebook and Google!!

They get together and off they go. End of story? No, only the beginning.

Today the anticipation, and longing seem to be missing. The imagination is also going by the boards.

Today it's hello and jumping into bed.

And it's not even with anyone close to a prince, usually.

The real work or discovery comes AFTER the wedding. This is true even with couples who have known one another a long time or have lived together. There is NOTHING like marriage but marriage.

It's as if the event now makes anything okay and you can in a sense, let it all *hang out*. Taking one another for granted comes into play. Here is the dirty little secret; no one prepares you for this turn of events and attitude. Too bad. A lot of problems could have been nipped in the bud right here.

Being polite, looking good, smelling nicely, and so on needs to happen all along; not just before marriage!

Life then takes over. Sex which is the yummy glue gets perfunctory and boring. Especially if you are trying to conceive and have to check a thermometer beforehand!

Money and how it is spent may be a big difference between two people. Just their different backgrounds and values and ideas may be too difficult to compromise and understand.

Social life and friends and maybe in-laws who can't tolerate one partner can take a toll. Children and rearing them is another wonderful area for disagreement.

Having crises in health, or finances, job problems, and so on get in the way.

If Cinderella and her Prince are not joined together as strong as iron they will drift or fall apart.

The relationship will change, and they may look elsewhere, or stay and be unhappy.

Monogamy is not a natural state. Basically, the Gibbon is a rare creature who is monogamous.

The Bonobos however, are the least warlike and most contented creatures and are close to we humans biologically. They have sex anytime with anyone!!

We might learn from them…

They of course, did not read Cinderella.

Our cells change every seven years. Our desires seem to do about the same. Maybe, just maybe, we should decide every seven years whether we wish to continue with the current partner. I believe in love, and I know great sex is necessary for it. With time and age or health, relationships can change but they can still be warm and gratifying. It takes insight and a willingness to address the issues with a partner. Cinderella would have to open up and she and her Prince would have to talk.

Happily ever after is possible but the definition of *happily* might have to be altered!

"Love does not recognize the difference between peasant and Mikado." - Japanese Proverb

Choose Your Battles

"Sometimes, silence is the best way to win an argument." - Jorge P. Guerrero

What do you argue about? With whom? What is the outcome?

All good questions to begin looking at this.

Now there are arguments that are based on facts. They can be easily checked, and they are not open to much opinion. You do however have to *fact-check* and trust and regard the facts as legitimate and trustworthy from someone respected. These arguments go on all the time and they can arouse heated banter back and forth. They can engender strong feelings and can alienate you from another person if you violently disagree. This happens with the areas of politics or religion or other firmly held beliefs.

Often you hear people say, let's not talk about those two issues.

Often one of the parties is usually on safer ground and has facts that are convincing and bear out as truth. There are however *super salesmen* who can convince others of almost anything, no matter what the truth is.

Now the more important side of all of this has to be within family systems, and then this gets translated into couples.

Growing up we all learn who is the boss. The parent is powerful and never seen as wrong when we are children. This then becomes how we relate to authority figures and others who hold some power over us.

When a parent is really tough and dominant the child may never be able to challenge anyone in authority. These people are docile and good employees who do not cause problems, following whatever that *boss* demands.

When in an intimate relationship the whole picture changes.

Here there are strong emotions and feelings get in the way.

Coming from two backgrounds automatically means you have different ideas and ways of behaving as part of who you are.

In the beginning of these relationships everything is honky-dory. All sweetness and light and overlooking whatever the differences may be. Sex and love cover up and mask a great deal.

Whatever glimpses or signs that are there are usually brushed aside or not heeded until later. Then when the ugly head is reared, the sex and love may not be enough to get through it and move on.

The patterns of behavior that each partner comes with is usually the one that will be there forever.

You always hear about the couple who broke up after many years because he left the cap off the toothpaste.

Don't laugh; those little actions can add up or become large in a partner's tolerance level.

The things couples argue over and disagree about can be anything. No one on the outside has to understand it; it just IS.

Maybe one has to always be *right*. Maybe one is the decision maker, maybe one is more accomplished or successful in the outside world. Maybe… fill in the blank.

The problem then becomes; is there any way for both to save face, feel valued, or see the other's side of things? Maybe yes or maybe no.

That will determine where the relationship ends up.

Now some couples have one person who says what goes and the other is the, *yes, dear* one. Maybe he is the father authority figure and she likes that or is just used to it.

If the differences get too heated it can cause BIG problems. In some it can lead to violence. That can be acted out inside the family or outside. Either way the *loser* of the battle feels badly, and the *winner* also feels badly that they caused hurt; usually but not always.

There is no problem having different ideas or ways of behaving if the differences are aired and dealt with in a respectful manner. There is no problem if they are really nasty and yelling or cursing is involved, IF they can then talk about it and move on. Some differences can mean change, or at least laughed about, or ignored, with time.

Some people use conflict just to have attention or to feel SOMETHING in the relationship, even though it is not positive, it is feeling, and a connection of sorts.

So, look at the battles you choose, and see if the conflict is really important and if things can be better as a result.

If not; wave a white flag!

"Discussion is an exchange of knowledge, argument is an exchange of ignorance." - Robert Quillen

Attention… Attention

"A celebrity is a person who works hard all his life to become well known, and then wears dark glasses to avoid being recognized."- Fred Allen

Cute!

It's the truth, too.

We all want attention about different things at different points in our lives.

Some people need it ALL the time. Look at any number of 'famous' people. They need adoration, and acclaim from the world at large. Movie stars, sports figures, and certainly politicians.

Most creative people struggle for it and they want the attention but all too often it alludes them. Some of them, as a result of powers that be, not because they have no talent struggle forever.

As children, we often have parents that give us undivided attention and often make us feel we are VERY special. When we scribble we are thought to be Picasso, when we read we are thought to be geniuses, and when we get a good grade in school we are told we will conquer the world. Ha!

When the truth finally comes out and we discover we're merely human and not so special to anyone else it can be a huge shock. We may then go on with the false premise that we are VERY special and that the world is wrong not to recognize it. Bad road ahead there. We truly have come to believe what we heard in childhood. Unfortunately, the world is not our doting parents giving false claims.

To come to terms with reality at any juncture is not easy. To accept who we really are with our plusses and minuses is never an easy or fast route.

Now when it comes to intimate relationships it gets a bit murky and in some cases downright ruinous.

A male or female partner that needs attention in its' variety of forms may be impossible to live with over time.

In the beginning, we all give our loved one lots of attention. We listen to every word they say, we try to give attention with actions that please them. Their opinions matter first and foremost. Sometimes we forfeit our own needs for attention to satisfy their needs.

That's all well and good in the beginning.

HOWEVER, after time it can be wearing, demanding, and outright unreasonable.

We can begin to resent it all and want something for ourselves. TOO LATE!!

The pattern has been set. It usually cannot change. Not always but for the most part it has been set and can't be undone.

As you begin to NOT give the attention demanded you will be the 'bad' one.

Often other family members will be told 'stories' and they will take sides. The situation can become so toxic there is no way out. Ignoring the partner may lead them into others' arms. If children are involved it can be a truly sad state of affairs as they are often taking one parent's anger as the right one to protect.

Neglecting the need for attention is a dangerous slippery slope in a relationship.

The signs are there in the beginning but few heed them and that is the reason the escalation when it is no longer, 'cute' becomes unmanageable. It can force the relationship to end, no doubt about it.

We all need attention and loving care from the people close to us and there is nothing wrong with that. At times, we need more than at other times and we can make those needs known. Communicating clearly is the key and hopefully a loving partner will rise to the occasion.

But, when the attention is needed constantly and in one direction and maybe even escalates, that is when it usually becomes intolerable.

There are instances however, and I have worked with individuals where one partner delivers and delivers and it goes on for years. Some of these people are true martyrs and like it that way.

Now I am not talking here about the need for attention when one is physically or mentally ill; that takes a different breed of caring.

In the end, attention is a necessary part of any relationship and getting the balance is the trick. Put the spotlight, if you will, where it belongs when it is needed!

Oscar Levant is said to have once asked George Gershwin, "Tell me George, if you had it to do all over, would you fall in love with yourself again?"

Beware Of Sensitive Men

"Men are not stupid, or at least not too stupid to realize that if they didn't get sensitive real fast, they weren't going to get laid anymore." - Cynthia Heimel

Funny?... Is this a true statement? What do you think?

It may be true in many instances, but here I want to address the really sensitive man issue.

Do women want a guy who cries at tender movies? Do they want a man that is *putty* in their hands? Some do. Some women are *strong* and there is a traditional reversal of roles. They go out to work and their partner takes care of the house and maybe children. That can work for some couples.

However, there is a disconnect when a man is a *success* outside the home, and he has had to *fight dragons* to get there, and then he is not a *marshmallow* when he comes home and relates to his partner.

It is almost impossible.

In some rare cases, some men can inhabit both sides of their nature and pull out what they need in each situation. They are very special people.

Being sensitive embodies a great deal.

It means you are wearing your feelings on your sleeve and maybe only sensitive about yourself. It can also mean being alert to another's feelings. That's the good part in a relationship.

We cannot put ourselves in another's skin and feel what they feel completely, but we can have empathy and caring that allows us to be there emotionally to offer what we can.

It is putting someone else's feelings before our own. That takes a heap of doing and a pretty fulfilled self to let it happen.

If we are *needy,* we are only interested in OUR feelings and slights, and hurts. Sometimes this type of person has the proverbial 'chip on the shoulder' and is always looking for problems. Sometimes they can manufacture things up that really don't exist. Big problem. A book titled, 'The Highly Sensitive Person In Love' by Elaine N. Aron talks about a lot of this.

Some fascinating research was done that showed that as many men as women are born sensitive and that women remain that way while 'real' men do not. Women like dating and being friends with sensitive men but want to marry a different type man.

They prefer the sensation seekers, if you will. Different genes seem to govern these two types.

As a result, marrying a different type than yourself, can lead to a lot of misunderstanding and indeed maybe half of all divorces.

Sensitive men are cautious about commitment and being hurt or overwhelmed by another's needs.

Sensation seekers are also cautious, but they fear it for loss of variety, and fear of boredom.

A pairing of these two types is not an easy road to long-term togetherness.

Two sensitive people may find the initial attraction quickly leads to disappointment and boredom.

They can find sex to be mysterious and powerful, and they are turned on by subtle cues.

Sensation seeking men and women seem to enjoy sex more, want new partners, have had more sex, and can enjoy sex without love. Different.

A sensitive person will demand more depth in their relationships, see more threatening consequences in their partner's flaws, reflect more, and worry about how things are going. Because they pick up on so much, they are prone to overstimulation and stress and they need *down* time. The partner can then feel left out. They also find different things enjoyable as compared to others.

All in all, it is good to be sensitive, whether man or woman, but like with much else in life, it can be too much.

So, Goldilocks what's *just right* You have to decide for you; AND your partner.

"It is hard to believe that anything is worthwhile, unless there is some eye to kindle in common with our own, some brief word uttered now and then to imply that what is infinitely precious in us is precious alike to another mind." - George Eliot

A Big Deal Is No Deal

"Most of the bad guys In the real world don't know that they are bad guys. You don't get a flashing warning sign that you're about to damn yourself. It sneaks up on you when you aren't looking." - Jim Butcher

So that this is not sexist it should say guys and girls!

There are so many things that can be a big deal in any relationship that they are too numerous to mention.

However, there are some that stand out, and over the years I have heard many of them repeated so often, that what I write may help others avoid the pain, misery, and depression, that warnings could have been foreseen and maybe big problems prevented. Watch any murder story involving couples and see what might have been prevented.

Now this is not to say that time and circumstances could change, and new issues present themselves that were not there earlier.

Usually what we are for the better part of our lives is set by the time we are young adults.

We fall in love with people, not by chance, but by our backgrounds and emotional needs. Often, we accept things we see and don't like as something else that is important is being offered overall.

The problem is that if the core of your emotional, and sexual needs is not being followed, you will probably be *in trouble* at some point. You can only compensate so much and for so long.

The big warnings have to do with your background and values.

What is important to you? Does your partner share those values?

What do you most like about this person? List one to ten.

What habits do you see and not like?

Are there secrets that make you suspicious?

Are you more important than his/her family? Friends?

Is affection shared?

Are your sexual desires similar?

Are there children from another relationship? Do you agree about how they are treated?

Lynn Hubschman

How is money used?

Are your goals the same?

Have you heard rumors you ignore?

Do you totally trust one another?

Are you shown you are cared about?

Do you really listen to one another?

How do arguments get resolved?

Do you respect one another?

What do you do for fun?

How many intimate relationships has the partner had and for how long? Why did they end?

Are you able to show anger and move on?

What is the use of alcohol? Drugs?

Are you both physically well? Is the immediate family healthy?

Has there been mental illness in the person's background? In the family?

Is there any criminal history?

Have you checked the educational and employment history to be sure it is true?

Do you like each other's friends?

Is he/she lazy? Too ambitious?

Who is in control and how is it displayed?

How compulsive is the partner?

Again, all of these ideas can be running through your mind with any partner and no one is perfect. The thing here is to be aware of the extent of your concern, share it, and see what happens. Time will give you an answer. No one can be putting on an *act* forever. Our pasts can predict our future in many significant ways. We need to heed our instincts. We should not poo-poo what goes on in our minds. Trust your feelings.

Jumping too fast because we need to be loved and love in return is a formula for danger. The recipe for happiness is never guaranteed, but there are ways to be prepared, and asking these questions is a good start.

I say to clients, that I want to meet their *intended* and have them fill out my questionnaire before they take a leap. It can be a leap of faith, when more is necessary.

The more time the better, to explore who this person really is under a variety of circumstances.

The heart has to lead but the head needs to do a bit of work as well!

If it's a BIG deal, please make it NO deal!!

"Life is warning you to get rid of an addiction every time you are emotionally uncomfortable in any way." - Ken Keyes Jr.

Getting Rid of Love Is Never Easy

"Lips that taste of tears, they say are the best for kissing." - Dorothy Parker

You've loved him/her with all your heart, (and body), for a long-time... years maybe, but the problems have always been there and dealt with.

In the beginning the thrall of love blankets everything. The drive to be together in every way pushes you toward one another. You can't be apart long or you do just that; long.

Getting rid of love is never easy. The issue or issues keep coming up and guess what; you make excuses, overlook them, talk yourself out of them, and the sex drive cures all.

Well, guess again; the problem or problems, will NOT go away.

When you 'sober' up and face reality you may in fact see that you have a toxic reoccurring unsolvable problem. Yes, the *love* will carry you through a lot of crap, a lot of hurt, and a lot of unsatisfied needs.

However, and it's the big however, if the same damn thing keeps upsetting you, you may in fact be in a TOXIC relationship that really is not good or healthy for you to continue.

Realizing it may not make you ready to act. The pull of passion and true caring will carry you along, but just like in ALL relationships, the hurt, and either lack of sensitivity, or inconsiderateness, that cannot be altered will do the thing in... maybe after many years.

Why do people stay in such situations? Lots of reasons, but the only one that matters is that you CARE.

Caring is the core of life and it doesn't merely disappear, even with facts in front of your face.

You can call him/her all the names in the world, tell them to go f... themselves, and so on, but in the end only you can make the decision to move on.

If you believe you deserve better, you will have to keep reminding yourself about that. The fact of the matter is; YOU DO!!!

Being constantly hurt and upset and communicating it, which is necessary, in any relationship worth its' salt, maybe doesn't change things. The pattern may be too well set to be able to be changed.

Holding on to hope won't do it.

Wishful thinking doesn't do it.

Being a *victim* is solely your fault. Give it up!!

Face it head on.

Now it is true, there is no perfect relationship, and no one can exhibit love the way you might like all the time. There are times when you or your partner may need more. There are times when you are both at a *bad* point. It's all part of the package.

The real bottom line is when the pattern just gets to a point where you want to die, kill them, or know you have to move on; you need to DO something.

The something is to get to NOT CARING! This is not automatic or fast, and you will waver, and be tempted to stay or go back, or try this or that. All normal. It is work to push the negative constantly into your brain and thoughts. You have to WORK at it.

The fact of the whole business is that you are not alone, and you have probably been through other challenges before, and guess what? You survived, and most likely lived to tell the story, and love again.

Love has a shelf life. After time, relationships do change and should.

The really good ones have passion forever.

The ones that are toxic can have that passion fail and change so that you move to; INDIFFERENCE.

You don't care where they are, who they're with, or what they're doing.

You don't look to see if they have texted or called.

You are not tempted to go back and be a *used* person again.

It is THEIR problem now, in your eyes. They cannot replace you, and they will not know the love you offer again. Let them try to replace it. You will find better.

Water always finds its' level emotionally. Those that have experienced and opened themselves up to love cannot live without it, and it will usually happen. You will be cautious to be sure, but that's okay. Talk and talk some more, to anyone who you care about, and who cares about you.

It is awful to get rid of a relationship that had meaning and yes, real love at some point, but not impossible. Impossible is living without love!!

"Let no one who loves be called unhappy. Even love unreturned has its rainbow." - J.M. Barrie

That Was Then

"Regret for the things we did can be remembered by time; it is regret for the things we did not do that is inconsolable." - Sydney J. Harris

How much time do you spend thinking about something from your past?

Most of us spend a considerable amount of time doing just that.

It's the things that made us feel badly. The what ifs. And also, the happy times.

There is nothing wrong with any of it. But it is the amount of time and the degree to which it uses your emotions that matters.

The thing about it is that it cannot be changed. Nothing can make any of it different.

If you had a rough period in early years, that can haunt you and *eat* you up for years, and maybe forever. That past has wounded you mortally.

It is not uncommon to be someplace and see really old people still talking about their parents.

Many times, it can be good memories, but frequently the bitter part is still there.

Early relationships can linger in one's mind and they can even consume thoughts.

Things about any part of life; work, school, friendships, and activities are all included in this return in time.

Choices that were not what you hoped would turn out well, can take up a lot of space in the head.

It seems that the negative aspects of life control more of our thinking than do the good parts we have experienced.

Regret for those paths not taken, those experiences not lived, the frittering away of time, money, and risks that frightened us, come into play here.

With age, and hopefully wisdom, we can evaluate our lives and how we have used our time and talents. We can honestly assess what we are and what we have done with the time allotted us here on this planet.

Learning from experience is a fine outcome of this. Staying stuck does not move us forward. We can remain in a rut, so to speak, and then we can't stand ourselves, and others do not want any part of us.

Now when it comes to relationships it is a tender area.

If we have been rejected, we can spend a great deal of time trying to figure it all out. What did I do wrong? What might I have done differently? We can blame the other person or dream up all sorts of excuses and scenarios where it might have turned out differently.

If we have been the one to reject a partner, we can be adamant about the reasons and feel fine.

Sometimes we can change our mind and the feelings will be strong. We may want them back.

We can then think of ways to change the decision.

Regret is a bad feeling. It can be crippling.

To wallow around a bit is normal, but after a short period of time we should move on and live in the present.

One of the really difficult areas occurs when a partner dies. Sometimes when they are ill, or not the person they once were, we are left with remembering the past and wanting to stay locked in it.

There are people who do stay and talk about the past constantly. Other people usually do not want to linger there forever.

That was then, and this is NOW!

At times you really must force yourself or push hard to stay in the present. It is especially hard when the present is not so wonderful.

Reverting to the past is easy. You can just reinforce the positive times and soft peddle or even deny the hard parts. It is up to you and you can make it whatever you choose.

At times others can remind you it was not all peaches and cream, and you can accept that, or fight it off or even become angry that they said it.

There are momentos, pictures, cards, voices on phones, and so on, to remind and keep the past fresh and alive. The person is not with you, but they are; in a sense. You are holding on to them.

The memories have *legs*.

The best way to deal with any of this might be to savor the memories and hold on to the good parts, and be grateful for them and maybe, just maybe, use the experience with a new person.

Keep the flame going as you wish but be aware that today does NOT return!

"Time is a storm in which we are all lost." - William Carlos Williams

We All Have Loss

Brahms' gold watch was stolen one day from his rooms which he never locked. When the police came and urged him to take the matter up officially, he simply said, "Leave me in peace! The watch was probably carried away by some poor devil who needs it more than I do."

That's a good attitude in the face of misfortune.

It is true we all face loss in a variety of forms; some more onerous and sad than others.

Many people feel *lost* in the world as they have never felt grounded or that they matter.

That is a tragic way to go through life. It would take a heap of work to turn that beginning, around.

Then there are the realities of life, and losses that occur sometimes through no fault of one's own.

Loss of a job, loss of a friend. Stolen things.

The facts of just living, always include loss.

Loss of good looks, a pleasant figure, one's hair, strength and so on. Aging brings with it a slew of changes that are felt as loss.

Sometimes there is a loss of faith in a variety of sources. What we once counted on or held dear may be seen as different at some point, and we shed that part of ourselves. When strong values or areas, such as religion, are involved, that may be a yeoman's task. That stuff is so ingrained from childhood that to get rid of it, seems almost sacrilegious, or a betrayal of sorts. It can leave us unsure, and even guilty, for quite a while.

Not having the skills and quickness we once enjoyed can be a big sense of loss.

The issue of memory and forgetting invariably comes up.

The whole business of self-esteem gets caught up in these changes.

We feel diminished. Maybe even irrelevant. Depression is not unusual as all of this takes place.

We are no longer who we used to be.

Now when it comes to our close and loving relationships any loss here can be all consuming.

If the loss is temporary, due to a misunderstanding or hurt feelings, that can be worked on. When people care about one another, they figure it out.

If the loss is permanent, as through a death, that loss is not getting fixed so quickly or easily.

Have you ever heard a widow speak badly about the man she loved, who is now dead?

Not usually.

They all become *saints*. No matter what they were in real life.

Getting over that kind of loss, is for some, monumental, and for some others, it is never going to happen.

Their lives revolve around that person, the past, and all the memories.

Often, they become almost obnoxious, and you want to scream, *Get over it!*

For another group, they live with the memories and go through the motions of day to day living. Their heart is never totally in anything, as before.

When in love, the connection and joy of life is there. When that goes, it feels like a death of self.

For some, like when a dog dies, they get a *new* one. But for many, and depending on the age, often life is never the same. There is a loss, and part of the living heart goes with it.

While I am not addressing the loss of parents, or heaven forbid, a child; they are separate and unique difficult situations.

Life dishes out *junk* and we all have to deal with lots of it from time to time. Loss can offer an opportunity to develop and grow and change. It can open new doors. It can show us strength we didn't know we had.

We can put it to good use to help others as well.

Shared grief and bad times offers us a closer bond with other people, and they may come closer to us as a result.

So, fear loss not... you're still HERE!

"You cannot prevent the birds of sorrow from flying over your head, but you can prevent them from building nests in your hair." - Chinese proverb

Being Dumped Hurts

"When someone leaves, it's because someone else is about to arrive." - Paulo Coelho

There is not a person alive that hasn't been *dumped* by someone. It's part of the human experience. If it happens time and time again in romantic relationships the question is; why?

The first thing to examine is how long was the relationship, and what was shared?

If it happened after a relatively short period of time and perhaps after meeting through technology, there probably wasn't a whole lot of *you* involved.

Knowing someone for a brief period usually doesn't get you too emotionally invested in them and the relationship. What is possible with the flick of a finger on a keyboard makes some pairings flighty from the get-go. Some people even end the whole thing that way; on the Internet!

Even though that may be the case; if you are *dumped* you feel badly. You wonder what you did, what you said, or did not say, and what went wrong. If you thought there was a real connection, and *chemistry,* the breakup will be one that haunts you for reasons about why it happened. Going over the details will probably not give you answers. It may however, if it happens often enough, give you pause to wonder about your capacity for real love. That is a good thing.

Gaining insight, even through pain, will help you in the long run.

If the person who left doesn't give you any reason about the *why,* you may want to discuss the situation with close friends, or a professional therapist, who can throw light on the subject; the subject being, YOU.

There are no perfect people and no perfect relationships. It is better to find out that the one that ended was not for you in the long run. That is a good thing, and the sooner the better.

If sex was involved that puts another light on the subject. It is not uncommon for that aspect to cloud other issues and areas that should be given attention.

Trying to not just understand your role and part in the whole affair is not enough. Trying to understand the other person is also a good exercise. Now, maybe there will be NO answers but that's okay. You still should move on and learn from it all.

If you have never been able to sustain a relationship that is romantic, then indeed you need to try and ferret out the reason.

If it all puts you into a depression turning to drugs or alcohol you need to get help as that will be a self-defeating pattern.

Now if the relationship was of long duration, and you truly shared yourself and your secrets and your body, getting dumped can feel devastating.

Pulling yourself together after that takes a lot of work and time. Fantasizing about the person, and maybe even accepting them back, will be a big hurdle. Trust will not be the same. Wanting to *pay them back* after being hurt is not uncommon. This too does not help you move along.

Life happens, and much of this is unplanned.

Love should be a matter of strong feelings, and when real, there is no *other* as you have chosen, and you are the choice of a partner. There is no looking any longer, and no one that comes along can replace what you share with that special someone. It is not just a habit; it is a genuine choice.

True love accepts you and the other with all the faults. The relationship is strong enough to withstand anything. You don't have to fight for love. It's there or it isn't. Even with the ups and downs; it's what you want.

Omnia Vincit Amor, Or Love Conquers All

"To penetrate into anyone, you find madness or dullness so most stay on the surface." – Tennessee Williams

I believe most of this is true. How many people do you know who are intimately tied together and enjoy a full and complete life; physically and otherwise?

Does love conquer all? It was the Roman poet Virgil who said it.

In many instances, it can.

Of course, there are all sorts of *love*.

The love of a parent for a child is usually unconditional and shows caring. Look at the parents who care day in and out for children with handicaps; physical or mental.

The love of siblings, if they have been raised well, is a close bond.

The love of children for parents is up and down but, in the end, should be two adults who respect and love one another. When the parent is, old and needs their help, they do it with kindness.

There is friendship love and the non-people loves; of country, work, pets, creativity, nature, art and so on.

The love I address here is between two people who share a physical aspect. This is intimate love.

It is not an easy connection by any means. It takes time and constant vigilance, knowledge, practice and a lot of understanding.

With all that life dishes out how can love blossom and flourish? Can it conquer differences and at times even hate?

The answer is a resounding…YES!

The bond that connects those lucky and fortunate enough to experience real love know that at times the negative can come in between. It can be in-laws, child rearing, money issues, differences of background and culture and even basic values.

The conquering all gets healed with talk and in bed!!

As long as those areas work there will be healing.

As long as those two areas are practiced there will be love.

We love in and out of bed but the drive to connect in these two ways will allow love to conquer all.

It may not always be fast or automatic but one or both need to say let's talk or let's go to bed.

That giving of oneself is what makes love worthwhile.

It is the reason for all the poetry, songs, literature, paintings, and drive most humans have to find the real thing.

If it was easy it would not be what it is; a struggle to find and then hold on to. It is that *magic* that most people strive for and long for.

While it may not last a lifetime whatever time you have it; nothing can replace the feelings involved; hence the need that is being sought for fulfillment. The thing to remember is that you are responsible for your own happiness.

If you are smart in the only way that smart matters, you will learn how to feel good about you, and then accept and share the heart you have with another.

There is a sweet ring that was used years ago, that used stones to spell out, *dearest*.

It had a diamond, emerald, amethyst, ruby, emerald, sapphire, and topaz. If you had and wore that you knew you were adored.

There are any number of ways to feel loved and each of us shows It In our own way. You need to only remember the ways when other negative feelings or issues come to the forefront.

Then love will truly take over and indeed, conquer all!!

"Take away love and our earth is a tomb." - Robert Browning

Printed in the United States
By Bookmasters